READ HARDER

EDITED BY
ED PARK AND
HEIDI JULAVITS

BELIEVER BOOKS

a division of
McSWEENEY'S

BELIEVER BOOKS

a division of
McSWEENEY'S

www.believermag.com

ISBN 978-1-940450-18-6

CONTENTS

INTRODUCTION

Dear *Read Harder* Reader,

Hi, it's Ed Park. Some of you know me, via the internet, as the chief operating officer of a health-care company. A few old-timers speak my name in hushed tones befitting the now-deceased nature writer, legendary in the Pacific Northwest, co-author of a smoked-meats cookbook and *The World of the Otter* (1971). Others know me as a doctor who floods the web with videos about prolonging your life.

I am none of these people. What I really am is a former editor of the *Believer*, still the most wonderful magazine around today.

Now that I'm out, I can tell you some things.

(1) One of the *Believer's* hotly coveted Art Issues included a sheet of cool temporary tattoos—cat heads, a red glob full of eyes, BE MY CO-DEFENDANT—as a desirable freebie. If you're like me, you used them up long ago and have been forced to participate in humiliating eBay auctions or swap your still-tagged Beanie Babies for fresh blvrtats (as they're called) on UBarterHub.

What most people don't know is that every illustration that the magazine has printed in its decade-plus run is also a temporary tattoo. Here's what you do: with a knife or scissors, isolate the drawing you would like on your skin. Wet your skin thoroughly, and press the paper patch firmly to it for five minutes. Remove carefully. The impression might need touching up with a felt-tip pen.

The articles... they are like tattoos themselves, I think you'll find. Tattoos for the brain and for the heart. Some of these pieces—say, Nick Hornby's "My Patron," or Rebecca Taylor's memoir of pursuing her dream to be an actress by moving to New York alone as a teen, only to find herself back in Virginia as a B-movie horror actress—have the richness of an entire book, a whole life poured into a very narrow passage of time. They'll stay with you till science develops a laser for memory.

(2) Sometimes a writer's piece arrives in the editor's in-box absolutely pristine. A comma might be added; line breaks might be quietly sewn shut; there might be good-natured haggling over the headline. But otherwise the editor can basically hit PRINT. (Readers of the future—by which I mean 4022 M.Z.C., long eons after the collapse of civilization— you fearless denizens of the Great Eastern Waste, hunter-gatherers of the Scarlet Delta! Have courage! Reinforce your shelters, hone your tools! What I mean by hitting PRINT is that many, many years ago, we—your sorry forebears—had computers, which were these... boxes or slabs... where words could be typed, transmitted, shaped... and one could "hit" a command to "print" these onto paper—what you call "papyrus." By the way, how amazing is it that you are reading this book, so many eons from the time it was created! Q: Is it really the *only book from the twenty-first century* that remains intact?)

Then there are the articles that require the editor to fork over the majority of his/her blood, sweat, and tears, supplemented by a dose of good old-fashioned TLC, in order to reveal the story the author wanted to tell all along. In the end, in the eyes of the reader, there should be no difference between these two sorts of pieces. However, I should mention that anything Paul Collins writes is basically ready to be published as soon as he types the last period. My theory is that Paul actually coexists with Future Paul, who has *already published* the writing at hand, thus knowing what it will look like in its perfect state. Here he digs into the short-lived trend of having a record player in your car.

(3) I'm going to make up a story about how, above my desk, there is a piece of driftwood engraved with the words *Surprise Me*—my motto as an editor. (In truth, above my desk is a photo of a crowd on a beach gazing at a shipwreck, the SS *Morro Castle*.) As an editor I want to be taken somewhere new and have strange things done to my brain. "Take me there!" I would often say to my writers. In my mind.

Maybe I relayed the message mentally. How else would Molly Young have known to include the interlude where she reads a weird, interminable PDF from Abercrombie & Fitch that says, "Introduce Fifth Concept"? How else could Zach Baron, Megan Abbott and Sara Gran, and Annie Julia Wyman get me so excited about books (*The Wheel of Time*, *Flowers in the Attic*, and *Mimesis*, respectively) that I otherwise had no interest in reading? The funny thing is, now I have those books but actually prefer the articles about them. That's how good these pieces are.

(4) Confession: even though I helped edit the magazine for eight years, I didn't always have a chance to read every issue cover to cover, thus missing some of the great stuff that my delightful teammates were bringing in. So there are pieces here about which I recall thinking, upon initial publication, Oh that looks really good…, before losing track of them as the grind of daily life took me away. Then there are a handful of pieces here that I don't remember at all but are total knockouts. But I am like that with my own children—I have fathered, by some estimates, twenty-five sons and daughters in three different countries, many named Ed or its variations—Edward, Edna, Edwin, etc.—with certain sources putting that number closer to a hundred and twenty-five (!). It's very likely that Ambien and excessive video-game play contributed to these apparently fecund fugue states, but I will not blame these factors—I am "owning" my problem.

We are excited to share this selection of beautifully mind-bending, surreptitiously smart-making pieces from the second half of the *Believer*'s history to date. They will make you laugh and a few of them will, I swear, break your heart. (You might as well download that box of Kleenex before you start Jeannie Vanasco's "Absent Things as If They Are Present.") The magazine continues to amaze—I can say this objectively now—and I'm confident that in 2020, you will see a third anthology, *Read Hard with a Vengeance*. After that, we'll consult Harrison Ford movies for title ideas—*Edwina! Give your brother his mitt back! No, not that mitt. Not that brother. The other brother, Edmund. I mean Edgar!*

Your friend,

Ed

Manhattan

March 2014

MICHAEL PAUL MASON

THE DISAPPEARANCE OF FORD BECKMAN

DISCUSSED: *Tulsa, The Perfect Golf Swing, Ralph Lauren, Televangelism, Minimalism, Paternal Estrangement, Relentless Artists, German Castles, Cy Twombly, The IRS*

hen the economy sours, news anchors talk of housing and manufacturing, of hedge funds and barrels of oil. They generally don't discuss the lives of artists, and how their careers are crushed into a dull oblivion. If artists survive the fiscal and emotional shakedown, they steady themselves as adjuncts in the Midwest; they design for architectural firms. They take corporate commissions and they sit on city planning boards. They might show up again, but this time in coffee shops or farmers' markets.

Artists fade, but they don't disappear. Not the way Ford Beckman disappeared, at least. Beckman enjoyed heights few artists attain, and then no one in the art world could find him.

When Beckman's name surfaced at showings, it was met with shrugs.

Photograph by Jimmy Bloyed

Dealers scanned floors, looking for Beckman's trademark velvet slippers, which he wore to exhibitions. They'd heard about financial issues, but they knew him as a man of resources. Where, they wondered, was Ford Beckman?

Beckman, now fifty-six, has been hiding in Tulsa, Oklahoma, where, until recently, he has been serving doughnuts for seven dollars an hour. A look into his eyes will tell you what you already know: there isn't a more punishing zero than the sugary naught of a Krispy Kreme Hot Original Glazed. And yet Beckman is emerging, and doing so in one of the worst economic climates of our times. It's a move that he feels particularly prepared to undertake.

To most in the art world, Ford Beckman came out of nowhere, when in fact he had been a lesser star in two different realms: golf and fashion.

Born in 1952, "Clancy" Beckman, as he was then known, was raised in a world of extremes. As a child, he and his brother ping-ponged between their divorced parents. His mother, an artist, lived in a meager two-bedroom bungalow in Florida; his father, "Spook" Beckman, an aloof, gum-chewing radio personality, owned a mansion in Ohio. Early on, Ford found peace in the midst of polarization, and one could argue that he even learned to generate the effect—a rhythm that still dictates his life.

Throughout his adolescence, painting came so naturally to Ford that he didn't think much of it. His art teachers marveled at his propensity for abstract work. Beckman says he has always sensed a complex relationship between colors, textures, and shapes. But instead of yielding to the siren's call of aestheticism, he chose to perfect his golf swing. For years, Beckman practiced daily, and played in junior tournaments all over the world.

Just like his paintings, Beckman is something of a contradiction. He's a heavyset man, yet he gestures lightly and speaks quickly, like an excited teenager. He tells me that in the early '70s, the televangelist Oral Roberts was building an athletics program at his university, and the school offered Beckman a golf scholarship.

"Oral and I used to hit golf balls at night together, up there on campus," Beckman says. "I caddied for him on Saturdays, and he was the real deal. He taught me about faith and it changed my life." Roberts's influence is most apparent in the religious titles of Beckman's work. One of his panel series is called *Holy Ground*. Another later work—a solid white rectangle dividing a yellowed canvas—is called *Salvation Painting: At the foot of the cross: To God Be the Glory*. Beckman employs similarly evangelical titles across a majority of his work; he believes his paintings belong in churches rather than galleries or museums.

His current studio is a large green Dutch barn in Tulsa. It sits off a bypass near the middle of town, backed up against a residential area and nestled among business offices. It's the only building in the area with a gravel parking lot. The ground floor is dark and cluttered with a renovation-in-process, but the top floor is Beckman's brightly-lit studio, a crisp, open space that gives his new series of drip paintings ample viewing room. Some of the works feature Beckman's familiar colors— waxen yellow, slick black. Others are strikingly neon. Several of them have already been sold, one to the Armand Hammer Collection.

Beckman comfortably plants himself in the center of the room with his hands in the pockets of paint-splattered khakis. The series, Beckman estimates, might bring in two or three hundred thousand dollars—less than he would normally command, thanks to a newly depressed market.

While a student at Oral Roberts University, Beckman majored in art, but instead of channeling the impulse onto canvas, he entered the world of fashion. In 1972, he opened a small apparel shop in Tulsa called Clancy's, and took joy in orchestrating ensembles. He married Cynthia Harmon in 1973, and the couple devoted themselves to the business.

Throughout the '70s, Beckman began to experiment with fashion by putting together his own designs. He paired colors like peach and teal; he added stripes to sportswear. The resulting displays grew Clancy's in size and reputation—enough to attract the interest of New York silk dealer Dick Jacobson, who had mentored Ralph Lauren. In 1980, Jacobson arranged a meeting between Beckman and Lauren. The two spent an entire afternoon poring through Beckman's portfolio, which consisted of more than twenty complete lines of fashion illustrations.

"Ralph told me I didn't need to be there, and I wasn't sure what he meant," Beckman recalls. "Then he asked me to stay in New York for a couple days, while he made some phone calls."

Lauren opened doors for Beckman—not as a merchandiser, but as a designer. Within a matter of months, the client representation company International Management Group put Beckman under contract, and for the next eight years managed the licensing for the Ford Beckman label. After relocating to Connecticut, Beckman began visiting European textile mills and creating new patterns and color combinations that designers such as Armani and Lauren snatched up.

Beckman's designs moved beyond ties to full wardrobes, and his label found homes in retail department stores like Bergdorf Goodman, Harrods, Macy's, and Dillard's. In 1986, he was nominated for Cutty Sark's most promising US menswear designer prize—at the time, the fashion world's equivalent of an Academy Award nomination. Beckman estimates that he was pulling in an annual salary of six to seven figures throughout the '80s.

Beckman began painting again, in private, in the mid-'80s, his florid personality oddly gravitating toward the confines of minimalism. In addition to running a business, he was whetting his interest in the art world by collecting. As his fashion fortune grew, he invested in works that appealed to him. He bought sixteen paintings by Jean-Michel Basquiat before the artist's death, as well as a number of pieces by Jeff Koons, Julian Schnabel, and other notables. His art collection was exhibited around the world, and came to be a source of enormous pride for Beckman. It would also one day be the cause of his public undoing.

In 1988, Beckman's paintings appeared at the Craig Cornelius Gallery, in New York. He had opened a studio in Manhattan to work on his art while maintaining his home base in Connecticut for his fashion-world dealings. The idea that an artist could be a businessman in an altogether different industry was still a foreign one, and Beckman thought it prudent to keep his two worlds separate. It proved unnecessary. In 1988, a large textile company called Coloroll acquired Beckman's fashion business in a larger purchase, and it promptly discontinued his line. The Ford Beckman label dissolved, and from the ashes, a new Ford Beckman identity arose.

At the start of his new career, Beckman created *The Black Wall Paintings*, which depict deep black squares against yellowing backgrounds that pour over canvassed plywood platforms. Good minimalist art teaches you subtlety. Beckman's early paintings evoke a tension between antiquity and modernity, expansion and contraction. Layered with up to sixty coats of industrial varnish and lacquer, the heavy wooden squares deliver an austere visual mass.

The Black Wall Paintings caught the attention of Giuseppe Panza, a fastidious collector who was among the first to purchase works by Robert Rauschenberg and James Turrell. As was Panza's custom, his secretary relayed strict instructions for his arrival. When Panza entered the studio, Beckman and all personnel quietly moved to the back of the room, where they would stand in silence, watching Panza inspect each work.

Impressed with the work's human, flesh-like appearance, Panza bought several paintings from Beckman that day, and over the next several years, he accumulated dozens more. While he has given sizable portions of his collection to the Museum of Contemporary Art, Los Angeles, and the Guggenheim Museum, Bilbao, Panza keeps Beckmans in his permanent collection.

Getting bought so deeply thrust Beckman into the limelight of the early '90s art-world scene. Beckman had shows at the Whitney, and his paintings hung alongside those of Andy Warhol and Cy Twombly.

Reviews during Beckman's epic rise in the late '80s and early '90s contain all the promise of a legend in the making: "[Beckman's] work draws heavily on the artist's own self-assurance, and is in this way reminiscent of Julian Schnabel's paintings from the early '80s with their can-do-no-wrong bravado," proclaimed *Art in America*. *ARTnews* raved, "Though Beckman's work is engaged in a dialogue with the past, his paintings prove that powerful and engaging work can still be produced within the world of geometric abstraction."

In the throes of his feverish success, an image appeared to Beckman in a dream one night: a grinning clown. In Beckman's mind, his deceased father, who once performed as a clown, kept blurring into the image. Hours after waking, Beckman began scanning through library books for clown portraits. Finding them, he began the process of exorcising his feelings of paternal estrangement onto canvas, making a radical departure from his austere squares to representational pop paintings. Viewed casually, pop-art portraits depict a merely reproduced image, but closer study reveals the stamped-on figure fading in the viewer's consciousness like a watermark, so that the work's emotional resonance transmits through its backdrop. Beckman's clowns, for example, hover like ghosts over a field of black, from which the dolor of materials such as dirty linoleum kitchen tiles and cheap bedsheets cry out.

In 1991, Beckman produced his first series of silkscreens, none of them bearing the spiritually histrionic titles of his previous work. Instead, to the ire of his dealers, he called the entire series by their reflexive names: *Pop Paintings*. (Given the dream of his father, perhaps *pop* might carry an alternative meaning.) When the paintings premiered the same year in New York, Beckman received a studio visit from the art dealer Leo Castelli—tantamount to a papal blessing—which led to even more hangings throughout the world.

That same year, Beckman took a sizable and private risk. He suspected that his career, like that of every other artist, would fluctuate, and he wanted to protect himself against financial upheaval. He knew that his art collection would provide a buffer against hard times, so he invested heavily in more works to round out his collection. He targeted pieces by David Salle, Jeff Koons, Sean Scully, Keith Haring, and Ross Bleckner, taking out a multimillion-dollar loan to finance the acquisition. Less than thirty days later came what the history books call the art-market crash of 1991, a phenomenon directly attributable, in theory, to a 74 percent drop in Sotheby's shares, as well as a mass exodus of Japanese art investors. Even with the newly acquired paintings, Beckman's collection was now worth only a fraction of what it had been two months earlier.

Every artist saw a major devaluation of their work. It wasn't a lucrative time for Beckman to be popular, but it was an important time. One of Beckman's clown portraits made the cover of the popular German magazine *ART*. He agreed to showings by the European dealer Hans Mayer, who represented Andy Warhol, Cindy Sherman, and other artists. Beckman didn't admit to anyone that he needed the success in order to meet his basic financial obligations. Demand for his work seemed to outpace his prolific output, yet he began to feel commodified by the experience.

It was then, in the early '90s and in the midst of rocketing fame, that Beckman found a close friend in the reclusive Cy Twombly, who had long since achieved recognition as one of the preeminent artists of his time. Through his connections in Rome, Twombly helped Beckman land a big show at the Galleria Il Ponte in 1993.

Time spent with Twombly in Italy introduced a shift in Beckman's work. His abstract *La Roma* paintings reveal a soft luminescence and levity absent from his previous pieces. Shortly after creating the series, Beckman learned that his wife, Cynthia, was pregnant with their first child. He started another set of paintings, *Mon Jardinet*, which feature blooms of warm colors abstractly rising from light backgrounds.

Beckman's friendship with Twombly continued across continents and expanded to include a tight circle consisting of Donald Baechler, Julian Schnabel, and the collector Douglas Andrews. The friends often met in Florida, where Twombly would frequent flea markets for two-dollar purchases that he would transform into million-dollar sculptures weeks later.

Twombly's influence amplified the sense of artistic merit that Beckman craved; his paintings were still being sold in galleries, even though Beckman urged his dealers to pursue placement in museums. At the same time, Beckman was also feeling the pinch of his art-collection loan, and worried that he couldn't sustain the heavy debt if his own sales dropped even slightly. With a daughter on the way, he felt an even greater sense of duty to provide financial security. The predicament gnawed at him until he received a phone call from a virtually unheard-of German art dealer: Adolf von Ribbentrop.

Ribbentrop explained how he had been following Beckman's career with great interest, filling up his mansion with Beckman's *Pop Paintings*.

Hoping to strengthen his presence as a competitive art dealer, Ribbentrop asked Beckman if he wouldn't mind meeting him the next morning.

"He was calling me from Frankfurt," says Beckman, who was in New York at the time. "And sure enough, I went to my studio the next day, and at nine o'clock, there's a knock on my door, and here is a man with a hat on, and his arms are full of gifts."

Enthusiasm was a big part of Ribbentrop's appeal, but so was his generosity. On the spot, Ribbentrop wrote a check for all the works Beckman had available in his studio—about thirty-five paintings—and offered to visit him and his wife in Connecticut. Upon meeting with Ribbentrop, Cynthia Beckman was equally charmed. During the visit, Beckman learned that most of Ribbentrop's clientele came from the German aristocracy, and that he mainly dealt in paintings by modern masters like Picasso and Warhol. More important, he seemed wholly committed to Beckman's work.

"He wanted to buy each one for himself—he was that pure," Beckman says. "That is such a compliment to an artist of any kind. That is what you dream of hearing. And I said, 'Let's do it.'"

Beckman called his other representatives across Europe to inform them he had chosen Ribbentrop, and the response was icy for reasons Beckman guessed were obvious. They had made fortunes from him, he reckoned, and they were mad about being shrugged off.

It wasn't until later that Beckman learned from a friend about Ribbentrop's legacy. His father, Joachim von Ribbentrop, was the foreign minister of Germany and Hitler's most dutiful aide; he was the first politician executed at Nuremberg on October 16, 1946. His son—named after Hitler—was eleven years old at the time. Ribbentrop may not be the most popular person in the art world, Beckman's friend suggested.

In Beckman's spiritual worldview, the sins of a father aren't enough to condemn a son. By visiting Ribbentrop in Germany, Beckman would be able to judge for himself whether Nazi history had morally poisoned the art dealer. When he arrived at Ribbentrop's castle, overlooking the Rhine, Beckman found the family full of warmth and love. More important, they shared common ground in their religious faith. Ribbentrop, pragmatic and earnest, suggested that he and Beckman load a moving van full of paintings and visit his friends.

"And so we start selling paintings, and we go from castle to castle, literally," recalls Beckman. "Dukes, earls—these are serious people." Beckman was pleased to see his paintings sell well over the next several years. The kestnergessellschaft, in Hanover, where Klee, Kandinsky, and Picasso had also made appearances, showcased a Beckman exhibition in 1996, bringing him the level of recognition he had long sought.

Returning to America, Beckman couldn't have been more pleased—that is, until he heard the rumor that Ribbentrop was being denied entry into some of Europe's most critical art fairs. Beckman placed calls to Germany and learned even worse news: Ribbentrop was seriously ill, his family said, and he needed ample time to convalesce. Just when Beckman was poised to become a museum-level regular, he was on the brink of financial mayhem. Paying off his debt required steady income, but Beckman had no product to offer. The majority of his work was tied up in Ribbentrop's inventory.

So began Ford Beckman's dissolution. His former dealers ostracized him. His possessions began to slip away from him. First, he lost control of his beloved art collection, painting by painting, until a bank ultimately acquired the remaining works. Then he sold his home in Connecticut to pay off the outstanding debt. And finally, there was the IRS, which sought its due on the heavy revenues.

The Beckmans moved into an apartment in Connecticut and scraped by on a few meager shows until 2002, when Cynthia's father in Oklahoma became ill. They planned only a short visit, but due to his father-in-law's deteriorating health, Beckman found himself stuck in Tulsa and financially unable to return to the East Coast. Beckman left his remaining belongings in storage there, and aimed to find work in Oklahoma, but the search proved fruitless. What kind of income can a top-tier artist find in a small Midwestern city? Beckman scratched together money from the occasional show in Europe, but the rare royalty checks hardly sustained him. Most of his income was garnered by the IRS.

Despondent and beside himself with stress, Beckman was driving along Tulsa's strip-mall-laden Seventy-First Street in 2005, when he pulled into the city's only Krispy Kreme franchise and filled out an application. Under "previous experience," he simply wrote "artist." He was hired on the spot. For a year and a half, Beckman worked forty hours a week serving doughnuts, then took on an evening shift packing ham at a nearby deli. He had no time to paint, nor the money for basic supplies.

"Well, it was very humbling, when you're working with a bunch of high-school guys, and they're asking you, 'Where'd you come from?' and 'What did you do?' You don't tell them at first," says Beckman. "Well, I did painting. 'What kind of painting?' And you start to talk."

"He paints, like, modern, abstract stuff. I saw some of it on the Internet," said Kimberly Grimes, recalling her months working along-side Beckman. "He was a real whiz with donuts—a real cool dude, too."

Humiliation fathers the reclusive, and Beckman was no exception. He stopped communicating with the art world and left his mail unfor-warded and lines disconnected. Beckman thought he might remain in anonymity, until he was working the drive-through one day in December 2006. An old college pal, Ben Farrell, pulled up to the window and reached for his order. Farrell had followed Beckman's rise in the art world and was flabbergasted to see him in a local doughnut shop. He immediately offered him a job redesigning the offices for his adver-tising agency, and helped Beckman set up a studio in an unused barn he planned to remodel.

Although the salary allowed Beckman to quit Krispy Kreme and the deli, the hardships persisted. Six months into his consulting work, on May 25, 2007, Beckman suffered a massive heart attack at a Tulsa restaurant.

Fortunately, a woman sitting nearby was a nurse and responded immediately. Beckman regained consciousness in the ambulance, but the experience alarmed him. "Your body can only take so much pres-sure," Beckman says.

Soon after, Beckman suffered what he considers a final emotional devastation. The IRS held a public auction for all of his remaining items in storage—forty crates in total—and raised about two hundred thou-sand dollars. Beckman lost his personal treasures—gifts from friends, furniture, even his clothing and his library. (Today, he still owes the IRS, but the debt is only a fraction of what it once was.)

The art world is once again in financial upheaval—the worst since 1991. The Mei Moses All Art Index estimates a 35 percent drop in sales this year. In the middle of the turbulence, Beckman stands undaunted and productive. He walks a few steps into his Tulsa studio, turns, and faces a large work, a six-and-a-half-foot-square drip painting. Drip works are a litmus test for a painter because they reveal so much about an artist's maturity and skill. Beckman's piece has a surface texture as smooth as a printed poster, a subtle boast that contributes to its contained but balanced gyroscopic whir.

"What you see here is that the black has now exploded," Beckman says, pointing to *Rhythm Painting #1*. The famous black square is gone, replaced by swirls of black paint looped over a glazed, yellowing background. It looks heavy and solid, and although the painting appears to be moving, it also seems to have captured a moment in Beckman's evolution as an artist and his journey as a human. His *Black Wall Paintings* depicted a psychological pressure that gave rise to the tortured *Pop Paintings*. Then came the intimate *Mon Jardinet* and the *La Roma* works, exuding the kind of warmth and conviction brought about by companionship and fatherhood. Beckman's new work is that of a mid-career artist who has been severely tested. His *Rhythm Painting #1* evokes uncertainty and discomfort, or a chase between unraveling and becoming.

"All my paintings are self-portraits," Beckman says. ✷

ZACH BARON

THE END OF THE STORY

DISCUSSED: *Comical Hats, Tertiary Characters,*
Conan the Barbarian, The Dark One,
Typologies Within Typologies, Moral Predicaments,
Braid-Yanking, Rhapsodies Over Brocaded Silk,
Arcane Metaphysical Theology, Clark Gable

Robert Jordan, born James Oliver Rigney Jr., in 1948, sold more than 40 million books in his lifetime. His Wheel of Time series, a still-unfinished multivolume epic spanning, at last count, thirteen books, more than 10,500 pages, and approximately 3,734,312 words, is among the world's most popular fantasy series since J. R. R. Tolkien's *Lord of the Rings*. You would have every reason to expect this level of authorial accomplishment to be accompanied by an onset of false modesty—the one-sentence life story, say, graven casually on the back flap of a dust jacket. Yet in nine of the eleven Wheel of Time novels Jordan wrote before his death, in 2007, we're presented with the portrait of a man looking to get lucky at a Renaissance Faire:

Robert Jordan was born in 1948 in Charleston, South
Carolina, where he now lives with his wife, Harriet, in a
house built in 1797. He taught himself to read when he was
four with the incidental aid of a twelve-year-older brother,
and was tackling Mark Twain and Jules Verne by five. He
is a graduate of The Citadel, the Military College of South
Carolina, with a degree in physics. He served two tours in
Vietnam with the U.S. Army; among his decorations are the
Distinguished Flying Cross, the Bronze Star with 'V,' and two
Vietnamese Crosses of Gallantry. A history buff, he has also
written dance and theater criticism. He enjoys the outdoor
sports of hunting, fishing and sailing, and the indoor sports
of poker, chess, pool and pipe collecting. He has been writing
since 1977 and intends to continue until they nail shut
his coffin.

Jordan's biography is typical of his work: verbose but vivid, tenden-
tious but still somehow charming, and threaded throughout with equal
parts valor and invention. (Pipe collecting, after all, was not a sport until
Jordan made it one; nor, for that matter, was Robert Jordan a fantasy
author before Rigney rescued him from a prior career as an explosives
expert in Hemingway's *For Whom the Bell Tolls*.)

Real-life combat experience is something that Jordan, a former helicopter gunner (he claimed to have once shot a rocket-propelled grenade
out of midair), shared with Tolkien, who witnessed all but one of his
closest friends die in World War I. But where the don of modern fantasy
boasted a dusty, Oxford-certified facility with language, philology, and
the Middle Ages, Jordan made himself over after Vietnam in the classic
mode of the American genre-fiction author. A bearded man with a pen-
chant for elaborate canes, chunky rings, and comical hats, he favored the
look of a Southern general. He admitted to being a Freemason. At Q&A
sessions, he would not hesitate to interrupt a small child's incorrect pro-
nunciation of a tertiary character's name. He wrote the series for which
he became famous in an old carriage house cluttered with swords, axes,
crossbows, spears, knives, and a human skeleton.

In 2006, Jordan became sick with a rare blood disease called cardiac amyloidosis—a condition in which misshapen proteins, produced in bone marrow, come to be deposited in the walls of the heart. Faced with a median life expectancy of only four more years, Jordan channeled *The Good, the Bad and the Ugly*'s Eli Wallach, writing on his blog: "Don't talk to me about no stinking odds, gringo. I've got promises to keep."

What promises? After a post-Vietnam career that included a stint as a nuclear engineer, an early foray into historical fiction, under the pen name Reagan O'Neal, for publisher Tor (where he was first edited by Harriet McDougal, who would later become his wife), and three books' worth of pinch-hitting in the house's Conan the Barbarian series, Jordan began the Wheel of Time series in 1984. He'd pitched Tor on a six-book cycle. A little over twenty years later, when Jordan received his diagnosis, he was at work on the Wheel's twelfth volume, and seemingly no closer to finishing the series than he had been a decade earlier. Rigney's bio suddenly looked all too prophetic. They nailed shut his coffin the next year.

"I can almost *feel* that moment, standing and holding the book in my hands, listening to someone play an antiquated upright of Cadash in the background," read the online eulogy penned by a then thirty-one-year-old Brandon Sanderson, a burgeoning fantasy novelist and former Mormon missionary. He was talking about his first encounter with the Wheel of Time, which he stumbled upon in a comic-book store. "The cover screamed epic," he recalled. McDougal, now a widow, was in the midst of a search for a replacement when she read Sanderson's tribute online.

In this, as in most matters relating to the couple's happy marriage and the books it produced, she had her husband's blessing. Jordan, who once spoke so cavalierly about dying with a pen in his hand, had come to realize, at the end of his life, that his series needed a resolution, whether or not he was around to write it. His treatment left him strong enough to work two hours a day, and Jordan skipped ahead, wrote the series's final paragraph, then began working backward. In his last weeks, when his strength failed him entirely, Jordan summoned his family to his deathbed and narrated aloud the fate of a world he knew he wouldn't live long enough to realize. They made tapes for posterity. In September 2007, eighteen months after first receiving his fatal diagnosis, Jordan was buried at Charleston's Saint Stephen's Church. McDougal wore one of her husband's black, wide-brimmed hats to the ceremony. The Citadel sent a bagpiper. In the graveyard parking lot, his family gathered around Jordan's Porsche and listened solemnly to Samuel Barber's *Adagio for Strings*. The memorial program read, "He came like the wind, like the wind touched everything, and like the wind was gone." Once Jordan's assembled friends, family, and admirers finally cleared out past her home's dragon-carved gates, McDougal grieved. Then she went looking for a writer to finish what her husband had started.

After stumbling across Sanderson's wonkily sincere paean to Jordan ("You go quietly, but leave us trembling," the younger author had concluded), McDougal picked up one of his books, read forty-five pages, and fell asleep. But when she awoke, she later told the *Charleston City Paper*, "All the book's elements were perfectly clear" in her mind. Sanderson had the job.

Brandon Sanderson was born in 1975. His young-adult exploits, as he recalls them now, consisted mostly of piling up rejection slips for the seven fantasy novels he wrote while at Brigham Young University (where his roommate was the soon-to-be famous *Jeopardy!* champion Ken Jennings), and serving as a missionary for the Church of Jesus Christ of Latter-day Saints in Seoul. His dense first novel, *Elantris*, was brought out by Tor, Jordan's publisher, in 2005; *Mistborn: The Final Empire*, the book that McDougal read, came out in 2006, and was followed by two sequels, another stand-alone epic, *Warbreaker* (2009), and a series of books written for the young-adult market. A Wheel of Time reader since age fifteen, Sanderson initially reacted to McDougal's offer with skepticism, followed by stuttering. Later, he wrote her an email that began: "Dear Harriet, I promise I'm not an idiot."

His first spoke in the Wheel of Time, and the series's twelfth, came out in 2009. To write it, Sanderson had to contend with a character count that, by the time McDougal handed over the books to him, had climbed well into the high double digits. Jordan's heroes were spread out across more than fifteen different nations, each with its own intricate cultural mores, political systems, styles of dress, and ways of speaking, occupying regions vaguely recognizable as feudal England, eighteenth-century France, contemporary Tibet, and imperial Japan. (In a letter, Jordan once instructed a correspondent to read the slurry accents of one warlike people from across the ocean as if they came from Texas.) Knights in body armor straight out of the Middle Ages ride to battle alongside Native American–style warrior societies that shun horses and swords in favor of stealth and spears. In a city called Bandar Eban, citizens eat with chopsticks (*sursa*); in the nearby state of Tarabon, the men favor fezzes.

Not content with the standard dwarf-elf-mage fantastic calculus, Jordan also invented Green Men and gentle giants, ferocious desert clans, roving pacifist bands of Gypsy-like Tinkers, a magic-wielding female-centric nation-state, foxes who wear human skin, and a race of people who look and sound like snakes. Arrayed against the Wheel of Time's heroes was an almost comically infinite variety of evil: half-human Trollocs, eyeless Myrddraal, vampiric Draghkar, slavering Darkhounds, soulless assassins called Gray Men, thirteen Forsaken (powerful humans who serve the Dark in exchange for eternal life), and, perched above them all, the Dark One himself, sealed away at the moment of creation, and trying to break free ever since.

Then there were the still more esoteric kinds of knowledge a Wheel of Time author was expected to be fluent in. A scene involving magic might include gateways, balefire, skimming, shielding, inverting, delving, "Deathgates," fireballs, and lightning. That most basic unit of the fantasy novel, the sword, developed in Jordan's hands every bit as many codified forms as it did in twelfth-century Japan: "The Falcon Stoops," "The Creeper Embraces the Oak," "The Moon Rises Over the Lakes," and so on. Even Jordan's typologies had typologies.

Proust, you imagine, would've been spared the indignity, should he have expired after *La prisonnière*, of having someone else attempt

La fugitive. But Sanderson's Jordan imitation, when it was published, in 2009, wasn't bad. Like most writers in his genre, Sanderson's own books tended to fly by in a blur of action and curt, expository dialogue. Consequently, despite the complexity of a world the author had had very little time to master, Sanderson's Wheel of Time debut, *The Gathering Storm,* accomplished in 765 pages what it typically took the more garrulous Jordan three or four books to do.

For those who had grown attached to Jordan's characters, the emergence of a successor was a mixed blessing: it was a relief to find ourselves on our way to something recognizable as an ending, after two decades of waiting. At the same time, it was hard not to wish we were headed there with the people with whom we started the journey—Jordan very much included—and not their sometimes indifferently written, fast-talking facsimiles.

In the early going, Jordan explicitly patterned his story after Tolkien's *The Fellowship of the Ring.* In place of the Shire, Jordan created a town called the Two Rivers, an allusion to the two real-life tributaries, the Ashley and the Cooper, that meet in Charleston, near Jordan's South Carolina home. His Frodo was a teenage shepherd named Rand al-Thor; his Merry and Sam, Rand's two best friends, Mat Cauthon and Perrin Aybara. In the first book, *The Eye of the World*, a Gandalf figure named Moiraine Damodred—an Aes Sedai, in Jordan's parlance, gifted with the ability to "channel" the One Power, a mystical force that underlies all life—arrives just ahead of the forces of evil and takes our heroes away from home, likely for good. Rand, as he comes to find out, can channel as well, though the male half of the One Power is tainted, and thus fated to make those who use it go mortally insane. This would become the series's defining theme: the poison needle lurking inside the gift.

To create his main character, Jordan drew from a long and varied history of fantastic archetypes: Jesus, King Arthur, the Fisher King, Luke Skywalker, the one-handed Norse god Tyr. In the books' mythology, Rand emerges as the latest iteration of a soul that's immortal, a hero destined to be spun out again and again as the light's champion in times of need. Known as the Dragon Reborn—after his immediate predecessor from an earlier age—Rand is, like those who have come before him, fated to die in order to save the world. From the bit of prophecy Jordan uses to open the series's second book, *The Great Hunt*: "Like the unfettered dawn shall he blind us, and burn us, yet shall the Dragon Reborn confront the Shadow at the Last Battle, and his blood shall give us Light. Let tears flow, O ye people of the world. Weep for your salvation."

Blood, salvation, eternal life in posterity. Though he couldn't have known it at the time, Jordan had written his own mortal predicament into the Wheel of Time. The series's most poignant paradoxes—the taxing wear of responsibility on those who influence the weaving of the world, death as precondition for redemption—seeped into Jordan's real life at its end, as he belatedly faced a mockingly close approximation of the same ambivalently grim fate as the characters he wrote about.

Throughout the novels, Mat, the trickster and gambler of the group, favors the same sort of funny hats—and pitched battles—that Jordan did. Perrin, with his stolid temperament, beard, blacksmith's shoulders, and fierce, proud wife, can be read as the series's closest physical and romantic analog for its creator. But it's Rand's path that Jordan ultimately walked. Both men labored to succeed in spite of bearing an affliction that would presumably kill them; both faced an uphill battle to the finish—Rand, to unite the Wheel of Time's various nations and peoples against the forces of evil, and Jordan, in his last eighteen months, to get Rand's story on paper before it was too late.

Most heartbreakingly, Jordan slowed the pace of his novels down to a crawl toward the end, as if keeping his imaginary world alive might keep him alive, too.

Weaving the ever more complex strands of plot and characters was a task that increasingly defeated the Wheel of Time's author. Simultaneously, his fictional proxy's early triumphs (pulling an Excalibur-like sword from a fortress called the Stone, killing about one bad guy per book) shaded, in time, toward the ambivalent, the incomplete, and the downright disastrous. As the series wore on, the pace of the installments became sluggish as Jordan's attention divided. His main characters, Rand foremost among them, began disappearing from the books in which they were ostensibly the heroes. In one notorious instance, the tenth book in the series, *Crossroads of Twilight*, began, chronologically, in the middle of the ninth. Jordan then followed those two volumes with 2004's *New Spring*, a prequel.

At the time, this combination of events nearly sparked a full-scale rebellion in the millions-strong community of readers who were used to waiting patiently for up to four years for the emergence of the next book—and who in exchange expected the series to move forward, not backward. Said one typically disaffected critic, *SFSite.com*'s William Thompson, on the release of *Crossroads of Twilight*: "After several thousand pages of buildup, Robert Jordan has arguably abrogated his side of the bargain, leaving his audience stalled in details and descriptive sidles that have done little to move his primary plotlines forward, despite promises that the series is nearing a conclusion.... One must assume that the author had desired something more than being remembered only as having written the longest story in genre history."

This moment—roughly, books seven through ten (*A Crown of Swords, The Path of Daggers, Winter's Heart*, and *Crossroads of Twilight*), plus the prequel—is arguably one of the most bizarrely boring stretches in any kind of contemporary fiction. Rand dallies with a lover, and deals with various tepid rebellions, humdrum political complications, and distant foreign incursions. Mat, a lothario and gambler who at this point has emerged as the books' most entertaining character, gets stranded in a city and hangs out there. Perrin, whose wife is captured by an unfriendly army in the eighth book, spends the next 1,600 pages or so trying to get her back. Together, the four books are a study in inertia, and they prompted many to suggest that Jordan was intentionally drawing out the series for cash or, worse, that he had absolutely no idea how to end what he'd begun.

But though it is absolutely true that these two thousand–plus pages could've been compressed by an editor less kind than his own wife into a single book, it would be wrong to suggest Jordan dilated this series out of avarice or lack of preparation. The problem was that Jordan's strengths as a writer were also his weaknesses. He abhorred instrumental characters, the stock pawns of the genre, there to be set up and knocked down to move the plot along. And he hated being obvious, choosing instead to subtly foreshadow plot developments whole books in advance (then ridiculing readers who couldn't quite put the pieces together). Most of all, Jordan loved his own creations, good and evil alike, and wrote circles around them, developing their respective psychologies and romantic entanglements at what became a laughably immersive, infinitesimal pace. The rest of the world, he seemed to be saying, would just have to wait.

In fact, it ended up outlasting Jordan himself.

Despite the Wheel of Time's impressively vast mythological scope (Christianity, Arthurian legend, Buddhism, Norse mythology, and Japanese samurai culture, for starters) and strange, emergent parallels between its author and his characters, there remain a few major barriers to entry. Some of the bulk of Jordan's novels can be attributed to the breadth of the storytelling; much of it is the result of sheer, mindless, infuriating repetition. In the Wheel of Time, people tend either to faint, vomit, or burst out laughing at any significant dramatic turn. A big nose is pretty much the guarantee of an evil man. Literally hundreds of wine cups are inadvertently destroyed as characters receive bad news and then look down to see liquid slopping over the ruins of the goblet they've just crushed. Tics—braid yanking, maintaining an expressionless face, dry-washing of the hands—harden into characterizations by sheer virtue of being mentioned so many times.

Even more problematic, Jordan possessed an understanding of women so bankrupt it would make a seventh-grade boy weep. It was admirable that he tried: Jordan's heroes were as liable to be female as male—more so, even—and most of the societies he depicted were either matriarchal or, at worst, equal opportunity.

But Jordan's women do a lot of "sniffing," usually loudly. They cross their arms under their breasts. Men to them are "wool-headed lummoxes" or "wool-brained mules." (A disproportionately high number of women in the Wheel of Time are also lesbians—make of that what you will.) Jordan was not above describing rivals for the same man as "two strange cats who had just discovered they were shut up in the same small room." That is, when he wasn't making Borscht Belt jokes about their bad cooking, or spending pages describing their dresses. (In this respect, Jordan put romance novels to shame: the Wheel of Time without a doubt holds the record for inexplicably extended rhapsodies over brocaded silk, embroidery, hemlines, and necklines.) Mostly, what Jordan's women are is the same: some combination of cold, willful, quick to take offense, and—around the right man—weak in the knees.

Jordan was never anything but unapologetic. "I've seen a lot of comment, apparently from men, that my female characters are unrealistic," he once wrote. "That's because women are, for the most part, consummate actresses who allow men to see exactly what they intend men to see. Get behind the veil sometimes, boys, and your hair will turn white. I've been there, and mine went white and didn't stop there; a great deal of it actually turned dark again, the shock to my system was so great. Believe me, I mild it down so as not to scare any males into mental breakdowns." This is as indicative as any other passage Jordan penned regarding women: he seemed to regard a healthy mix of fear and condescension as a decent proxy for respect, and left it at that.

Sanderson, once he decided to take the job, was a blessing as far as females in the Wheel of Time went. His own Mistborn trilogy has a woman as its main character, and Sanderson is patently more familiar with a feminine psychology that flesh-and-blood humans might actually recognize. In Sanderson's hands, Jordan's women stop scolding each other and their men so much, fuss less about their wardrobe, and generally behave like rational adults rather than spoiled children. It is a relief to finally like the other half of the characters you've spent twelve books with.

So why read four million words about arcane metaphysical theology, battle after battle, the mundane, angst-ridden thoughts of hundreds of people you don't know, and sex scenes that involve sentences like "He cupped the back of her head and barely had the presence of mind not to finger her ear"? The vast majority of Wheel of Time fans will wax nostalgic for the first three novels of Jordan's trilogy, each of which is a comparatively compact, self-contained marvel of storytelling. The fourth book is the first to carry an ongoing arc into the next volume. After that the characters begin to spread out and, in some cases, stop accomplishing all that much; the pacing grinds to a halt entirely by the time we reach the infamous seven-through-ten stretch. But that still leaves the eleventh book, *Knife of Dreams*, the last Jordan wrote before his death. And it's this final volume, according to one devoted reader—who has lived with the Wheel of Time since childhood and the series's first book, and who has bought each successive sequel on the day that it came out—that is Jordan's unlikely masterpiece, and justification enough for what's come before it.

The book is the Wheel of Time's most frankly romantic installment: Mat, who has emerged from the last four novels to make an escape from an invading army, has taken Tuon, the heir to that army's throne, hostage. Both were told separately, long ago, that they were fated to marry one another. But they fight prophecy and each other with all the verve of Clark Gable and Claudette Colbert in *It Happened One Night*. Mat calls Tuon "Precious"; she calls him "Toy." They exchange gifts, insults, and test one another relentlessly; eventually, they save each other's lives and, at the end of the book, wed.

The absurdly huge scope of Jordan's series delivers on its promise at the exact paradoxical moment it starts taking seriously the individuals at the heart of the books. Mat and Tuon's belated union trumps the furious battles, wide-screen set pieces, and epic clashes between Dark and Light it takes place among, precisely because of how long the union took to arrive—through all the delays, detours, and dallying their creator increasingly couldn't resist. Part of the magic of Jordan's last effort derives from sheer relief at the resolution of several long-running plotlines. (Perrin finally recovers his wife; Rand finally moves to forge peace with the army he's been battling for the past three books; and so on.) But there is also, in the microcosm of Mat and Tuon's romance, the thrilling rekindling for readers of a long-dormant wish: that the books never end at all.

Once so focused on the end and the coming cataclysmic clash between an overarching good and a gathering, implacable evil, Jordan came to write his most stirring scenes with just one or two people in the frame. The end readers have anxiously awaited for twenty years is revealed to be a kind of MacGuffin—better a perpetual present in which Jordan, his characters, and his world live on than a speedy resolution and the subsequent loss of it all.

This, of course, is not an option: Jordan is gone. With him go the finely detailed characters it took thousands of pages for their own author to even begin to understand. The books roll on—*Towers of Midnight*, the series's thirteenth and penultimate book, is due in November. The series's final installment, *A Memory of Light*, was published in 2013. Inside the novels, time is circular: "There are neither beginnings nor endings to the turning of the Wheel of Time," goes the incantation that has opened each book since Jordan began the series more than two decades ago. But outside the Wheel of Time, time is an arrow headed only one way—into a future in which Mat, Perrin, Tuon, Rand, and the rest of Jordan's characters must live on without their creator. The ending will mean less without all of them there to see it. ✶

SUSAN STRAIGHT

TRAVELS WITH MY EX

DISCUSSED: *The Scholar, The Baller, The Baby,*
A Favorite Phrase, The I-91, Feets and It-Z-Bits,
A History with Cops, The Land of Uncool, A Large French Poodle,
The Short Blond Mom, Braids, Revenue

Southern California in mid-July. My ex-husband and I were headed to Huntington Beach because that's where The Baller, a shooting guard who'd been playing basketball since she was seven, wanted to celebrate her eighteenth birthday.

(We have three daughters—herewith known as The Scholar, The Baller, and The Baby.)

"I hate Huntington," I said. "My least favorite beach."

"I didn't want to go either," my ex-husband said. We were driving behind my van, the dark green Mercury Villager I. Today my van was packed with teenagers. Behind the wheel was The Scholar. Next to her, The Baller. In the backseat, The Baby, along with Neka, one of our daughter's high-school teammates. And in the middle was Bink, another

Illustration by Tony Millionaire

former teammate, and The Baller's boyfriend. We call him our Laurie. My house, full of my little women (though they are all taller than I am), has for years seen various successions of boys who have tried to be the equivalent of Louisa May Alcott's Laurie. This one seems close. Our Laurie is willing to sit on the couch with all three girls and any attendant girls and watch *She's the Man* or *Fired Up!* He cooks for himself. A lefty quarterback, he throws the tennis ball accurately and untiringly for the dog. His favorite phrase, uttered with deadpan sympathy: "That's unfortunate."

"Look at this traffic," I said. "This is why I hate going through Orange County."

The I-91 freeway. Four lanes *each way*, often the most congested in the nation.

My ex-husband and I have known each other since the eighth grade, when he was a basketball player and I was an ex-cheerleader. (My mother had run me over, accidentally, with her own 1966 Ford station wagon, effectively ending my career two weeks after it began.)

I looked at his foot on the gas pedal. He hardly ever wears sandals. Regulation boots at his corrections officer job. Size fourteen. When we were in high school, and he was an All-County power forward, one of his nicknames was Feets. Mine was It-Z-Bits. He's six-four and weighs 305 pounds. I'm five-four. 105.

We have been divorced now for twelve years. But we still see or speak to each other almost every day. Where we live, in the easily jeered-at Inland Empire, we know countless ex-couples like us. Whether it's because we can't afford to move away after we divorce, or we're just too lazy to dislike each other efficiently and permanently, it seems to work.

The Scholar would be a junior at Oberlin, and this summer received a research fellowship at Cal Tech. The Baller would start USC in weeks, with nearly a full scholarship. The Baby had just won a DAR (Daughters of the American Revolution) award for her history scholarship at her middle school.

But that's why I was broke. Two kids in college. A California economy in shambles. My upcoming pay cut: 10 percent. Feets: 14 percent pay cut from the county juvenile institution.

He works graveyard. That meant he'd slept for two hours, after spending the night watching two teenage boys charged with a gruesome murder.

By 2 p.m., we'd gone about thirty miles in traffic that was now, unbelievably, stop-and-go. We talked about how many police cars we'd seen that summer, how everyone we knew was getting tickets, how The Scholar and The Baller had both gotten their first citations this year under dubious circumstances. "Revenue," Feets kept saying. "The state is broke. They have to make money, and it has to be on us."

A California Highway Patrol car drove past us on the right, then pulled alongside the green van. The cruiser slowed, at the rear of my van's bumper, and then pulled back up to the side and hit the flashing lights.

"What the hell?" I said.

"He's pulling her over," my ex-husband said, resigned. "Of course he is. Car full of black kids in the OC."

The patrolman was shouting at The Scholar through the loudspeaker. My ex-husband said, "I'm going, too. He's not gonna pull any shit. I'm not having it."

My husband has a history with cops. He's the six-four Black Guy, the one that fits the description, the one who was seen carrying the shotgun earlier, the one the gas station attendant saw and accidentally stepped on the silent alarm, the one who "attacked" a campaign worker in Pittsburgh, the one who carjacked Susan Smith, the one you make up, but in reality the one who gets out of his car to help a woman change a tire and she nearly falls into a ditch, she runs away so fast.

"He better not mess with her," my ex-husband said.

"It's D——," I said. That's Our Laurie's name. "He's gonna make D—— get out of the car."

Our Laurie is the six-five Black Guy, the one with elaborate braids under his New York Yankees cap, the one wearing size-thirteen shoes and a South Carolina T-shirt because he'd just gotten a scholarship offer from the Gamecocks, the one who'd returned only the day before from the high-school All-American basketball camp in Philadelphia, the one with brown skin almost exactly the same shade as my ex-husband's, the one we tease our daughter about because she always said the last thing she ever wanted to do was replicate my life.

* * *

"Where you from?" one officer yelled at us, and another held the barrel of his shotgun against Feets's skull, pushing it farther and farther until the opening seemed to be inside his ear, under his huge Afro. It was August 1979. Westwood, California.

"Where you from? Where's your license? Where's your car? Is it stolen? Why are you here? Why aren't you in Riverside?"

We'd driven eighty miles from Riverside, the land of uncool, of orange trees and dairy farms and a tiny downtown. I was ready to begin my sophomore year at USC. Feets played basketball for Monterey Peninsula College, and our friend Penguin was a line-backer for a junior college in Riverside County. After the beach, they wanted to cruise the streets of Westwood, the paradise we'd seen only in movies.

Feets wore tight khaki pants, a black tank undershirt, and a cream-colored cowboy hat on his big natural. Then two police cruisers sped onto the sidewalk where we walked, blocking our path. Four officers shoved us against the brick wall.

I remember how it smelled.

He was their target, I realized quickly. Power forward. His shoulder blades were wide, dark wings; he was spread-eagled against the wall.

He fit the description.

"A black man with a shotgun and a cowboy hat was seen threatening people at UCLA," one of them shouted.

The cop who'd taken me aside looked at my license. "Why'd you come all the way from Riverside to LA? Where's your car? Whose car is it? Does your mother know you're with two niggers?"

Penguin was talking back to the cops, refusing to give them his license, and I thought they were going to shoot Feets. Through his ear.

They said a few more things to him, things I couldn't hear. They lowered the shotgun. He lowered his arms. They told us to find our car and leave L.A. "Go back to Riverside!" They said they'd follow us, and that if they saw us walking again, they would shoot on sight.

The patrol car shadowed us as we walked. My boyfriend walked slowly, slightly ahead of me. I knew he was afraid of the bullet that might still come, if he moved wrong. We went back to where we belonged.

What did the highway patrolman want? The Scholar had been going thirty-two miles an hour, between stops. She had always signaled.

"The right taillight's going out again," my ex-husband said.

"My seat belt is still broken," I said.

My ex-husband fishtailed in the dirt of the shoulder, trying to pull ahead of the van and the cruiser. The patrolman was yelling louder, his voice echoing off our door. "Ignore the white truck!" he shouted.

"Pull behind him!" I shouted.

"No, then he'll get scared!" my ex-husband was shouting.

I knew what he thought: if the officer got scared, he might shoot us.

The Scholar stopped, and the cruiser stopped, and my ex-husband accelerated and went around one more time, a terrible dance which wasn't funny but it kind of was when the highway patrolman leaped out of his vehicle then, agitated, staring at us, holding both arms wide in the air, saying, "What the hell?"

He had reddish blond hair, big shoulders, sunglasses.

He looked straight at me, and frowned. And that was good.

Oddly, this summer I read *Travels with Charley*: John Steinbeck, riding in his truck, named Rocinante, with a camper shell on the back, with his large French poodle, named Charley, who is "bleu" when clean, which means black. When they hit New Orleans, a man leans in and says, "Man, oh man, I thought you had a nigger in there. Man, oh man, it's a dog. I see that big old black face and I think it's a big old nigger."

Once Feets and I were camping across the country in a different truck—a blue Toyota with a camper shell—and we spent an uneasy hot night in McClellanville, South Carolina. At dawn, he got up and took a walk beside the Intracoastal Waterway. While we slept, the campground had filled with hunters. I lay in the camper, and from the open window near my head I heard a father say to his young son, "See that big nigger?

That's a big nigger, right there. When you get older, I'm gonna buy you a big nigger just like that."

I never told Feets exactly what the man had said. I just said there were scary people here and we should pack up and leave. We did.

If there's anything scarier than Fits the Description, it's Routine Traffic Stop.

The names or faces we've learned over the years. A brother in Signal Hill. Rodney King. The Baller's basketball coach's brothers, *both* of them. My younger brother's best friend. Shot nineteen times in his white truck as he maneuvered on the center divider of the freeway, having refused to pull over. He might have been high. Either hung up on the cement or trying to back up. No weapon. A toolbox. He'd just delivered a load of cut orangewood to my driveway.

"I ain't getting out," Feets said. He had his hands on top of the steering wheel.

"I know! I'm going," I said. I needed to get my wallet.

"He better not mess with her," he was saying.

"I'm going!" I said. We both knew it was my job. I bent down to get my pink leather tooled wallet. My job is to be the short blond mom. At school, at basketball games, at parent-teacher conferences, in the principal's office when a boy has called The Baby a nigger and the male vice principal sees my ex-husband—BIG DOGS shirt, black sunglasses, folded arms the size of an NFL linebacker's, and a scowl—and looks as if he'll faint.

My job is to smile and figure out what's going on.

By the time I got out of the car, the patrolman was looking at me, and The Scholar was pointing at me.

The traffic roared past on the freeway, twenty feet away from the silent weigh station. I took my sunglasses off and felt my mouth tighten. Who had smiled like this? (A foolish smile that angered someone. Custard inside a dress. What?)

"Why did you stop? What are you doing?" the cop said loudly at me.

"That's my mom and dad," The Scholar said, aggrieved. She wasn't scared. She was pissed. Her default setting.

"We're on our way to the beach for a *birthday party!*" I said, cheery and momlike. "Her dad and I didn't want to get separated, 'cause in this traffic we might never see each other again!"

The little women hate when I do this. They imitate me viciously afterward. They hate that I have to do it, and that I am good at it.

"What's the problem?" I asked. "Is it that darn seat belt?"

(Who smiled like this?)

The officer squinted at me, then at the van.

"One of the male passengers wasn't wearing his seat belt." But then he said drily, "He's wearing it now."

He asked for license and registration and insurance, and I made jokes about how deep in the glove compartment the registration might be, and I pulled the insurance card from my wallet, and the registration was outdated and he glared at me but went back to his patrol car.

The Scholar started a low invective about California's urgent need for revenue, and I leaned into the window to say to our Laurie, "You weren't wearing your seat belt? You always wear your seat belt!"

He said, "It wasn't me. It was Bink."

Bink is darker than he is, nineteen, wearing her hair tucked into a black cap, wearing a huge black T-shirt. She rolled her eyes, furious.

"He's coming back," someone said. The officer approached the other side of the van. "I need the male passenger to open the door. Open the door," he said.

Bink opened the door slowly.

He asked Bink for her license. He didn't let on that he'd thought she was a guy. He didn't ask her or our Laurie to get out of the car. I stopped having visions of people lying on their faces in the dirt. He wrote the ticket, our Laurie looked straight ahead, at The Scholar's hair, and The Baller looked straight ahead, out the windshield, and I knew Feets was watching in the rearview without moving. I stood awkwardly near the driver's-side window until it was done.

It wasn't until that night that I felt my mouth slide over my teeth again and I remembered. A foolish, dazzling smile. Custard.

Toni Morrison's novel *Sula*. The mother and daughter are on a train traveling from Ohio to Louisiana, and when the white conductor berates them for being out of the Colored car, the mother smiles at him, a placating, unnecessary show of teeth, and the black passengers hate her, and her daughter is ashamed of her custard-colored skin, and her weakness.

About twenty miles earlier, outside Corona, I'd been telling my ex-husband what I'd heard three days ago. I'd given one of our many nephews a ride home after football practice, with The Scholar. We'd spent a long time in the driveway of my father-in-law's father's house, talking to two of his brothers, three cousins, and a family friend. There is always a crowd in the driveway, because the house is not air-conditioned, and the beer is in a cooler, and there are folding chairs, card tables, and stereo speakers hung on the wrought-iron supports for the carport. It's the nerve center of communication for the entire neighborhood.

We talked about the newspaper article about the police review of the 2006 shooting of our coach's brother. The commission had found no fault, though the brother was pulled over three times in thirty minutes, the first time because "he had a weird look" and the second time because after the patrol car continued to follow him, he ran a stop sign and made a U-turn. The official report said he had struggled when the officers attempted to put him in the back of the car for questioning. Witnesses said he was trembling, his hands shaking, and that the officers said they were arresting him. His brother had been shot by deputies when he was very young. One officer said the man's brother reached for his Taser; the other officer shot him. The witnesses, who spoke mostly Spanish, said the man's brother did not reach for the Taser.

Mr. T, a friend, said he'd been pulled over this year in the mostly white neighborhood where he'd lived for a decade. The officers said he fit the description of a robbery suspect. He gave them his ID. The suspect was described as six feet, 185 pounds, and in his thirties. Mr. T is five-eight, rotund, and in his sixties. He was told to get out of the car and lie on his stomach on the sidewalk. He refused repeatedly, and was kept there for over an hour while the officers berated him and asked him questions.

One brother-in-law was stopped while riding his bicycle to work at 5 am. He is a custodian at the community college. He was told drug dealers often use bicycles now. He was given a ticket for not having reflective gear. The father of a basketball teammate was made to lie handcuffed in his own driveway for an hour by city police, who'd been called because his neighbors didn't recognize him when he sat on his block wall. He was wearing sweatpants, working in the garden. He is an LAPD officer. Every single friend and relative in the driveway had a story.

The Baller got her first citation earlier that year, in January. The highway patrolman followed her for five miles on the highway and had her pull over into the parking lot of a strip club. Our Laurie was in the passenger seat. He was questioned at length, about his identification, his address. The patrolman didn't believe that he was seventeen. When our daughter called me, she was crying. She said she was afraid of what I would say.

She was right. I was furious, but not about the ticket. "When you get pulled over, you put D—— in danger!" I shouted at her. "You're risking his life. Don't drive even four miles over the speed limit! He could have been shot and killed!"

Only some mothers say that to their children.

It took two more hours to get to Huntington Beach and find a parking space.

The six-four Black Guy and the six-five Black Guy arranged themselves on chairs. They were surrounded by us and six more girls on the blankets now, friends of The Baller's, eating chicken and watermelon and cupcakes.

Feets didn't go into the water, as he usually did when the girls call him the whale and, even now, try to jump on his back. He read and dozed. He had slept two hours.

Our Laurie went into the water. He was alone for a long time, the farthest out in the powerful waves of that day, and because he was so tall the water reached only his chest.

Feets had a huge natural. We used to stand in the mirror together, back in 1979, and with his ancient, tiny black blow dryer I did my hair like Farrah Fawcett and then he blew out his Afro.

His hair is short now, with a lot of gray, under his ballcap.

Our Laurie always has braids, under his ballcap. It's the braids that make people nervous. The hat. The long shorts. The intricate tiny braids that his mother makes every week, that cross his skull in complicated patterns and just touch his shoulders.

The Baby said, "Why does everyone make fun of watermelon and fried chicken anyway? Why did people always talk about Barack and watermelon?"

The Scholar said, "Oh my God, could you be any more annoying? Learn your history, OK?"

"Why don't you ever eat watermelon, Daddy?" she asked him.

"'Cause it's nasty," he said. "Just like green peas. They made me eat it when I was a kid, and I ain't a kid now."

He was slumped in his chair, half-asleep. His feet were covered with sand.

When I was pregnant with The Scholar, everyone in the driveway teased us. "You got size-five feet and he got them size-fourteen boats. What the hell is that baby gonna look like?"

Who said it? Him, or one of his brothers? Or did I dream it? "What if it's a short baby with his feet? It'll be like one of those plastic clowns—you can punch it and punch it and it'll pop right back up, on them cardboard feet."

That night, he called at eleven fifteen. He was on shift. "They make it back OK?" he said, quietly, anxiously, in the echoing vacuum of the cement walls.

We had left the beach in his truck after only two hours. He had to sleep before work.

"They came back about forty minutes after we did," I told him.

"For real?"

"I guess they got cold," I said.

Maybe they had been nervous. We didn't talk about it. "You working security?" I said. "You gonna fall asleep?"

He said he had court calendar, making the schedule for juvenile offenders who would be escorted in in the morning. He has to shackle and prepare them. He'd already told everyone at work about the seat belt. A lot of coworkers had gotten tickets this summer. "Revenue," he said. Then he said, "I just wanted to know they made it back," and hung up.

I stood in the kitchen doorway. Our Laurie was on the couch, with the little women heckling him while he took out his braids, which were full of sand. They had never seen his shoulder-length curls before, and they kept trying to take pictures with the cell phone. ✶

MOLLY YOUNG

SWEATPANTS IN PARADISE

DISCUSSED: *Nice Girls Who Like Stuff, Abercrombie & Fitch, One-Armed Push-Ups, California Adolescence, Weed, The Redemptive Quality of Sensory Exploration*

1.

I t is sometimes possible to define the depth of an experience by means of how radically it slows or hastens your sense of time. Swimming, fighting, nightmaring, enduring a migraine, having sex: these are all activities that move at exceptional rates. Shopping, too, and if you don't believe me, just enter a mall before sundown and see how you feel a few hours later when you reemerge into darkness. Depending on your mien and mood, this reemergence will feel sharply good or bad. The shopping wormhole affects everyone differently.

My father and I drove the other day to a mall in downtown San Francisco in order to exchange a pair of velour pants. San Francisco Centre contains more than 170 boutiques and is built like a gastropod

Photograph by Rebecca Smeyne

shell with spiraling escalators and a white interior. There is a concierge and a family lounge. In some ways it's a fancy mall, but mostly it is like any other mall, with a food court and a lot of bathrooms and the smell of Bath & Body Works fragrances colliding in midair. "I feel like a robot," my dad said as an interactive map guided us to the correct store. All around us were young men and women moving slowly, and I was reminded of the fact that malls function secondarily as retail centers and primarily as promenades for people under thirty-five. Coupled or single, male or female: it doesn't matter. A day at the mall reveals display behavior as colorful as anything you'd see on safari.

We passed two chocolate boutiques and a place called The Art of Shaving on our way to the pants store, which was packed with shoppers and decorative jugs of candy. Painted in curly letters high on the wall was the phrase FOR NICE GIRLS WHO LIKE STUFF. While I waited for a new size of pants to be retrieved, I thought about this statement of purpose, and how blurry it was, and how accurate in its blurriness. FOR NICE GIRLS WHO LIKE STUFF exactly summed up the feelings of anticipation and anxious self-regard that a mall coaxes from shoppers. I thought of horoscopes and fog and mingling crowds while waiting for the pants to come out. Vague things. I felt united with every other customer in the mall, committed as we were to the promenade. It was soothing and stimulating at once.

This feeling, the communal purpose and the sense of display, points to what a mall has going for it that a website, for example, does not. A mall has the sound of music, the smell of Cinnabon, the knowledge of a shared experience, the social excitement of seeing and being seen. It is a place of latent sexual promise; the teenager's alternative to a bar. It is FOR NICE GIRLS WHO LIKE STUFF. People dress for the mall like they dress for a date.

2.

When I zipped into my velour outfit for the plane ride back to New York, it felt good, like wearing a caterpillar. Throughout the flight home I thought about the malls I was leaving behind and the mall-like stores that lay ahead of me in Manhattan. Bona fide malls do not exist at the center of New York City, but mall-size stores do, and of these there is one in particular—a new one—that interests me. I learned about it through a friend who had gotten stoned, wandered inside, and entered the shopping wormhole. She called me in San Francisco and said I should go straight to the Hollister Co. flagship store as soon as I got back to New York, and to go alone, which I did.

The Hollister store sits at the corner of Broadway and Houston Street in SoHo, a forty-thousand-square-foot block full of California-themed apparel. Topless men and girls without pants stand at the entrance, some wearing zinc oxide smeared across their noses. The employees are selected for their insane good looks and friendliness, which creates the disorienting customer experience of receiving attention from people way out of your league over and over again. You can't avoid having a sexual experience at Hollister, even if it's just to stare at a greeter's bullet-hard nipples. Hollister's strategy may not be subtle, but it is clever. By literalizing the mall's sexual promise in actual naked flesh, the brand makes it unnecessary for shoppers to wander elsewhere. Rather than provide the neutral spaces of food courts and lobbies for promenading, the store offers a prefab (and make-believe) environment of sexual opportunity. It's the whole mall in one store!

There is a name for this tactic. Abercrombie & Fitch, which owns Hollister as well as the abercrombie and now-defunct Ruehl brands, is among a growing corps of stores intent on targeting a customer's in-store experience as the main vehicle for its brand promotion. Abercrombie's 2009 annual report describes a shopping experience designed to stimulate "senses of sight, sound, smell, touch and energy by utilizing visual presentation of merchandise, in-store marketing, music, fragrances, rich fabrics and its sales associates to reinforce the aspirational lifestyles represented by the brands."

In practice this means a few things. It means that the Hollister store on Broadway is cramped and dimly lit, with narrow wallpapered rooms converging at a mezzanine lit up with live projections of Huntington Beach (waves waist-high and closing out). It means that a low-output fog machine pumps mist from the rafters while potted palms obstruct the floor at random places, both ingenious ways to slow down foot traffic.

The store's official theme is "EPIC," and this is also the name of the brand's newest men's cologne, which hangs thick in the air. Things to buy at the store include distressed cargo pants, sweatpants embroidered with VARSITY CLUB SURFERS, sweatshirts designed to look like Spicoli's drug rug, and flip-flops on sale for $11.90. The tags on the women's clothing say BETTYS and the men's tags say DUDES. Music is a big deal at the store, almost a physical presence. A customer-service rep named Danielle told me that company policy dictates that the in-store music should hover between eighty and eighty-five decibels. (The level at which sustained exposure may result in hearing loss is ninety to ninety-five decibels.) The actual store soundtrack is unrecognizable yet generic; it is the music heard from the cars of popular kids in high-school movies.

3.

The real Hollister is a small California city in San Benito County, about forty miles inland, just west of Interstate 5. In 1868 it was named for Colonel W. W. Hollister, who drove a flock of sheep across the country as early as 1851. The land was considered sacred by the Chumash Indians and is currently known for its business-friendly environment and mild winters. Though Hollister Co. displays the year 1922 on its logo, the brand was in fact launched in 2000 in Columbus, Ohio. It is not clear why 1922 was selected as Hollister's origin point. Many things happened that year, none related to logo sweatpants: the Eskimo Pie was patented; Ernest Shackleton died; Hungary joined the League of Nations. If I had to guess at the significance of 1922 regarding Hollister, I'd point to three events that also occurred that year: the California grizzly bear was declared extinct, Helen Gurley Brown was born in Green Forest, Arkansas, and a meteorite landed near Blackstone, Virginia. In these three events we have the death of something authentically Californian, the birth of a woman who would encourage sartorial expressions of sexuality, and a random occurrence that no one could explain.

If Southern California surf culture is Hollister's guiding mythos, it is odd, too, that the company should have named itself for a town twenty miles inland with declining home sales and greater-than-average earthquake activity. Did a lot of thought go into the choice? Or possibly none at all? It could be that "Hollister" just sounded more marketable than the nearby towns of Chualar and Molus. A fake testimony delivered by an imaginary dude on the Hollister website confirms the authenticity of the brand and its flagship:

> I headed out to SoHo to see what the EPIC Hollister store was all about. Born and bred in Southern California, I was curious to see what's up. As soon as I came in I was like—oh, this is gonna be big….
>
> Everyone who works there is hot as hell––it looks like how you wish everyone looked on the beach. No grumpy old ladies screamin' at kids. The place is hooked-up, it's got everything. Dude, it's pretty spot-on to SoCal…. I got all mesmerized.…

But as its name suggests, "spot-on to SoCal" is exactly what Hollister isn't. What overwhelms a visitor more than the completeness of the flagship's fantasy is its specificity, first, and then its confusing lack of origin. To what movie, location, or lifestyle is Hollister referring with its potted plants and surf gear? How come we recognize it? Why is it cool?

4.

After I went to the Hollister flagship store for the first time, I woke up in the middle of the night, not sure whether I'd been sleeping or just lying prone long enough to feel like it. I got out of bed, turned on my computer, and opened a quarterly report for Abercrombie that I'd down-loaded earlier in the week—one of those million-page PDF files that you avoid on the desktop for days until moments like the one at hand, when factors of concentration and boredom align into a PDF-reading mood.

When I opened the document, I saw that it was not a quarterly report at all but some sort of marketing memo from 2007, seemingly origi-nating with Abercrombie but posted on Wikipedia without a source. Inside were bulletins about the company's financial performance and initiatives, including one designating ten million dollars for louvers and new signage. The document was illustrated with ad-campaign photographs and a picture of a bus. It contained bullet-pointed statements with nouns capitalized strangely, as though translated from German. For the quarter's accomplishments it listed:

- Introduce Fifth Concept in January 2008
- Currently implementing Core Retail Merchandising System
- Assembled strong and talented development team

and:

- Very excited about the business; great potential

I read the memo from start to finish and retained nothing, possibly because it meant nothing. But it meant nothing in relation to a retail giant with net sales in the billions and flagship stores in New York and London. What did it all mean? I went back to sleep.

5.

In 2008 IBM released an executive brief called "How Immersive Technology Can Revitalize the Shopping Experience." It outlined in lists and sidebars the future of shopping, and it accompanied a pair of stereoscopic goggles at that year's National Retail Federation Convention & Expo in New York City. The goggles were introduced as an in-store amenity that would allow customers to enter a 3-D virtual world when they visited their favorite store; for example, by viewing "a fashion show from Europe complete with music and smells," where, as a model walks down the runway, "her perfume will be noticeably in the air." IBM's brief poses the following questions:

> Do individuals feel like your brand is relevant to their lifestyle? Do they understand the value of your brand experience over the commoditized products that you are selling? Or, as they wander from store to store, do your potential customers forget your brand as it blurs in their minds with those of competitors?

The solution IBM proposes to these problems is immersive retail, a strategy that aims to destabilize a current trend in consumer behavior that management advisers call *commoditization*. Commoditization describes the circumstance in which consumers care only about an item's price, perceiving no other difference between competitors. For retailers like Hollister—brands that produce basic items of OK quality for not-cheap prices—commoditization is an unfriendly concept.

Immersive retail is also a way to counter the allure of online shopping, which boils down to its convenience (what you need: an Internet connection and a finger) and privacy. Stereoscopic goggles are a prediction that convenience and privacy will soon fail to be sufficient inducements to spend. IBM describes the goals of immersive retail the way a party planner might envision a successful bar mitzvah, aiming for a "memorable, interactive and emotional" experience full of "personalized dialogues." The paper explains that immersive retail "is more about involving the customer than it is about the merchandise." It is about shirtless male employees miming one-armed pushups on a rack of distressed jeans, yelling, "That's what I'm talkin' about!" and "Party at my house!" on a script every ten minutes. It's about filling a store with club chairs and issues of the *Surfer's Journal*, and about belly-button piercings that glint in the lights. "For stores in many retail segments to stay ahead of competitors," the brief explains, "they will need to generate the excitement of a theme park ride—and become a destination." Immersion retail presents clothes in the environment in which they are putatively designed to be worn, telling customers exactly what a product is supposed to mean.

6.

I do not think I am alone in recounting my teenage years in terms of things bought and the hopes invested in them. As a teenager in California, I wore sweatshirts and tight jeans like the ones Hollister sells, feeling always slightly paler and less experienced than the Kelseys and Jennifers of the world, as though the number of boys I'd hooked up with (zero) was embroidered across my trucker cap for all to see. These feelings rise anew when I enter the Hollister store, and I know why: despite its missteps, the brand nails certain aesthetic truths about my home state.

I attended community college with girls who resembled beta versions of the store's employees. To Mass Communications 110 they wore garments that insisted on comfort and conveyed the sexiness of total relaxation: sweatshirts, sheepskin boots, and thongs bisecting the slice of tanned upper butt that rose from low-cut jeans. It was a look of lazy, hygienic sexuality. The hottest girls always had brand-new socks, for example, and this was a key detail.

I'm lucky that I coincided with the trend. For one thing, it was an equalizing force. At a school made of both moneyed slackers and teenage mothers, the wealthy girls shopped at the same places as the non-wealthy girls. The former might have collected Tiffany bean pendants at home, but in the classroom it was possible for everyone to look basically the same.

Weed was another great equalizer. It is hard to overstate the importance of weed as a determining factor in the lives of West Coast teenagers. Weed was the reason girls selected clothes based on fuzziness, the reason boys sounded dumb, the reason we inflected every sentence as a question and used *like* and *you know* as phatic communications. In an era of T9 input, text messages begun with *I* would automatically fill in *mstoned*. Anyone familiar with the dim and spray-scented bedrooms of a weedy adolescence will recognize in Hollister's decor an environmental proxy of the average Friday night. Weed may not be for sale at Hollister, but its exigencies are everywhere.

One place we liked to visit while stoned was an interactive science museum in San Francisco called the Exploratorium. The Exploratorium is geared toward children but designed to be fun for adults, too, like a Pixar movie. It is vast, educational, and filled with exhibits that let you electrocute a pickle or dissect a cow eyeball. Inside the museum lies a geodesic structure called the Tactile Dome, which was introduced in 1971 as an experiment in sensory disorientation. The Dome is small, "about the size of a large weather balloon," and contains a three-dimensional labyrinth of pitch-black passages. A user takes off her shoes at the entrance, crawls through tunnels, climbs up a rope wall, and shoots down a slide into a pit of beans, all without the use of her eyesight. The passageway has thirteen chambers and no right angles, and various objects (keys, rubber toys) are hidden along the passageway for visitors to identify by touch. An early press release explained that visitors to the Dome "have compared the experience to being born again, turning yourself inside out head first, being swallowed by a whale, and, inevitably, being enfolded in a giant womb." The maze takes about ten minutes from start to finish and stimulates both fear and lust, each arising from the heightened sensuality of short-term sightlessness. The final descent into beans is Dionysian.

Dr. August F. Coppola, a scientist,[1] and Carl Day, an architect, are the men responsible for the Tactile Dome. They spoke of the project at its inception as part of "an art revolution which uses people as participants" rather than "as targets at which to hurl artistic messages." The press release explained that both men "believe the revolution, if successful, will greatly affect not only art, advertising and industrial design but even life styles and basic beliefs."

With nothing to see and only one direction to go, the Tactile Dome offers the purest antidote I can find for immersive retail. It stokes the senses where Hollister dulls them; it offers ecstasy followed by self-reflection rather than headache. I don't doubt that Hollister's dulling effect is strategic. Engineers of immersive retail must understand that we buy things when we are bored and not when we're excited, alive, and metaphysically horny—that these feelings are just promises to get us in the door. Hollister is dark, sexy, and stimulating, but it won't turn your head inside out. The store has no slides and no rope nets, only stairs and emergency exits. And there is no bean pit at the end. ✷

---

1. Coppola is the brother of Francis Ford Coppola and the father of Nicolas Cage. The November 4, 2009, obituary in the *San Francisco Chronicle* notes that "Professor Coppola was often referred to as someone's relative. But his own charisma and immense intellect left lasting marks on California and on San Francisco." It continues, "Fascinated by touch and its taboos—he told the Exploratorium that 'the first commandment in life is given: "Don't touch"'—Professor Coppola's exhibit [the Tactile Dome] made touch mandatory. He later wrote *The Intimacy—a Novel*, about a man who interacts through touch."

ANNIE JULIA WYMAN

A GLIMPSE OF
UNPLUMBED DEPTHS

DISCUSSED: *Fearless Graduate Students, Astroturf,*
Essential Inner Forces, Embarrassed Glee, Tintin in Tibet,
Swashbuckling, The Old Testament, Glittering Sobriety,
Spiritscience, Don Quixote's Questing Turkish Universities,
X-Men, Books with Long Titles

I.

Mimesis: *The Representation of Reality in Western Literature*: a relatively long title for a very long book. A pretty long, pretty boring, typically colonified title redolent of the very boring-est academic writing (boring at least for those readers who don't have a professional interest in, for example, *Insuring the Industrial Revolution: Fire Insurance in Great Britain, 1700–1850*, or even, somewhat more excitingly, *The Buried Book: The Loss and Rediscovery of the Great Epic of Gilgamesh*). There are those of us who claim not to be terrified by such titles, fearless graduate students that we are—since our careers usually depend on producing them—but the fact remains that most readers and writers secretly despise them. They seem to signify not

Illustration by Tony Millionaire

only overspecialization but some kind of hideous buildup, an intricate, inescapable clotting in the way we think and communicate to others what we're thinking about.

So I was terrified by *Mimesis*, its title and its heft, fearless Stanford graduate student that I was—and the fact of the matter is that the thing stuns me still. It is the very longest, most dignified, patient, and heart-rending work of intellect and soul I have ever encountered. Hyperbole may be the preserve of the young writer, a condition of semi-adolescent spirit not unlike that of a high-school quarterback pointing up at the Big Man in sheer giddy idiocy after the last-minute game-winning touchdown, when the floodlights in the podunk stadium still look like burning stars and the Astroturf still feels like the surface of an enormous planet whose inhabitants have been allowed, oh my god, an unfathomability of valor, of excellence for which one's heart could not ever be prepared—but in this ephebe's opinion Erich Auerbach earns his superlatives. His book is not a planet, Astroturfed or otherwise. It is a universe.

The range and the depth of Auerbach's argument are staggering in and of themselves. In just over five hundred pages he attempts a coherent account of the stylistic mechanisms operating behind the written depiction of human life from Homer to Virginia Woolf.[1] Along the way he hits the Old Testament (Genesis), Petronius, Tacitus, Ammianus, Ovid, the New Testament (Jerome, Job), Augustine, the *Chanson de Roland*, a handful of Provençal stories about Adam and Eve, Dante, Boccaccio, Rabelais, Montaigne, Cervantes, Shakespeare, La Bruyère, Racine, Saint Simon, the Goncourts, Schiller, Goethe, Stendhal, Balzac, Zola, Proust—to name only those to whom he dedicates at least half a chapter. Plus he reads them in their original language (Greek, Latin, Provençal, Old

---

1. He goes about this flabbergasting business armed with two main concepts: (1) *figura*, in which literary characters and situations represent—are *figures* for—larger human/ intellectual/spiritual truths that require the reader's interpretation (very, very broadly, this is how Auerbach thinks most Western literature works—it asks us to interpret, it makes *figuring things out* the essence of reading—which is a result of the religious/intellectual/historical impact of Christianity), and (2) the ongoing collapse and commingling of high and low styles throughout Western literary history (the more various, the more inclusive the style and the social and cultural subjects treated by that style, the more realistic any literary representation of human life will be).

French, Spanish, English, German, etc.), and he keeps at least one eye on each writer's cultural and historical context.

The goal of this massive erudition is, simply put, to better understand what it means to be alive—what truths, what hardships, what triumphs are specific to as well as shared by each moment of human existence. In life and history as Auerbach sees it, universal meaning "must not be sought exclusively in the upper strata of society and in major political events but also in art, economy, material and intellectual culture, in the depths of the workaday world and its men and women, because it is only there that one can grasp what is unique, what is animated by inner forces."

But I can't pretend that Auerbach's argument—whether in its granularity, its sweep, even its fundamental relation to the development of all kinds of progressive literary criticism after World War II, both inside and outside the academy—is why I wanted to write about *Mimesis*. The book is almost never taught anymore, even in comparative literature departments, though the more famous chapters are sometimes anthologized. Ideas about universal meaning and essential inner forces—about humanism, anthropocentrism (both not so much universal as Western), etc.—have taken their rightful knocks. Most people, academics or otherwise, don't believe in them anymore.

Why write about *Mimesis,* then? Well. It's just that I am very afraid that these days no one ever says—sort of offhandedly but with the kind of stiff sweet embarrassed glee one might bring to the recounting of a first kiss, even a lost virginity—"This book gave me joy."

II.

I read *Mimesis* as part of an independent study in literary criticism that can't be written anymore—the kind of seemingly eccentric, electric performances that thinkers as diverse as William Empson and Roland Barthes and Theodor Adorno left as their gifts to what has since become a much stodgier discipline. I was in the last quarter of my masters program, I was overloaded with other work, and if it hadn't been for my weekly foray into the strenuous glimmering of *Seven Types of Ambiguity* or *Minima Moralia*, I might have gone under.

But as might be obvious from the first paragraph of this essay, when the time came I was less than excited to crack open my Auerbach. My professor—a straw-haired, round-shouldered mutterer whose eyes sometimes started up from his desk or the wall or whatever he was staring at and sparked at the same instant that his head set itself to bobbing like mad and words came out of him that just shocked the perception—had for once deadened my enthusiasm. We'd just finished *S/Z*—which brags the briefest, sexiest title in the semiological canon—and now I had a week to plow through another *Something: The Somethingness of Something-Else at Some Historical Moment or Another* when I was already reading four or five of the same in other seminars. With *Mimesis* I was expecting to do no better than plow, than underline and dogear and then mutter through our session without ever lifting my eyes from my notes.

Or I would have done those things, if Amazon could have sent me a copy in time. My professor assigned it a week or so in advance of our regular Thursday meeting, but then it was some kind of school holiday and then I wanted to visit some friends in Los Angeles and then there was some movie I wanted to see (*X-Men Origins: Wolverine*) after that and then all of a sudden I sat down to order the book and realized it was Monday. I had three days.

The Stanford library had two copies of *Mimesis*—one uncirculating, one checked out until November of next year. The San Francisco Public Library had two as well. One was missing. The other was a third printing from 1971, also uncirculating but fifty miles closer to my apartment than the Stanford copy; it lived with the other valuable tomes in the Special Collections Room on the sixth floor of the main branch on Grove, up near where the light streams in pure and somehow fragrant through the apex of that nautilus dome. The Special Collections Room is an unbelievable treat, a secret; it is almost always empty and silent and still, save for the gorgeous bursts of color on the naked pages of the illuminated manuscripts in the glass cases lining the aisles.

An old librarian with two pairs of reading glasses dangling from her neck brought me my decidedly unfunny tome (I write *unfunny* because the book is cataloged in the Schmulowitz Collection of Wit and Humor, which I can't even begin to explain). I had a double handful of sharpened pencils—special collections rooms around the world have the best free pencils—and a notebook. I cleared my throat—I don't know why I always clear my throat before beginning to read silently, but I do—and then a little boy, maybe seven years old, came in and asked the librarian, "Can I see all the *Tintin*s?" This old woman grumbled a little and then brought him out a stack of treasures as tall as he was and he sat down near me and began reading aloud.

His voice was high and piercing and he made no effort to keep quiet. The librarian, who had taken out a pack of cards and was playing solitaire on her desk—I wanted to say, you know, your computer can do that for you, and much more discreetly—was totally oblivious. It was all I could to do to keep myself from heading over to the boy and leaning down and saying to him, *Excuse me, but this is supposed to be a quiet room, so I'm very sorry but can we just skip to* Tintin in Tibet, *the one with the teddy bear and the pickax and the lost Chinese friend and the St. Elmo's Fire? That's my favorite and we've got only a little while before somebody else comes in here and gets huffy and tries to shut us down.*

But such pleasures would have to wait for another, sweeter afternoon when swashbuckling—not *The Representation of Reality in Western Literature*—was the order of the day. I flipped open *Mimesis* and fiddled with the flyleaf. *Onionskin.* I turned the page. *Eight-point type.* I squeezed my eyes shut and then fixed them on the first word of the many, many, many thousands before me.

Auerbach begins by differentiating between the bright, neat articulations of Homeric style and the deep mystery of the Old Testament. By the third page, I knew that I was in rare company: Auerbach reads like a writer; each word, each sentence, each syntactical swoop and stop is scrutinized for its effect and reproduced in an effortlessly complex prose.[2]

On page three or so, he describes the *Odyssey* as follows:

---

2. *Mimesis* has been translated into English from the original German only once, by Willard R. Trask, in 1953. No one has seen fit to revise Trask's translation, since it is both incredibly readable and very faithful.

The separate elements of a phenomenon are most clearly
placed in relation to one another; a large number of
conjunctions, adverbs, particles, and other syntactical tools,
all clearly circumscribed and delicately differentiated in
meaning, delimit persons, things and portions of incidents
in respect to one another, and at the same time bring them
together in a continuous and ever flexible connection; like the
separate phenomena themselves, their relationships—their
temporal, local, causal, final, consecutive, comparative,
concessive, antithetical, and conditional limitations—are
brought to light in perfect fullness; so that a continuous
rhythmic procession of phenomena passes by, and never is
there a form left fragmentary or half-illuminated, never a
lacuna, never a gap, never a glimpse of unplumbed depths.

This is good, I thought. Um, this is real good. The contours of that sentence wrap perfectly around its content; the "procession of phenomena" described in Homeric Greek reemerges in Auerbach's syntax, persisting even through translation from German into English. The first list—an oh-so-orderly menagerie of the parts of speech—links so neatly with the second, with an almost giddy exhibition of every possible relation between those parts of speech. Together they precisely form a "continuous and ever flexible connection." The fluidity of the thought, its glittering sobriety! And the coyness—what provocation, to end a sentence about clarity with "a glimpse of unplumbed depths."

The little boy kept reading and I kept reading, too, and his voice rose up and around the manuscripts in their glass houses and I touched not one of those sharpened pencils for three hours.

III.

Back in the first half of the twentieth century there were people on this planet who could read seven or eight or twenty languages. These were the philologists, mostly German and Austrian, recipients of the finest gymnasium educations—which, of course, conjures up the sheer feats of athleticism performed by literal gymnasts. *In the center of the field house, Auerbach performs an entirely new interpretation of Chaucer on the much-pounded floor of Middle English criticism. Then, on the tangly rings of British modernism he gives us a series of hermeneutic somersaults rivaled only by yesterday's magnificent flip-flops along the narrow, leathery beam that is Tacitus.*

Auerbach and his philologist friends practiced what was called *Geisteswissenschaft*—in Edward Said's rather clunky phraseology, "knowledge of the products of mind or spirit." A better translation might be simply "spiritscience." *Geisteswissenschaft* is a kind of semi-intuitive, semi-intellectual activity requiring supreme academic preparation in linguistics and historical context. Etymology is at the root of the philological, mind-spirit-knowledge-o-logical endeavor—literally, to *love* the language so well that its smallest particles blossom into a more integrated, complex understanding of work, author, and world.

Emily Apter, a NYU professor of French and comparative literature, calls this "word histories as world histories," but it is also, essentially and perhaps most interestingly, a coupling, a friendship, a love relationship. As Said writes, the long-dead author and the insanely brainy philologist become "friendly, respectful spirits trying to understand each other" in "sympathetic dialogue… across ages and cultures."

This isn't as fluffy as it sounds. It's refreshing, even, when so many humanities programs, particularly at the undergraduate level, have taken to defending literary criticism as a science—when teaching students to "analyze" has become more important than teaching them that literature is worthy of love. And, of course, true love can be nasty—Auerbach dubs Ovid "full of fear, lust and silliness," and takes Cervantes to task as an inferior craftsman, implying that perhaps the most famous novel of all time was, in terms of social realism, a huge step backward, since it does no work to critique or even portray in any detail the brutal feudal system that makes Don Quixote's questing and Sancho Panza's toadying possible.

Nor is *Mimesis*—despite those heartwarming love relationships, despite the excellence of the prose—an easy read. Each chapter begins with either a long excerpt from a primary text followed by a translation, or with a short historical preamble immediately followed by a long excerpt from a primary text followed by a translation—Auerbach always forces the reader to immerse herself in the writing in question before he begins his own reading. *Here,* he seems to be saying, *what do you think?* This is at first flattering, seemingly very generous—but after two or three chapters it can induce severe nail-chewing and frowning and other such symptoms of intellectual despair. Let me say only that it very quickly became apparent that I do not possess the makings of even the most junior philologist. Approaching, say, a chunk of Shakespeare, I had to work myself up to my own amateurish conclusions, all the while knowing they were going to be blown apart.

But if, as heretofore claimed, Auerbach is such a great writer—so magnificently capable of complexity and clarity in the same breathless instant—why would he allow his readers such insecurity? Leaving even the bravest reader on uncertain footing thirteen times, at the beginning of each new chapter, is certainly not the way to tempt anyone through five hundred pages—unless that anyone is a lonely, self-conscious young someone at the top of the SFPL, someone who remembers that books are, as Sartre said somewhere or other, long letters to unknown friends, and clings to that half-remembered, probably misremembered maxim as a sign that by falling silent from time to time, Auerbach offers his readers—his friends—not insecurity but profound respect; taken with a little confidence, a little grit, the book reveals itself as a bracing dialogue between Auerbach's and our own experience of literature.

Which is obvious—but there's more to it than that. At the end of *Mimesis,* Auerbach admits that "a systematic and complete history of realism" would have been "impossible" and labels his own language, even in its patient complexity, a system of "unusual and clumsy terminology." *Only connect,* said Forster, and insecurity, lacunae, uncertainty are exactly what make us feel the urgency of his command—it is only at the edges of such a self-induced muddle, when all is clumsy, amateurish, impossible, and our reassuring conclusions are blown apart, that we feel we are or can or need to be a part of something larger, some higher system. Unplumbed depths must surround the blaze of the lights above—so that we can look up and judge their glory, wince at their brilliance, point skyward.

IV.

"For if it is true that man is capable of everything horrible, it is also true that the horrible always engenders counterforces and that in most epochs of atrocious occurrences the great vital forces of the human soul reveal themselves: love and sacrifice, heroism in the service of conviction, and the ceaseless search for possibilities of a purer existence."

Auerbach did, in fact, know everything horrible—much more horrible things than a lonely somebody for whom Tintin and *Howards End* represent meaningful indices of personal identity. Auerbach's world, like ours, was one in which human beings seemed intent on proving just how much inhumanity they were capable of. The seeming naïveté in the passage above is a direct, life-affirming response to world war and to atrocity, a word that means not so much these days unless the people who use it know, as Auerbach did, how to speak—or who at least try to speak—joy when they feel it.

In 1936, Auerbach arrived in Turkey to take over the direction of the University of Istanbul from Leo Spitzer, a friend and fellow philologist. At the time, Atatürk's modernization projects were in full swing, the westernization or Romanization of higher education included. In 1933, a Swiss flunky named Albert Malche had been given the task of evaluating Turkish universities. He reported that they were backward, inferior, etc., and recommended a new university system with professors from "Berlin, Leipzig, Paris or Chicago." Hundreds of invitations were sent out across Europe; most of those who accepted were Germans and Austrians—including Spitzer and Auerbach—displaced by the rise of the Third Reich.

Auerbach was an exile, a German Jew who found himself in a land not quite Western, not quite Eastern. He had been cast out by burgeoning German nationalism, then had been granted by burgeoning Turkish nationalism a measure of security and the opportunity to teach. Auerbach never exactly reconciled his position at the University of Istanbul with that particular paradox (unlike Spitzer, who eventually wrote a long, moving essay on how much he loved learning Turkish). Auerbach led groundbreaking work in Western philology and advised students who were working on Eastern literature, but he never learned the languages they spoke. Perhaps this is a sign of prejudice, but the fact remains that Istanbul, where *Mimesis* was written, was not his home in any sense of the word. His mind and his heart lingered somewhere behind him, a thousand miles to the west.

Various scholars have various ideas about how difficult an experience exile might have been for Auerbach; Istanbul during and after World War II was a cosmopolitan capital, an East–West crossroads frequented by the likes of Béla Bartók, Bruno Taut, Leon Trotsky, and, later, James Baldwin, Sir Steven Runciman, and Michel de Certeau. But the fact remains that *Mimesis* expresses a deeply felt lack—of resources, of community, of a beloved homeland and culture now overwhelmed by murder and indifference to murder. Odysseus, *the* epic wanderer, opens the book, and is immediately joined by Abraham, who earns Auerbach's most tender treatment: "It is as if, while he traveled on, Abraham had looked neither to the right or left, had suppressed any sign of life in his followers and himself save only their footfalls."

Mimesis's epilogue is often called melancholic, and rightly; Auerbach lists almost all his book's flaws, catalogs all the critical tasks he should have liked to undertake—and then writes: "But the difficulties were too great…. I may also mention that the book was written during the war and at Istanbul, where the libraries are not well-equipped for European studies. International communications were impeded; I had to dispense with almost all periodicals, with almost all the more recent investigations, and in some cases with reliable critical editions of my texts. Hence it is possible and even probable that I overlooked things which I ought to have considered.…"

If Auerbach had had access to more books, perhaps his work would have been more thorough. Perhaps he would have been able to include scads and scads of helpful footnotes and could have initiated an extended engagement with other critics and the reams and reams of scholarship on each of the authors he chose. "On the other hand," he writes in *Mimesis*'s penultimate paragraph, "it is quite possible that the book owes its existence to just this lack of a rich and specialized library." He explains that if he had had the opportunity to read everything that had been written on the texts he chose to examine, he "might never have reached the point of writing." (The book's epigraph is Andrew Marvell's yearnsome "Had we but world enough, and time.")

Plainly put, *Mimesis* is a monumental, doomed effort—but it is my feeling that its failure is also its essence, its force, the gravity that secures its magnificence. It is a world, a universe of bright articulation and semi-submerged darkness—monumental and also a momunent. Without some deep loss—represented by the immolation of Jewish culture in the Third Reich, the growth of fascism, and Auerbach's own immersion in an unfamiliar world—such a work would not be possible.

On the last day of my time with *Mimesis*—the third day I spent up near the top of the nautilus dome in the silence and screaming color of the SFPL Special Collections—I made it to "The Brown Stocking," Auerbach's chapter on *À la recherche du temps perdu* and *To the Lighthouse*. The Proust excerpt he chooses is one of the more famous, perhaps second only to the thing about the cookie and the maiden aunt. The young narrator, suffering from one of his typical bouts of neurasthenia, wants his dear mother to tuck him into bed one last time. He stands in awe before his tyrannical father—who has just, quite surprisingly, allowed the boy's mother to sleep in his room to quiet him—on the staircase of their family home:

> *Je restai sans oser faire un mouvement; il était encore devant nous, grand, dans sa robe de nuit blanche sus le cachemire de l'Inde violet et rose qu'il nouait autour de sa tête depuis qu'il avait des névralgies, avec le geste d'Abraham dans la gravure d'après Benozzo Gozzoli que m'avait donné M. Swann, disant à Hagar, qu'elle a à se départir du côté d'Isaac.*

> I stood there, not daring to move; he was still confronting us, an immense figure in his white nightshirt, crowned with the pink and violet scarf of Indian cashmere in which, since he had begun to suffer from neuralgia, he used to tie up his head, standing like Abraham in the engraving after Benozzo Gozzoli which M. Swann had given me, telling Hagar that she must tear herself away from Isaac.

* * *

I include such a significant chunk above because it never hurts to read a little Proust—and I include the French as well, exactly as it appears in *Mimesis,* because it contains a killing error. *Disant à Hagar?* Telling *Hagar* she must tear herself from Isaac? Isaac's mother was Sarah, not this Hagar person.

After the delicacy, the tenderness (even when transmuted to biting critique) with which he treats every other author in the book, Auerbach reaches in and manipulates Proust—not only in his translation but in the original. Needless to say, this is an unforgivable trespass. Not only does it violate any dialogue between friendly spirits in a moment of sneaky prosopopoeia—he talks over Proust, and he doesn't excuse or explain himself, which is not only unethical but downright rude. He misrepresents *À la recherche*; his substitution changes the tenor of the passage. The heavy, threatening atmosphere that emanates from the implied violence of the sacrifice in the engraving disappears and is replaced by something stranger and even stronger.

You see, Hagar was Abraham's second wife, the mother of Ishmael— Ishmael the first, the quintessential wandering Jew, Ishmael who became a Muslim prophet, Ishmael who is the conduit between the Western Judeo-Christian tradition and Eastern Islam. Auerbach's error is not so much an error as a heartbreaking fudge—it makes the narrator of the passage as much Ishmael as Isaac, as much exile as sacrifice—as much Erich as Marcel. A new motif emerges: isolation, loneliness, and the simultaneous redemption of the same—a half-concealed bridging of two worlds by a writer who had found himself lodged between them.

At that point I stopped reading. I looked up. I was alone in the reading room. I felt alone, I felt how perfect and painful it is to be alone, and then I felt that I was not alone. Um, this is beautiful, I thought. This is very beautiful.

I would risk writing that this is what *art* does—not that it is necessarily autobiographical but that it appropriates, it expresses without apology and without proper permission. It is a violation, a rupture—an unwanted first kiss that nonetheless shocks the heart into a swifter, sweeter beat.

I did check a French edition of *À la recherche* (the SFPL had four copies in the international literature division on the third floor) to make sure I wasn't misremembering my Old Testament or my Proust. *Disant à Sarah* is the correct phrase. Which is to say that *Mimesis* is not a book of criticism; it gives us the joy that comes in recognizing another's suffering and the great beauty by which they have expressed and thereby surpassed it, even for a moment, even for one tiny, seemingly invisible moment.

But what happened to *Mimesis,* and to Auerbach? The book is dying out; as mentioned above, it's seldom taught, though the fiftieth anniversary of its publication in English sparked a series of conferences, several collections of essays, and a new edition of the book with an introduction by Said.

Auerbach himself left Turkey in 1947 for the United States, where he took a position at Yale. He began the work of establishing comparative literature as we now know it: the study of different national and cultural literatures in relatively broad perspective. At Yale he supervised Fredric Jameson's thesis, and it was through the work of Jameson and his colleagues that comparative literature became a departmental presence in many, though certainly not most, American universities. The comparativists have succeeded the philologists.

Jameson, like Hayden White, like Bruce Robbins, has been called a rock star in my presence (White wears a diamond earring the size of a pea). The comparativists are famous in all the ways academic critics can be famous these days, with their swagger, their vinegar, their various intellectual beefs. They are, of course, very important; Jameson in particular is a sort of galaxy of his own. I only wish every once in a while they didn't loom quite so large, so that we could see, just for a little while, the artistry, the vulnerability their predecessors possessed.

That is to say, Auerbach does something Jameson can't and won't: he misquotes Proust, executes his beautiful fault, and then writes, twenty pages later, "Hence it is possible and even probable that I overlooked things which I ought to have considered…" Such coyness, such provocation, to end a book of startling insight with a self-effacing admission of oversight and error—when it is a seeming error that makes the book more stunning than one thought possible. The only response is to be irritated, to be charmed, to be consoled, and to turn from the last page to the first and search again, through all the book's intellectual brilliance, for the moments when that light is paired with an ingenious artful depth. Some books, once opened, ought never to be shut—oh, had we but world enough and time.

When *Mimesis* does end, it ends with a wish: "Nothing now remains but to find him—to find the reader, that is." I finished my three days at the SFPL and I went to my regular Thursday meeting and my professor and I muttered at each other such words of enthusiasm that my face hurt, my heart hurt, my head hurt in a perfect and all-embracing way, and I had a funny feeling, somewhat stupidly put, that this was the kind of work I wanted to do for the rest of my life.

He said, "So did you check? Has anybody else noticed the Proust thing?" And I said, "I dunno. I should have checked. I didn't have time. I hope so."

I hadn't checked. Which was embarrassing. But sometimes, when there are no X-Men movies playing, I can be a good student. So I went home and searched the usual academic databases, and at least one other scholar—David Damrosch, author of the aforementioned *The Buried Book: The Loss and Rediscovery of the Great Epic of Gilgamesh*—had noticed the Proust thing. And learning that was almost as good a feeling as learning that a first kiss will of course be followed by a second, and a third—that the startling pleasures that come so infrequently in our lives do in fact repeat themselves, and are shared.

Find the reader—find him—well, there are at least two or three of us, Erich; in fact, I am certain that there are thousands and thousands of us, with our *Tintins,* our sharpened pencils, our professorships, our unfair prejudices against books with long titles about the politics of insurance in America, our brains and lusts and sillinesses and nearly—but not quite!—empty reading rooms, and for now and forever that is enough. ✳

LEV GROSSMAN

THE DEATH OF A
CIVIL SERVANT

DISCUSSED: *Cambridge Secret Societies, Complicated Smells,*
Boot Dealers, Poetry about Fairies, Freud's Theory of the Uncanny,
Virginia Woolf, Western Lordlings, Peter Pan, Death-Proof Elves,
Missionary Ladies, Trotting Knights, Murdering Beethoven,
The Antiquarian Revival, J. K. Rowling, Sexless Marriages

Before he became the husband of Adeline Virginia Stephen—later a novelist of some considerable reputation—Leonard Woolf was a cadet in the Ceylon Civil Service. At Cambridge, Woolf had been a member of the Apostles, the exclusive secret society that also included John Maynard Keynes and the philosopher G. E. Moore. But graduated from Cambridge without any particular distinction, and unlike his peers he didn't have very much money: he was one of nine children, and his father, a Queen's Counsel, had died when he was eleven, of tuberculosis and workaholism. Woolf couldn't afford to read for the bar himself—the registration fee alone was forty pounds— and he wasn't especially confident that, as a Jew and an atheist, he was cut out for school teaching, which would have been the other conventional

Leonard Woolf in Jaffna, Sri Lanka (photographer unknown)

option. So in 1904 he took the British civil service examination. He placed sixty-ninth out of ninety-nine.

That wasn't good. But it was good enough to get him a second-rate position: an Eastern Cadetship in the Colonial Service. He packed up his clothes and the complete works of Voltaire in ninety volumes and steamed off over the horizon, bound for Colombo, then the capital of Ceylon, aboard the SS *Syria* of the P&O line. The journey would take a month. Because the P&O line wouldn't carry dogs, Woolf's faithful wire-haired terrier, Charles, had to come on a separate boat.

At twenty-four, Woolf was both world-wearily cosmopolitan and touchingly innocent. As was the fashion among the Apostles, he was a misanthrope and a committed cynic—his personal motto was "Nothing matters." He was proud and touchy and sharp-tongued. He was also exceptionally brilliant; by the time he was a senior in high school he was already a first-rate classicist. (His poor showing in the civil service exam was the result of spotty preparation, not a lack of brainpower.) But Woolf was also a virgin who had never traveled farther from home than northern France. He was nowhere near as jaded as he liked to pretend to be. Fifty-five years later he would write in his second volume of auto-biography, *Growing,* that when he waved good-bye to his mother and sister on the London docks that morning, it felt like a second birth.

Ceylon was a giant step forward into adulthood and independence for Woolf, but it was also a great leap backward—backward in time. Ceylon had yet to enter the twentieth century, at least as it was known in the Western world. "Before the days of the motor-car," Woolf wrote, "Colombo was a real Eastern city, swarming with human beings and flies, the streets full of flitting rickshas and creaking bullock carts, hot and heavy with the complicated smells of men and beasts and dung and oil and food and fruit and spice." The alien heat and gargantuan insects appalled Woolf. The day after he arrived he was reunited with Charles at the docks. Charles promptly peed on a passerby, who seemed not at all troubled by this, then threw up from the emotion and the sun. Crows flew down to eat the vomit. Welcome to Ceylon.

Woolf's first posting was to Jaffna, a town at the very northern tip of the island. Arriving in January, he immediately set about learning

Tamil and acquainting himself with the local legal code. It would have been easy for his colleagues to underestimate Woolf. He was slightly built and cursed with an unintentionally comical appearance: he had a long face, jug ears, and an enormous caricature of a Jewish nose. But there was a steely mental toughness to him. At first his responsibilities were largely bureaucratic, but he complained to his superiors that he was bored, and over the course of his career his job would eventually be broadened to include everything from overseeing agricultural projects to investigating murders. Touring the outskirts of his district, he would sometimes bicycle thirty-five miles in a day. He discovered that he had a mania for efficiency. At Cambridge, Woolf and his friends had evolved something they called "the method," a kind of marathon interrogation technique that they used to break people down, take their measure, and expose their weaknesses. Woolf adapted "the method" for use in colonial bureaucracy—one of his innovations was the practice of answering every letter on the same day it was received. This dramatically improved his office's productivity while at the same time provoking his subordinates, who were mostly Ceylonese clerks, to the brink of mutiny.

After work came the colonial sacraments of tennis and bridge and tea and whiskey. It was the twilight of the imperial world of Kipling. The white population of Jaffna consisted of maybe two dozen people, a gossipy little cell that distrusted Woolf's intellectual airs, which he quickly learned to conceal (the Voltaire, he later recalled, was "a particular liability"). Needless to say, the social life wasn't everything Woolf could have wished for. "Lord!" he wrote to his best friend and fellow Apostle, Lytton Strachey, who was safe at home in England, having done even worse than Woolf on the civil service exam. "I'm damnably polite and nice and quiet but I feel at any moment I may get up and burst out against the whole stupid degraded circle of degenerates and imbeciles."

Woolf was an assiduous observer of human fauna, and an equally assiduous autobiographer, and it's possible even now to reconstitute the social structure of white Jaffna in near-molecular detail from his letters and memoirs. The molecule on which Woolf lavished the most attention, after himself, was Jaffna's police magistrate and the town's other would-be intellectual, a man named B. J. Dutton.

Most of Woolf's colleagues could at least pass for gentlemen, but Dutton couldn't. He wasn't a "pukka Sahib," in the parlance. He hadn't been to university, and his background was lower-middle-class. He didn't play tennis or bridge. Woolf described him as "a small, insignificant-looking man, with hollow cheeks, a rather grubby yellow face, an apologetic moustache, and frightened or worried eyes behind strong spectacles." He was nervous and socially awkward. He lived alone "in a largish bungalow with a piano, so it was said, and a vast number of books."

The other policemen hated Dutton. "A bloody unwashed Board School bugger, who doesn't know one end of a woman from the other" was how he was described to Woolf. But Woolf didn't hate Dutton. He was just baffled by him. And, despite himself, fascinated by him. That spring—May of 1905—Woolf found himself in need of a new place to live. Even though he knew his reputation would take a major hit, he moved into the largish bungalow along with the piano and the books and Dutton.

There the two men gradually got to know each other. Dutton was terrified of his peers but also considered them contemptible—vulgar and cruel and uneducated. He mooned over women, but the idea of actual sex repulsed him; it would be "impossible with anyone with whom one was in love." Nevertheless, Dutton was a kind man, and he had a gallant streak. In one case, when a prostitute was brought before him for sentencing, Dutton convicted her, but paid her fine himself and gave her client a stern talking-to. (Everybody else thought that this was incredibly funny, including Woolf, who was one of the girl's clients—in fact, he had surrendered his virginity to her.) "I have hardly ever known anyone so hopelessly incompetent as Dutton was to deal with life," he wrote. "He lived the life of a minnow in a shoal of pike."

Like Woolf, Dutton had literary aspirations. His bungalow was indeed entirely lined with books—cheap editions of the classics intended for popular improvement—and he spent every evening writing poetry; he'd amassed hundreds of thousands of lines of it. His verses were, in Woolf's opinion, "incredibly feeble." Woolf wasn't a cruel man, but he had after all been an Apostle, and he was a literary snob of the first water. The intensity of the revulsion he felt at reading Dutton's poetry took him to metaphorical extremes:

When later on in Ceylon I became an extremely incompetent shooter of big game, and, in cutting up the animals killed by me, saw the disgusting, semi-digested contents of their upper intestines, I was always reminded of the contents of Dutton's mind. As he not unnaturally disliked and temperamentally was frightened of the people and life which surrounded him, he very early escaped from them and it into books and the undigested, sticky mess of "culture" which they provided for him.

What Woolf saw on the onionskin that had passed through Dutton's decrepit typewriter left him literally incredulous. "Who could possibly imagine," he wrote, "that in 1905 an English civil servant, a Police Magistrate—what we now know to have been an imperialist—would sit hour after hour, day after day, writing poetry about fairies or, as he called them, fays?"

We know a lot about Woolf. He couldn't have realized it then (though he probably had his suspicions), but his destiny lay with the inner circle of the ruling literary caste of the twentieth century. He was a harbinger of modernism, the school of Virginia Woolf and Joyce and Faulkner and Hemingway. But who was B. J. Dutton? There was no word for him in 1905, but we have one now: he was a *nerd avant la lettre*. And he was a harbinger, too, in his tiny, ineffectual way, of another of the twentieth century's dominant literary traditions: fantasy.

So far as I can tell, Woolf scholarship, at least of the Leonard variety, has until now remained innocent of Dutton's full name, probably because nobody ever bothered to look him up. But he is eminently findable, even by an amateur literary sleuth. Woolf remarks in *Growing* that Dutton was four years older than he was. Woolf was born in 1880. Public records show many Duttons born in England in the 1870s, but only a handful of male Duttons, first initial *B*. And there is only one B. J.: Bernard Joseph Dutton, born 1876, bang on time, in Stoke on Trent. He is beyond a doubt, for reasons that will become clear, our B. J.

The 1881 census found Bernard at age five living in Whitford with his parents: Aaron Dutton, "boot dealer," and Anne Dutton, "wife of boot dealer." He was the oldest of four brothers. The 1891 census has him as a student at a Catholic boarding school called Cotton College near Stoke on Trent; Aaron is by this time the foreman at an enamel works in Burslem, and father to yet another son and two more daughters. Bernard Joseph Dutton is absent from the 1901 census, but he reappears, as Mr. B. J. Dutton, on the passenger list of the Staffordshire, a steamship that left Liverpool for Colombo on April 14, 1904.

Something strange passed between Woolf and Dutton in that bungalow. Later in life Woolf would become a good Freudian (as steward of the Hogarth Press, he would be Freud's first publisher of record in England). If he'd been one in 1905—and if Freud had invented it yet—Woolf might have found his theory of the *unheimlich,* the uncanny, useful in understanding his feelings about Dutton. Freud explained this theory (which he didn't come up with until 1919) using an anecdote about an experience he had had on a train. A man walked into the compartment Freud was traveling in. Freud instinctively disliked him: "What a shabby-looking schoolmaster" was his internal comment. A second later Freud realized that he recognized the man: the man was Freud. A bathroom door had swung open, and Freud was looking at his own reflection in a mirror. He identified that unsettling, mystical, electrical sense of simultaneous recognition and revulsion as "the uncanny."

When Woolf met Dutton, the bathroom door swung open. Dutton was a mirror image of Woolf, both attractive and repellent, strange and strangely familiar at the same time. As his excellent biographer, Victoria Glendinning, puts it, when Woolf looked at Dutton he saw "a terrifyingly degraded version of himself." Both men were outsiders, of uncertain social standing, sexually inexperienced, who nourished secret dreams of literary glory. Woolf too felt contempt for those around him—he was afflicted with a mild congenital tremor in his hands that Virginia Woolf later recalled seemed to express her husband's barely contained loathing for humanity. Leonard himself compared Dutton to another Leonard: Leonard Bast, the working-class intellectual in *Howards End.* Dutton was a Woolf in sheep's clothing.

And there were those poems, Dutton's feeble fays. If they'd been just bad Woolf might have felt dismay or embarrassment. But Dutton's writing wasn't just bad. Woolf actually found it disgusting. Frightening, even. Like those dead entrails, heavy with food halfway on its way to becoming fecal matter, both filthy and fertile, Dutton was *abject*. He produced in Woolf a special kind of fear, the kind provoked by something horrible and infectious that implicates not only the other but oneself.

In a weird way, Dutton's poetry couldn't have been better calculated to prey on Woolf's buried anxieties. Both men were engaged in the work of Empire, vigorously superimposing a tidy bureaucratic English order on what to them was a primal and chaotic Tamil folk culture. By writing about magic and fairies Dutton was poking around in the shallow grave of England's own folk culture of magic and fairies. He was blurring the tidy line that was supposed to separate the colonizers from the colonized. To Woolf, fantasy must have seemed like a kind of treason, a betrayal of their shared allegiance to the modern era. If an Englishman can believe in fairies, how the hell can you tell him apart from the savages? The whole system comes crashing down! "If we have a tree in our back garden, there is no devil, no Yakko in it," Woolf wrote in *Growing*. But, he added, dropping his voice to a stylistic whisper, "very deep down under the surface of the northern European the beliefs and desires and passions of primitive man still exist, ready to burst out with catastrophic violence if, under prolonged pressure, social controls and inhibitions give way." In Dutton, Woolf smelled a literary Kurtz, in imminent danger of going native. (And lest we forget, Woolf was only two generations removed from the Jewish tailors of London's East End. He and his family were busily engaged in erasing any traces of their own indigenous culture, in an effort to attain some semblance of English respectability. At Cambridge he'd been almost as exotic to his fellow undergraduates as the Tamils of Jaffna were to him.)

Just as every Englishman has a savage somewhere inside him, watching and waiting for a chance to tear his way out, every adult has a child inside him, and in Woolf's case that child wasn't very far below the surface. At twenty-four Woolf was not yet completely grown-up. He was always waxing lyrical about his childhood, the time before his father's death, which he remembered as "the Platonic idea laid up in heaven of security and peace and civilization." Now he was barely out of college and clinging tenuously to adulthood, plugging his ears against the siren song of the nursery while trying to assert his authority in a strange land over men two and three times his age. There is an absolutely priceless photo of Woolf in Jaffna on a balcony in formal dress, with his hounds all around him, playing the role of the Western lordling and managing to look all of about fourteen years old. Dutton, a man who looked like a child, and who wrote about childish things, would have seemed to Woolf like a cruel parody of himself, a living image of the self he was seriously worried that he truly was.

But who was Dutton, really? Was he just a virginal boy-man who wouldn't grow up and put aside childish things? (*Peter Pan*, the epitome of this particular late-Victorian obsession, opened to massive acclaim in December of 1904, the very month Woolf arrived in Ceylon.) Granted, to a lot of people, Duttons and Woolfs alike, fantasy is the literature of childhood. Our reading lives don't begin on Earth, they begin in fairyland, or Middle-earth, or Narnia, or Earthsea, or Hogwarts; for Woolf it might have been Wonderland, or George MacDonald's fairy dreamlands, or the weird aquatic netherworld of Charles Kingsley's *The Water-Babies*. We know that at boarding school Woolf was a rabid consumer of early science fiction—he wrote about drowsing under the gas jets in the school library and being "transported from the rather boring and always uncertain life to which one had been arbitrarily and inexplicably committed, to the strangest, most beautiful, and entrancing world of *20,000 Leagues Under the Sea*, or *The Log of the Flying Fish*." (The latter is a long-forgotten novel about the voyages of a magnificent ship made of atherium, a material so strong it can travel underwater, and so light it can fly.)

It's odd that children are so interested in fantasy when they're still in a position to find the real world fresh and new. You'd think we'd raise them on Dreiser—they, unlike most people, might actually be curious about the gritty, naturalistic details of the life of Sister Carrie. It's possible that to children the world still appears to be mysterious and inexplicable and occasionally monstrous and thus best represented by narratives about the supernatural. It's also possible that, being closer to infancy, they haven't entirely shed a vision of a world that is not boring and uncertain, arbitrary and inexplicable—that is not indifferent to their needs, a world in which they are powerful, central figures. It has not yet been definitively demonstrated to them that their thoughts and words cannot alter the universe. Freud had an appropriately fantastical name for this childish delusion: he called it magical thinking.

Magical thinking isn't fantasy in the literary sense. It is *a* fantasy, in the psychoanalytic sense: a dream of a world where actions don't have consequences, where loss is an impossibility, where wishing makes it so, where one doesn't have to make choices, because all possible good things arrive at once, unbidden, with none of those nasty trade-offs that are so characteristic of real life. There is no either/or in a fantasy, it's all both/and. This is the world that Dutton's fairies evoked for Woolf, and that he was struggling so mightily to put behind him.

But fantasies aren't literature, and fantasies aren't fantasy. This isn't a distinction that Woolf would have made, but Dutton might have made it. Granted, fantasy literature, broadly speaking, tends to be set in worlds where magic is real. But that doesn't mean that anything is possible. Magic doesn't permeate those worlds completely. Magic exists, but only as a flash of vital light in a universe that is otherwise as dark and mechanical as our own—its presence casts the tragic, non-magical parts of life in higher relief. Magic tantalizes with the possibility that it might quicken the world back into life, restore the lost paradise of magical thinking, but ultimately it cannot.

The non-fan's idea of fantasy is like the Land of Do-As-You-Please in Enid Blyton's *The Magic Faraway Tree,* where children can drive trains and ride elephants and eat six ice creams at one sitting whenever they want to. But a much better example is Tolkien's Middle-earth: the Elves live there, and do not age or die, but mankind lives there, too. The two races, mortal and im-, coexist within a single cosmic continuum, and you'll never feel your mortality more keenly than when you're standing next to a death-proof elf. (Elves lose their immortality if they mate with a human, a deal it's hard to imagine any competent elf striking.) And even Enid Blyton's fantasyland isn't as innocent as it looks. Stay too long in the Land of Do-As-You-Please and it will rotate away from the top of the Magic Faraway Tree, with you in it. A chill wind will come up, the sun will go out like a candle, and the ladder back to everything you know and love will be whisked away forever. *Et in Arcadia ego.*

Woolf saw fantasy as a childish thing, a form of cowardly escapism, shameful in the way that childish things are. Life had taught him to see it that way. After his father died, at the age of forty-seven, Woolf's mother retreated into a domestic fantasy life every bit as fantastical as Enid Blyton's. She couldn't or wouldn't face up to the hard realities of daily life, and the contempt she inspired in Woolf ran so deep that it became a permanent feature of his personality. "She lived in a dream world which centred on herself and her nine children," he wrote in *Sowing*, the first volume of his autobiography. "It was the best of all possible worlds, a fairyland of nine perfect children worshipping a mother to whom they owed everything, loving one another, and revering the memory of their deceased father." This struck Woolf as sheer laziness, and cowardice. It enraged him, and he never stopped calling her on it, no matter how many unpleasant scenes he caused. There would be no fays for her. Glendinning reports that all the Woolf children had a special nickname for their mother: Lady. "All the children except Leonard, that is. He alone never called her 'Lady.' He called her Mother."

Woolf may have been right about Mother, for all we know, but he was wrong about fantasy. In the world of fantastic literature, emptiness and fullness are both present. Magic holds out the possibility that magical thinking will come true, that death is an illusion, and that all possible good things will in fact arrive in due course… but they never actually do. Harry Potter can summon his broomstick, but he can't bring his parents back to life. In that respect the world of fantasy isn't all that different from real life. Our world, Earth, is also a hybrid world, both quick and dead, fashioned from inanimate matter but haunted by a meaning that never fully manifests itself—the delusion that all will be well, because all should be well, because we want it to be well. It's a delusion that often seems strangely real even to grown-ups. Magical thinking is something we never quite shed. It's not infantile at all, it turns out. It's human.

Much of fantasy literature arises from this essential truth: that magic is not the end of all your problems; it's the beginning. Travel deeper into the realms of gold—further up and further in, as Aslan says—and you leave reality behind, only to reencounter it in transfigured form.

Reality in Jaffna wasn't easy. Woolf contracted malaria and eczema and dysentery, and he almost died of typhoid. Charles, his loyal wire-haired terrier, did die, from heat exhaustion. The bungalow didn't seem quite so large once they were both living in it, but Woolf and Dutton did their mutual best to rub along and find common ground. They made an odd pair, reminiscent in their way of Jake Barnes and Robert Cohn in *The Sun Also Rises*: Jake cynical and world-weary, taking pride in seeing things as they are, Cohn socially inept and unable to distinguish between life and the South American adventure novel *The Purple Land* (by W. H. Hudson, now as forgotten as *The Log of the Flying Fish*): "For a man to take it at thirty-four as a guide-book to what life holds is about as safe as it would be for a man of the same age to enter Wall Street direct from a French convent, equipped with a complete set of the more practical Alger books."

Like all great buddy-comedies, the story of Woolf and Dutton includes an attempted makeover. Woolf made Dutton take up tennis, at which he was hopeless; he mostly played with Jaffna's two missionary ladies, the virtuous Misses Case and Beeching. Woolf and Dutton threw a bridge party for which Dutton cleaned up the bungalow and made a mighty effort to decorate it. The event was a qualified success: the missionary ladies attended, as did the government agent, the ranking civil servant in Jaffna, but otherwise it seems to have been a grim affair. Dutton played his own arrangement of Beethoven's Fifth on the out-of-tune piano, which is something he apparently did on a nightly basis anyway, whether or not guests were present. Woolf immortalized the evening in a poem, addressed, perhaps, to one of the Misses:

> You listen, even as I do, to the notes
> The awful iteration of Fate's hand,

Hammer upon the tinkling cracked piano—
I wonder if you really understand.

You hear him sounding it out in the other room,
The bitterness, doom and mockery of each thing—
As you sit there silent, I wonder, do you hear
The exquisite note of degradation ring?

One hopes that Woolf, unlike Dutton, kept his poetry to himself. All Englishmen who were in their twenties in 1905 had at least one thing in common: they'd watched the world of their childhoods die. Just as they were coming of age, electricity replaced gaslight. Cars and buses replaced horses and bicycles. Urban populations were exploding, mass media and advertising were yammering, and mechanized warfare crouched in the wings, ready and waiting. The early twentieth century looked and sounded and smelled nothing like the late nineteenth. "In those days of the eighties and nineties of the nineteenth century the rhythm of London traffic which one listened to as one fell asleep in one's nursery was the rhythm of horses' hooves clopclopping down London streets in broughams, hansom cabs, and four-wheelers," Woolf would write, toward the end of his life, in the unimaginable year of 1960. "And the rhythm, the tempo got into one's blood and one's brain, so that in a sense I have never become entirely reconciled in London to the rhythm and tempo of the whizzing and rushing cars." Woolf felt displaced, like the hero of H. G. Wells's *The Time Machine,* exiled in the future. So did everybody else—Evelyn Waugh once remarked that if he ever got ahold of a time machine, he'd put it in reverse and go backward, into the past.

It's no accident that both modernism and modern fantasy made their entrances at that moment, in that same displaced generation. It's rarely remarked upon, but just as Virginia Woolf and Joyce and Hemingway were inventing the modernist novel, Hope Mirrlees and Lord Dunsany and Eric Rücker Eddison were writing the first modern fantasy novels, at least in the form most fans are familiar with. This happened for a reason. Modernism and fantasy were two very different responses to the same disaster: the arrival of the modern era and the death of Woolf's beloved nursery-world. Though like siblings—or roommates—who are mortally embarrassed by each other, they're not in the habit of acknowledging the connection. Like Woolf and Dutton, modernism and fantasy are each other's uncanny double.

The resemblance isn't immediately obvious. The modernists were interested in confronting reality directly, and meticulously documenting their experiences of it—like Woolf, they had no patience for those who dallied with fays. The modernists are the cool ones: modernism is the twentieth century's most canonized, most critically decorated literary movement, while fantasy remains one of the least assimilated and least critically understood genres. Over the years the academics who tend the canon have extended rope ladders down to some of the "lower" forms: science fiction, detective fiction, comic books. But never fantasy. High-status literary novelists love to dabble in genre writing—David Foster Wallace, Margaret Atwood, Doris Lessing, Kazuo Ishiguro, and Cormac McCarthy have all written science-fiction novels, for example. But by and large fantasy remains proudly, stubbornly culturally radioactive. The fantasist is not a pukka sahib.

But fantasy and modernism aren't just opposites, they're mirror images of each other. When the social, cultural, and technological catastrophe that inaugurated the twentieth century took place, leaving the neat, coherent Victorian universe a desecrated ruin, all that was left for writers to do was to sift disconsolately through the rubble and dream of the organic, vital world that had once been. Modernism was pieced together out of the jagged shards of that shattered world—it's a literature made of fragments, the better to resemble the carnage it represented. Whereas fantasy was a vision of that lost, longed-for world itself, a dream of a medieval England that never was: green, whole, prelapsarian, magical.

Here and there you can spot their shared heritage, the places where modernism and fantasy touch. Modernists and fantasists both rework myths and legends: you can watch King Arthur and his knights trot, obscured but still visible, through Eliot's "The Waste Land," Virginia Woolf's *The Waves* (in the person of the knightly Percival), and Joyce's *Finnegans Wake* ("Arser of the Rum Tipple") to emerge into the sunlit meadows of T. H. White's *The Once and Future King*. Modernism and fantasy are set against the same landscapes: verdant preindustrial hills and dark, broken ruins. *La tour abolie* of "The Waste Land" is the architectural double of Orthanc, the tower of Saruman the White in *The Lord of the Rings*. The green fields of Narnia abut the "fresh green breast of the new world" that Fitzgerald invokes at the end of *The Great Gatsby*.

But by the time we reach them, those green fields are always in decline. The spell never lasts. King Arthur is always dying, and the Elves are always shuffling off toward Valinor, where mortals cannot follow them. Narnia falls into chaos, then drowns and freezes, and the survivors retreat into Aslan's Land. We think of fantasy and modernism as worlds apart, but somehow they always end up in the same place. They are perfectly symmetrical. Fantasy is a prelude to the apocalypse. Modernism is the epilogue.

Woolf had a private fantasy that he cherished. It was about B. J. Dutton, and how, in another world, he might perhaps have found happiness:

> The only possible way in which I can imagine he might have cheated fate or God or the Devil would have been for him to have obtained a safe, quiet post in the Inland Revenue or the Post Office and to have lived a life bounded on the one side by Somerset House or St. Martin's-le-Grand, and on the other by a devoted mother and a devoted old servant in Clapham or Kew.

I have a fantasy of my own about Woolf and Dutton. It goes like this: after a couple of months living together, Woolf has a change of heart about Dutton's poetry. He experiences an epiphany. He grasps the deeper meaning of the fays, and the nature of Dutton's vision, however crudely expressed. He recognizes that this shy, awkward chap is at heart a fellow yearner like he is for the vanished past, the past that never was, and a mourner like he is for the world's fall from grace. One night the awkward chitchat and murdered Beethoven give way to a moment of spiritual recognition—*mon semblable,—mon frère!* They return to England the best of friends, Woolf to be reunited with the scattered Apostles, Dutton to take up his place as the poetical rival of Lewis and Tolkien. Both men achieve their share of peace and contentment.

It was not to be. He may have been touchy and funny looking but Woolf was, at heart, a winner. He made a great civil servant. He was transferred and promoted, eventually rising to the rank of assistant government agent for Hambantota, a region in southeastern Ceylon that encompassed about one thousand square miles, with a salary of 650 pounds per annum. In 1912, after seven years on the magic mountain of Ceylon, he took a leave of absence and returned to the chilly realities of England, where after a passionate courtship he made an excellent match with the sophisticated bourgeoise Virginia Stephen. He resigned his position and took his ordained place among the mandarins of the Bloomsbury group. In addition to nursing his wife through numerous breakdowns, to the infinite enrichment of English literature, Woolf cofounded the Hogarth Press—publisher of "The Waste Land"—wrote several influential monographs about the international economy, and played a key behind-the-scenes role in the founding of the League of Nations. He lived to be eighty-eight. There is a tiny but still satisfying bit of nerdy irony in the fact that after his wife's suicide Woolf lived out his last years in the loving company of a woman named Trekkie.

Dutton's story doesn't end as happily. He stayed behind in Ceylon, where he did not prosper—he "remained a failure in every direction," as Woolf put it—although he was eventually promoted from police magistrate to district judge in Matara. He married one of the missionary ladies, Miss Beeching, whom Woolf described as having "a curious face rather like that of a good-looking male Red Indian." (Like Dutton, Beeching is an extremely minor but still identifiable historical figure, a pioneer among women missionaries who worked in Canada before coming to Ceylon. Touchingly, in *One Hundred Years in Ceylon, or, The centenary volume of the Church Missionary Society in Ceylon, 1818–1918,* it is recorded that in 1906 she married one "J. B. Dutton.")

Dutton was a social leper, but as a writer he wasn't alone, though he probably didn't know it. If he'd had the Internet, he would have realized that back in England the Antiquarian Revival was in full swing. The future was before him. Hope Mirrlees isn't much read anymore, but from the moment their work was published, J. R. R. Tolkien and C. S. Lewis have never gone out of print, and the turn of the millennium has seen a massive resurgence of interest in fantasy. Since 1997 J. K. Rowling has sold 150 million Harry Potter novels, and *The Lord of the Rings* movies earned almost three billion dollars at the box office. So far in this millennium it's the Duttons, not the Woolfs, who are in the ascendant. (Woolf surely knew, when he compared Dutton's mind to the intestines of the beasts he killed, that the Romans used to read the future in the entrails of dead animals.)

As it happened, Matara was the next district over from Hambantota, and Woolf and the Duttons occasionally bumped into each other. In a memorable passage from *Growing*, they share a final dinner together under a wild tropical night sky, beside a sea out of which turtles poked their heads in the darkness. "The sky, the sea, the stars, the turtles, the bay, the palms were so lusciously magnificent at Tangalla Rest House that Nature seemed to tremble on the verge—I don't think she ever actually fell over the verge—of vulgarity." (Even in a state of ecstatic transport, Woolf the proto-modernist always had the question of good taste on his mind.) It was the last hurrah of the preindustrial nineteenth century, a world living on borrowed time. A few years later the automobile would arrive in Ceylon, and that was the beginning of the end of Woolf's clop-clopping nineteenth-century rhythm. The district of Hambantota would eventually be almost completely obliterated by the Indian Ocean tsunami of 2004.

Dutton was living on borrowed time, too. He would never see Middle-earth or Narnia. He couldn't catch a break for the life of him, though at least he was to be spared the horrors of World War I (unlike Lewis and Tolkien, who were both survivors of the Somme). His marriage had gone sour, and Mrs. Dutton, née Beeching, had gotten hugely fat. To Woolf's eyes Dutton seemed to have become even tinier and more insignificant, as if she were slowly devouring him like a monstrous parasite.

A few months after their dinner together, Woolf happened to be passing through Matara, but he found Bernard Joseph not at home.

Mrs. Dutton was there alone, in a house so obsessively neat and clean it reminded Woolf of an antiseptic ward at a hospital. She unburdened herself to him. "She told me that her marriage was a complete failure, that Dutton was so queer that he ought not to have married, and that she was completely miserable, and, as she spoke, the tears ran down her cheeks." Woolf goes on to describe a surreal scene in which Mrs. Dutton insisted that he take a tour of the house, and led him to her bedroom. "Whether my nerves had given way and I was no longer seeing things as they really were, I do not know," he wrote, "but it seemed to me that I had never seen a bedroom like it." It was full of yards and yards of clean linen and voluminous white mosquito netting that hung over separate beds. "It gave me the feeling of unmitigated chastity. It was the linen of nuns and convents rather than of brides and marriage beds." One wonders if, in writing this, fifty-five years later, Woolf cast his mind back over his own famously sexless marriage.

He wisely kept both beds between them, and made his escape as quickly as he could. "I never saw Mrs. Dutton again," he wrote. "And a year or two later, when I had left Ceylon for good, I heard in England that Dutton had died of tuberculosis."

The only other trace of Dutton's passing I could find is in the mid-summer 1912 issue of the *Cottonian,* the alumni magazine of Cotton College, his old high school. The lead story is a remembrance of Hugh McElroy, another old Cottonian, who was chief purser on the *Titanic,* which sank in April of that year. But a little farther down in the Old Boys' Corner there appears a notice of the death of Bernard Joseph Dutton ('93), former district judge of Matara, Ceylon. The magazine loyally praises him as a "brilliant scholar and linguist." The previous year he had given up his post and returned to England, and he died on April 21, 1912, in Holywell, aged thirty-six years. "In his office of Judge he was loved by the natives and respected by all Europeans in Ceylon. R.I.P." ✳

JEANNIE VANASCO

ABSENT THINGS AS IF THEY ARE PRESENT

DISCUSSED: *Being God, An Indefinite Definition, A Summer Home for Working Girls, Amazonian Plagiarism Hunters, Blatant Freudianism, Credit to Wavy Gravy, The Essence of Property, Passing Judgment on Coleridge's Penmanship, A Very Significant Omission, Differing Views of the Pope and the US Government*

I.

The night before he died, I promised my father I would write a book for him. I was eighteen and harboring profound confidence charged with profound grief. He was eighty, and under so much morphine I doubt he even understood.

Not only was I unable to write my father's eulogy, I was unable to write him a letter for his coffin. All week, in a depressed but strangely sleepless state, I filled a notebook with the same sentence: "A blank sheet of paper is God's way of saying it's not so easy to be God."

Image courtesy of the National Museum of American History

II.

The dictionary defines *erase* as "to scrape or rub out (anything written, engraved, etc.); to efface, expunge, obliterate." Its Latin root roughly translates as "to scrape away." These definitions imply loss and destruction. They call to mind Richard Nixon's audio-tape gaps, the photographic manipulations of Stalin, the Archimedes Palimpsest, the missing fragments of Sappho. Death.

Heidegger practiced erasure as a way to define nihilism (in an indefinite sort of way). In a 1956 letter to Ernst Jünger, Heidegger wrote the term *being*, then crossed it out: "Since the word is inaccurate, it is crossed out. Since the word is necessary, it remains legible." Here erasure, or what philosophers call *sous rature* ("under erasure"), illustrates the problematic existence of presence and the absence of meaning. Crossed out, *being* becomes unreliable and indispensable at once.

Literary erasure has its own definition. To erase is to create a new work out of an existing one: canonical, obscure, wonderful, terrible, it's the erasurist's choice.

When Mary Ruefle whited out select words from *A Little White Shadow,* an obscure nineteenth-century book published "for the Benefit of a Summer Home for Working Girls," lines of captivating poetry emerged: "It was my duty to keep the piano filled with roses." Wave Books brought out a facsimile of her erasure, preserving the appearance of her small, whited-out copy, under the appropriate (and appropriated) title *A Little White Shadow.* When Jen Bervin ghosted select words in Shakespeare's sonnets, her own free-verse poems rose to the surface in darker ink:

> Against my love shall be, as *I am* now,
> With Time's injurious hand crush'd   and o'erworn;
> When hours have drain'd his blood
>   and fill'd his brow
> With lines and wrinkles; when his
>   youthful morn
> Hath travell'd on to age's steepy night;
> And all those beauties whereof now
>   he's king

Are *vanishing or vanished* out of sight,
Stealing away the treasure of his spring;
For such a time do I now fortify
Against confounding age's cruel knife,
That he shall never cut from memory
My sweet love's beauty, though my
    lover's life:
His beauty shall *in these black lines*
    be seen,
And they shall live, and he in them
    still green.

Why erase the works of other writers? The philosophical answer is that poets, as Wordsworth defines them, are "affected more than other men by absent things as if they were present." The more practical answer: compared to writing, erasing feels easy.

But I am here to convince you: to erase is to write, style is the consequence of a writer's omissions, and the writer is always plural.

To erase is to leave something else behind.

III.

Let's start where most people think erasure starts. The year was 1966, the place was a furniture repository in London, and Tom Phillips had just bought a forgotten Victorian novel, W. H. Mallock's *A Human Document*, for threepence. Its narrator tells us that a Hungarian countess gave him the strange journal of a deceased, possibly Russian woman. At first, he says, it reads like your average journal, but suddenly, in bursts, it exhibits the qualities of a novel and a scrapbook: the woman writes of herself in the third person, describes the unspoken thoughts of a man, and occasionally breaks her narrative with letters and fragments of poetry evidently written by the man. "As they stand," the narrator observes, the journal's components "are not a story in any literary sense; though they enable us, or rather force us, to construct one out of them for ourselves." The narrator treats the journal as malleable; by chance, Phillips stopped by the bookstall with the express purpose of finding an old book that he could mold into a new one.

Phillips began by crossing out unwanted words with pen and ink. Then he turned to painting, typing, and collaging over words (he decided no material extraneous to the novel could be used, so all collage fragments came from other pages of the book). The resulting work explodes with colors and shapes. Some pages contain unmistakable images surrounding the remaining text: the flag of England, the outline of a moth, a dark rainbow. Others are spectacularly confusing: is that a ladder leading from petticoats into smoke on page two hundred, or a broken broom? My favorite ars poetica moment is when the words *the next lips* and *unfastened her lips* emerge from opposing sides of abstract lips. With visual eloquence, Phillips reminds us of the transformative power of any novel, and of how material, how thinglike, words can be. Folding one page over and flattening it onto the page below resulted in his erasure's title: *A Humument;* i.e., *A Hum[an Doc]ument.* The project began "as idle play at the fringe of my work and preoccupations," Phillips explains in his afterword. More than four decades later, he continues to erase *A Human Document.*

After Phillips embarked on *A Humument,* dozens of acknowledged erasures have been published, from *Radi Os* (Ronald Johnson's erasure of *Paradise Lost*) to *Tree of Codes* (Jonathan Safran Foer's erasure of Bruno Schulz's *The Street of Crocodiles*), and every so often Phillips's admirers deride these erasures as plagiarisms of his magnum opus. With unacknowledged irony, the accusers assume the role of nineteenth-century "plagiarism hunters," literary gumshoes in search of stolen lines, sentences, metaphors, allusions, plots, ideas, anything that could be considered another author's originality. In other words: everything. A plagiarism hunter would report such thefts in an article in order to embarrass the offender. These "thousands of feeble writers" who "subsist by detecting imitations, real or supposed" infuriated Thomas De Quincey. Tennyson deplored this "prosaic set" of "men of great memories and no imagination, who impute themselves to the poet, and so believe that he, too, has no imagination, but is for ever poking his nose between the pages of some old volumes in order to see what he can appropriate."

One contemporary plagiarism hunter, in his Amazon review of *A Little White Shadow*, implied that Ruefle should have credited Phillips: "I see no mention of the great artist, Tom Phillips." Another arraigned Foer's originality, arguing that *A Humument* long prefigured *Tree of Codes*: "More directly, could there be another form of unconscious plagiarism involved?" Foer did credit Phillips in *Tree of Codes*'s afterword, but what bothered this plagiarism hunter is that Phillips's erasure came first. OK. Let's splash back a decade or so before Phillips began erasing.

In 1953, over the course of one month and forty rubber erasers, Robert Rauschenberg erased a drawing by de Kooning and called it *Erased de Kooning*. Rauschenberg said he wanted "to purge [him]self of [his] teaching." Calvin Tomkins said, "What else, in God's name, could you think about his wanting to *erase* a de Kooning drawing? The implications were so blatantly Freudian, the act itself so obviously a symbolic (if good-natured) patricide." Jasper Johns called it "an additive subtraction." Had Phillips been aware of Rauschenberg's erasure? Is *A Humument* an unconscious plagiarism?

Phillips cited the newspaper-cut-up techniques of William Burroughs as a strong influence, just as Burroughs had cited those of Brion Gysin. No one cited Caleb Whitefoord. Who?

Does it matter?

As Emerson put it, authors do not weave "their web from their own bowels." Isn't every book an erasure?

IV.

A belief in the purely originating author underpins Anglo-American copyright law as well as the European *droit d'auteur*: to be protected under copyright, a work must prove its "originality." William Blackstone invoked originality when he wrote about literary property in his four-volume treatise *Commentaries on the Laws of England*: "When a man by the exertion of his rational powers has produced an original work, he seems to have clearly a right to dispose of that identical work as he pleases, and any attempt to vary the disposition he has made of it, appears to be an invasion of that right of property." The final volume of

Commentaries was published in 1769, the same year an English court ruled that no literary works could enter the public domain. In that decision, Justice David R. Aston expressed that a literary work embodies the personality of its author and therefore belongs only to that individual: "I do not know, nor can I comprehend any property more emphatically a man's own, nay, more incapable of being mistaken, than his literary works." Exactly two hundred years later, in his essay "What Is an Author?," Foucault questions our tendency to think of authors as isolated individuals, but suggests that if we stop thinking of authors as individuals, we may stop thinking of other kinds of people in that way.

We may want to regard an author's style as a palpable, individual thing, but writing reveals style to be a nebulous aggregation of other influences. Allen Ginsberg openly credited his influences: everyone from William Shakespeare to Wavy Gravy. Drafts from his time as a young poet include imitations he made of William Carlos Williams, William Blake, even the seventeenth-century metaphysical poets John Donne and Andrew Marvell. Ginsberg began writing *Howl* by imitating Williams's stepped triadic form. In the middle of typing the poem, a new style emerged, with long, incantatory lines (influenced by Whitman) and imaginative leaps and fractured syntax (influenced by American modernist giants such as Hart Crane). The San Francisco authorities who prosecuted *Howl* as obscene were likely unfamiliar with Catullus or Rimbaud, two poets Ginsberg devotedly studied.

Ginsberg shows that by imitating the style of other writers, as well as by resisting them, a writer develops his or her own style. Erasure is simply an exaggerated form of writing. "We say that an author is *original* when we cannot trace the hidden transformation that others underwent in his mind," Valéry wrote. "What a man does either repeats or refutes what someone else has done—repeats it in other tones, refines or amplifies or simplifies it." But instead of concealing or denying their influences, erasurists acknowledge that they have come from somewhere, not nowhere, and make clear the chaotic process of creating art.

Mary Ruefle openly disclosed her process not with an afterword but by publishing *A Little White Shadow* as a photographic reproduction of her whited-out copy. Even though she erased select words from a Victorian book, the result is stamped with her unmistakable voice: pared-down statements that at first sound emotionally removed but express profound emotion: "other people read / sonnets / but / my cousin Suvia / never cared for / blood / and in this as in / most things I agreed with her." Compare those lines with lines in her recent poem in *Poetry* magazine, "White Buttons": "I like to read in tree houses / whenever I can which is seldom / and sometimes never." In both instances, her casual tone is deeper and more heartbreaking than it sounds. Even a century-old book can generate modern poetry.

But by referencing their sources, erasurists risk criticism and even legal action. The copyright lawyer Augustine Birrell argued in 1899: "The essence of Property is an unwillingness to share it, but the literary art lives by communication; its essence is the telling of a tale with the object of creating an impression and of causing repetition… the author's rights are not based on a desire to exclusive possession of that which he has written." However, not all copyright lawyers agree. In general, if an author quotes a significant portion of another author's work that lies outside the public domain (published after 1923), our legal system considers it copyright infringement. Even if someone considers an erasure an act of plagiarism, which is not to be confused with copyright infringement (no current statute, criminal or civil, mentions the word *plagiarism*), some lawyers treat plagiarism cases as cases of unfair competition or of violations of the doctrine of moral rights. Because erasures are often unrecognizable from their sources, or use sources in the public domain (*Paradise Lost,* for example), they for the most part have avoided the courts. Foer's publisher wrote to the Bruno Schulz estate, and the estate gladly approved the project and charged no permission fees. When Joshua Beckman, however, erased *Poet in New York* by Federico García Lorca, its American publisher at the time—Farrar, Straus and Giroux— sent an order to Beckman's tiny (now-defunct) publisher, Left Hand Books, to stop the printing of the book. Ultimately, Beckman and his publisher complied. In effect, his erasure was erased.

What makes erasure unsettling is that one author is appropriating one text. The nineteenth-century novelist and unblushing plagiarist Charles Reade discriminated between heterogeneous and homogeneous works of literature. "There is a vital distinction," he wrote, "between taking ideas from a homogenous source, and from a heterogeneous source; and only the first mentioned of these two acts is plagiarism: the latter is more like jewel-setting." Would Reade consider erasure plagiarism? I don't think so. Appropriation proponents like Reade believed that appropriation depended on how successfully the writer integrated the appropriated material. If plagiarism is to steal the style or expressed thoughts of someone else, then erasure is a psychological lobotomy of personal identity. The erasurist can change another writer's work until it is no longer itself.

V.

Creating ex nihilo is a romantic, but not an entirely Romantic, conceit.

In 1759, Edward Young published *Conjectures on Original Composition,* a manifesto for Romantic poetic theory. "An *Original,*" Young wrote, "may be said to be of a *vegetable* nature; it rises spontaneously from the vital root of genius; it *grows,* it is not *made: Imitations* are often a sort of *manufacture* wrought up by those *mechanics, art,* and *labour,* out of pre-existent materials not their own." The nineteenth-century English Romantics, those thought to be the heresiarchs of originality, repeated Young's claims, praising the originating hero-artist. Spontaneous, unbidden creation reigns above all, they preached.

Supposedly.

In "Essay, Supplementary to the Preface," Wordsworth claimed the writer should "owe nothing but to nature and his own genius." Coleridge lauded Wordsworth's poetry as "perfectly unborrowed." Shelley wrote in *A Defence of Poetry* that poets possess the power to make "forms of opinion and action never before conceived." Did the Romantics popularize originality, or have we erased their contradictions in favor of a more compelling story?

Wordsworth borrowed descriptions of daffodils from his sister Dorothy's diary when writing his famous poem "I Wandered Lonely as a Cloud," and even credited its two best lines to his wife, Mary: "They flash upon that inward eye / Which is the bliss of solitude." Coleridge translated German idealist philosophers, particularly Schelling, and presented their writing as his own in *Biographia Literaria*. (Coleridge's defenders call it accidental and not dishonest, as Coleridge, they explain, was a messy note-taker.) Wordsworth and Coleridge even developed (with Dorothy's help!) ideas for what would become Coleridge's *The Rime of the Ancient Mariner*, which he based on a book by an English privateer: "Much the greatest part of the story was Mr. Coleridge's invention," Wordsworth would later write, "but certain parts I myself suggested."

But let's make a lengthy example of Shelley. Shelley wrote that originality "arises from within, like the colour of a flower which fades and changes as it is developed, and the conscious portions of our natures are unprophetic either of its approach or its departure." Yet if you read his letters chronologically, you can see that his anxiety to be original caused him severe writer's block. In 1818 he wrote to William Godwin, "I exercised myself, in the despair of producing anything original." That same day, he wrote to Thomas Love Peacock, "I have lately found myself totally incapable of original composition." The next year he wrote to Leigh Hunt, explaining that he had begun translating Latin because he "could absolutely do nothing else… original." Two years later, jealous of Lord Byron's success, he wrote to Peacock, "I write nothing and probably shall write no more."

Yet in 1820, in the preface to *Prometheus Unbound*, Shelley called complete poetic originality a ruse: "As to imitation, poetry is a mimetic art. It creates, but it creates by combination and representation. Poetical abstractions are beautiful and new, not because the portions of which they are composed had no previous existence in the mind of man, or in nature, but because the whole produced by their combination has some intelligible and beautiful analogy with those sources of emotion and thought, and with the contemporary condition of them." He continued, in the preface to *The Revolt of Islam*, "There must be a resemblance, which does not depend on their own will, between all the writers of any particular age," acknowledging "an influence which neither the meanest scribbler, nor the sublimest genius of any era, can escape, and which I have not attempted to escape."

A book that perfectly encapsulates the contradictions and complexities surrounding the English Romantics is an erasure of their works: *Gentle Reader!* by Joshua Beckman, Anthony McCann, and Matthew Rohrer. If you think erasure is valuable as an exercise but lacks literary merit, then I strongly recommend this book. You will find surreal images ("if you would knock at my door / you would hear / a bee pray to god and / the rose take apart the horizon") and straightforward but astonishingly expressed statements ("I would write / myself into the university / and be invincible / which was fatiguing"), evidence that erasure can achieve what Wordsworth called "the spontaneous overflow of powerful feelings," even though the process is influenced by prior work.

Only the title appears on its otherwise drab gray cover. The authors credit themselves alphabetically on the book's spine, a reminder that all writing is collaborative; however, they quietly wait until the last pages to cite, poem by poem, the works they erased, such as Wordsworth's "Michael," Shelley's "Julian and Maddalo," and Coleridge's "This Lime-Tree Bower My Prison." Never are we told which poet made which erasure. The book's semi-anonymity denies the concept of a singular author, telling us that originality begets originality. A traditional author biography—which ticks through awards, previous publications, and degrees, and lists where the author teaches and lives, another way of saying "Look at me! I exist!"—is printed nowhere in *Gentle Reader!* Its absence is an affirmation: the poem is more important than the poet.

Of course, a perfect affirmation would have been to publish it anonymously, the way Wordsworth and Coleridge's *Lyrical Ballads* first appeared, in 1798. (Coleridge, however, had urged his publisher to issue their work anonymously not for any idealistic reasons but because "Wordsworth's name is nothing—to a large number of persons mine stinks.") Wordsworth, in the preface to the 1802 edition, explains that he asked Coleridge to furnish him with poems for the book. "I should not," he wrote, "have requested this assistance, had I not believed that the poems of my friend would in a great measure have the same tendency as my own, and that, though there would be found a difference, there would be found no discordance in the colours of our style." Like Wordsworth and Coleridge, Beckman, McCann, and Rohrer's tendencies are very similar—all three demonstrate an uninhibited play of the imagination—but each possesses a voice recognizably his own. (When Beckman and Rohrer collaborate, as they did with 2002's *Nice Hat. Thanks.*, they write poems recognizably their collective own, a little lighter and more playful than their other work.) In the lines I am about to quote, unusual claims are made believable by their creators' intimate tones. Listen to Rohrer in his poem "Childhood Stories" as he expresses a sophisticated but naive wonder at people's reluctance to accept magical occurrences in life:

> They learned to turn off the
> gravity in an auditorium
> and we all rose into the air,
> the same room where they
> demonstrated
> pow-wows and prestidigitation.
>
> But not everyone believed it.
> That was the most important
> lesson
> I learned—that a truck driven
> by a dog
> could roll down a hill at dusk
> and roll right off a dock into a
> lake
> and sink, and if no one believes
> you
> then what is the point
> of telling them wonderful things?

Now observe Beckman assert innocence and then undercut it with guilt in "Final poem for the gently sifting public begins on the streets…":

> I am not greedy.
> I will do what I am told.

> I will not attempt to create the
>   eucalyptus tree
> or steal the lines of other poets.
> Oh Peter, I stole a tree from
>   your poem
> and now it is gone, and you
>   at home
> and me without your number.

Finally, compare those passages to the simultaneous clarity and ambiguity in lines by McCann. (He achieves this effect by making an assertion in each line, while avoiding end-stops.)

> I came out of the past, with
>   fingers all stained
> Behind my face my brain glows
>   like carp
> It's like this, you'll see, even
>   in pictures
> Leave it to someone to figure
>   that out

Not that this is required knowledge in order to appreciate *Gentle Reader!,* but you might find it interesting: Rohrer has said that his most personal poem appears in its pages. It isn't surprising if you believe empathy is the cornerstone of most great art. To quote Emerson again: "Every man is an inlet to the same, and to all of the same… What Plato has thought, he may think; what a saint has felt, he may feel; what at any time has befallen any man, he can understand. Who hath access to this universal mind, is a party to all that is or can be done, for this is the only and sovereign agent." This is what I love about the genre: the words the poet writes (by virtue of erasing others) may well be much more acute and crucial than what the poet thought he or she wanted to say. I won't tell you which poem Rohrer considers his most personal. Correctly guessing each poem's author isn't the fun of *Gentle Reader!* Reading the poems is.

VI.

Erasurists "submit" to new associations, assume the language suggested to them, and their work comes to life fecund with dynamic visions. Published last year by McSweeney's, *Of Lamb*, by Matthea Harvey and Amy Jean Porter, shows how amazing the visions can be. Harvey erased a biography of the English essayist Charles Lamb into a warped retelling of the celebrated nursery rhyme "Mary Had a Little Lamb." *Of Lamb* follows the tragic romance between a mercurial Mary and a lovesick Lamb. Told in a set of linked poems by Harvey and paintings by Porter, the words and art sustain each other, like a pair of trees grown together. After Mary rejects Lamb, Harvey's tropes and the changing colors of his wool show Lamb's overwhelming heartbreak: "He could hardly support his shadow," Harvey writes. "A dismal tide rushed in. Lamb turned to drink." Lamb is sent to a madhouse, where his delusions manifest: "I have sometimes in my dreams imagined myself as King Lamb, Emperor Lamb, higher than which is nothing but the Lamb of God."

No visual trace of the erasure's source, David Cecil's *A Portrait of Charles Lamb*, appears in *Of Lamb* (in this instance, erasure is less about the reader seeing absence and more about the writer using it to inform the creative process), though Harvey does credit the biography in her afterword. She explains that because the essayist had a sister named Mary, almost every page contains the words *Mary* and *Lamb*. As Harvey whited out Cecil's book, the nursery rhyme emerged, and dark descriptions of Charles's life with his sister quietly entered. Mary Lamb, at the age of thirty-one, went floridly mad, murdering their mother and wounding their father. Three years after their father died, Charles brought his sister to live with him, and they spent the rest of their lives together. Even though I began *Of Lamb* aware of the biography, I found myself forgetting about it for pages at a time, knowing only that I was enjoying a book of phenomenal originality and strangeness. With each re-reading, the biography became beside the point. After all, a book should stand on its own. Shouldn't it?

Tree of Codes disproves that. "For years I had wanted to create a die-cut book by erasure, a book whose meaning was exhumed from another book," Foer writes in his afterword. "I was in search of a text whose erasure would somehow be a continuation of its creation." He chose his favorite book, Bruno Schulz's *The Street of Crocodiles*, a collection of linked stories about, most memorably, the narrator's mad father. Rather than ghosting the words he wanted to erase, as Bervin did, he physically removed them to write a story that, instead of skipping forward and backward through time (as *The Street of Crocodiles* does), focuses on one day. Here the exclusion is not a matter of arbitrary formalism but the very heart of the book's meaning: after the Germans seized Drohobycz, Schulz's hometown, in 1941, he distributed his art and papers—which are believed to have included his unpublished novel, *Messiah*—to his gentile friends for safekeeping. The next year, a Gestapo officer killed Schulz on the street. He was sixty years old, and the bulk of his unpublished creative work has never been recovered. Only two slim story collections—*The Street of Crocodiles* and *Sanatorium Under the Sign of the Hourglass*—survive. Foer writes in his afterword, "Schulz's surviving work evokes all that was destroyed in the War: Schulz's lost books, drawings and paintings; those that he would have made had he survived; the millions of other victims, and within them the infinite expressions of infinite thoughts and feelings taking infinite forms." The holes in *Tree of Codes* intensely, persistently remind you that something is missing. You can peer through them to see words, sometimes entire sentences, printed pages later. No longer solid and immutable, words on page 44 are now neighbors with words on page 59. From page 15, you can read a sentence printed on page 29: "I heard the windows shake." Foer turned Schulz's songful sentences of prose into piercing lines of poetry. Using Schulz's own words, Foer writes, "The last secret of the tree of codes is that nothing can ever reach a definite conclusion." His words encapsulate the genre: erasure is never final.

Because the "original" is partially present in an erasure but entirely present somewhere else, some readers may find erasures, especially ones as visual as Foer's, inauthentic. In his 1936 essay "The Work of Art in the Age of Mechanical Reproduction," Walter Benjamin explains the concept of "aura," writing that "the presence of the original is the prerequisite to the concept of authenticity." Printed in Belgium, die-cut in the Netherlands, hand-finished in Belgium, bound in the Netherlands, and published by Visual Editions, a London-based book publisher, *Tree of Codes* has been mass-produced, though each copy—with the physical removal of select words—gives the illusion of being the original. Ironically, the first English translation of Benjamin's essay is inauthentic because it contains a (maybe) accidental erasure. First published by Jonathan Cape in 1970, and later by a branch of HarperCollins, the English translation is missing twelve words. Their absence collapses two sentences into one that botches a very important point by Benjamin. The last two sentences of Benjamin's original introduction should read, in English: "The concepts which are introduced into the theory of art in what follows differ from the more familiar terms in that they are completely useless for the purposes of fascism. They are, on the other hand, useful for the formulation of revolutionary demands in the politics of art." However, the words *purposes of fascism. They are, on the other hand, useful for the* are missing. The resulting sentence is grammatically correct but drastically changes Benjamin's meaning: "The concepts which are introduced into the theory of art in what follows differ from the more familiar terms in that they are completely useless for the formulation of revolutionary demands in the politics of art."

A mistake in translation, or a typing error? It is impossible to ask the translator, because the translator's name, strangely, remains unmentioned.

VII.

For some erasurists, the method is to begin with a minor model—an inadequate or middling book—and then, absorbing its nutrients, give birth to a better book. Ruefle did this, and the result was extraordinary. Other erasurists select a literary work they want to engage with rather than improve. In *Tree of Codes*, Foer erases Schulz's words to write, "The tree of codes was better than a paper imitation." It is not an imitation, but a new work that speaks to the "original" without imitating it.

The perfect example of engaging with a book some might consider impossible (or unethical) to improve is Thomas Jefferson's erasure of the Bible. In 1804, during the evening hours late in his first term as president, Thomas Jefferson began erasing the Gospel of Matthew. "In the

New Testament there is internal evidence that parts of it have proceeded from an extraordinary man," he wrote, "and that other parts are of the fabric of very inferior minds. It is as easy to separate those parts, as to pick out diamonds from dunghills." With the help of a razor blade and six books of the New Testament in four different languages (English, French, Greek, and Latin), Jefferson removed the supernatural aspects of the Bible (miracles, angels, the prophecy surrounding Jesus's birth), and anything he believed Matthew, Mark, Luke, or John had misinterpreted. (He does include references to the Great Flood, Noah's Ark, and the Second Coming, as well as to heaven, hell, and Satan.) Next, he collaged fragments together, chronologically arranging excerpts from the separate books of the Four Evangelists, to create one single narrative. To understand the doctrine of Jesus, he wanted to legitimize the Bible's more-believable claims. At times he made quiet edits that he felt would improve the text: for example, he removed the *as* in the construction *for as in a day*. By 1813, he had completed his erasure. He bound the final copy in Moroccan leather, titled it *The Life and Morals of Jesus of Nazareth,* and shared it with friends but never allowed it to be published, likely worried that he would again face accusations of being a non-Christian. After he died, it stayed in his family until the Smithsonian purchased it, in 1895, for four hundred dollars. That year, it was displayed at the International Cotton Exposition in Atlanta, and attracted so much attention that the Government Printing Office made lithographic reproductions that, for decades, were given to new congressmen. Commonly referred to today as the Jefferson Bible, it is being studied and conserved at the National Museum of American History. What he once called his "wee little book" is valued for its creative approach to reading the Bible.

The contemporary writer and visual artist Jen Bervin also edited a literary work some may consider it taboo to erase: Shakespeare's sonnets. Rather than seeking to improve the sonnets, Bervin wanted to understand them through erasure. As I fell into [Shakespeare's son]*Nets*, I felt as if my bifocal vision had failed: two poems appear on each page, hers overlapping Shakespeare's but both readily apparent. The conflicting dark and light print and her anxious tone ("I / use / the whole, and yet

am I not") deepen the erasure: a young poet's struggle against her mas-
terful forebear becomes an homage to his indispensability.
Cue Harold Bloom. "The largest truth of literary influence," Bloom
writes, "is that it is an irresistible anxiety: Shakespeare will not allow
you to bury him, or escape him, or replace him." Bloom more generally argues that "the poet in a poet" finds inspiration by reading another
poet's work, but almost always produces poetry that is derivative of the
existing poetry. If poets subscribe to Bloom's theory, they may descend,
as Shelley did, into unbearable writer's block. So instead of *derivative*,
let's use the word *different*. It is great if a poet improves a work, but I find
erasures interesting because their authors make existing books new.

That celebrated directive, the motto of modernism, Ezra Pound's
"Make it new" (a translation of Confucius, who borrowed it from
Emperor T'ang, who inscribed on his bathtub "Every day make it new"),
helped give birth to fresh styles of writing. Indeed, one of the most prominent themes of modernism is the shadowy yet influential character of
the forebear. Modernism has been accused of ignoring the past, but
really it's about first examining the past and then wiping it out through
intense revision as a way to push forward. Modernism could not exist
without tradition. The modernists understood that in order to be a great
writer, one must first be a great reader. Similarly, Bloom offers hope:
only through creatively misreading the old masters can young poets
"clear imaginative space" for themselves. Erasurists find their imaginative space by reading creatively.

One of the genre's most creative readers is Srikanth Reddy. Not only
is his erasure, the book *Voyager*, conceptually captivating, but the writing
is amazing. Let me repeat that: the writing is *amazing*. Here's an excerpt:
"As a child, spelling out / *world* was to open a world in myself, private and / byzantine, with mountains by a pale fragile sea, / the coast
stretching southwards in the curtained / evening hours."

If you think erasure easily results in writing this good, consider
this: *Voyager* took Reddy seven years to produce. When I explain his
reasoning and method, you'll understand why.

Its title refers to the *Voyager* spacecraft, which launched in 1977
when Reddy was four years old. A golden record affixed to *Voyager*'s

side contained a friendly greeting from Kurt Waldheim, then the secretary general of the United Nations: "We step out of our solar system into the universe seeking only peace and friendship, to teach if we are called upon, to be taught if we are fortunate. We know full well that our planet and all its inhabitants are but a small part of the immense universe that surrounds us and it is with humility and hope that we take this step."

Eight years after his words were sent into space, Waldheim was accused of having served as a Nazi SS officer. He maintained his innocence, but admitted that, as a young member of the military staff, with no authority on the army level, he had known about German reprisals against partisans: "Yes, I knew. I was horrified. But what could I do? I had either to continue to serve or be executed." With that silence in mind, Reddy erased Waldheim's memoir, *In the Eye of the Storm,* which, remarkably, never addresses the scandal surrounding his war years: the memoir itself is a form of erasure.

Crossing out Waldheim's words, sentences, and sometimes whole paragraphs (and preserving the remaining words in their original order), Reddy erased the memoir three times—once for each section of *Voyager.* The first section addresses, with clipped poetic lines, the silence and complicity enmeshed in all of us: "The silent alone lie united," Reddy writes. The second section explores, in the form of prose poems, *Voyager's* composition and Reddy's own silence and complicity as a scholar opposed to the Iraq War: "As / I write these lines, people with pictures of / fighters killed in action run through New York's / traffic-choked streets, rising to the spirit of the / occasion, while I, sitting in my second-floor / office connected to various communications / cables, maintain control over some very unruly / emotional forces."

The third section inhabits Waldheim's voice with poems that preserve the spaces left by Reddy's deletions from the memoir: "I was led to a globe, / beholden / to its vast revolution / —a revolution living eyes / could hardly credit— / my life diminishing in scale."

For the rest of his life, Waldheim was praised and vilified. Pope John Paul II awarded him a papal order of knighthood. The US government banned him. But never does Reddy judge Waldheim: "The failed idea repeatedly described in this book," Reddy writes, "is *alter ego.*"

Janet Holmes also used erasure to write a deeply political book. She found a way to write about the Iraq war by erasing the poems Emily Dickinson wrote during (but not directly about) the Civil War. "I couldn't have engaged in this process without a deep reverence for the work of Emily Dickinson," Holmes has said of *The Ms of My Kin* (the title is an erasure of "*The Poems of Emily Dickinson*"). "My intention was to share both her language and her tone in poems that reflect a substantially different war than the one that raged during her lifetime. In my ideal imaginary, a reader would feel compelled to go back to the original poems, and would experience some resonance between the originals and the erasures. I hope the layout of the poems, with Dickinson's originals floating, ghostly, behind them, encourages such reading." Dickinson's poems are already so condensed. Their contours and organizations of sound have about them an air of having been foreordained. Yet Holmes condenses them into succinct descriptions of 9/11: "a feeling / Yesterday / Of Ground / letting go—." Dickinson's capitalization of *Ground* enriches the erasure, linking the described feeling to what physically happened at Ground Zero. This is precisely what makes *The Ms of My Kin* so ambitious.

Another Dickinson devotee (author of *My Emily Dickinson*) and practicing erasurist is Susan Howe. Howe begins her recent collection, *That This,* with a lyric essay that contains a willed erasure of select memories of her deceased husband: "Now—putting bits of memory together, trying to pick out the good while doing away with the bad—I'm left with one overwhelming impression—the unpresentable violence of a negative double." She asks if a trace of something can become the something it traces, "secure as ever, real as ever—a chosen set of echo-fragments?" For the second section of *That This,* Howe used scissors, tape, and a copy machine to collage an eighteenth-century woman's diary: "Even the 'invisible' scotch tape…" Howe observes, "leaves traces on paper when I run each original sheet through the Canon copier." The most powerful absence, she shows us, is visual.

*　*　*

VIII.

After my father died, men removed his body from our home. They left the bed.

Hospice had loaned him the bed to die in. His last days were the only memories the bed offered me. One night I stood in the doorway and imagined him still breathing in his room.

A week later, different men returned and wheeled his last days from our home. I can't decide what filled me with more emptiness: the empty bed, or the empty room.

I wanted to convince you that "to erase is to write," but more than that I want to remind you of my father's absence. He is the reason behind most of what I write, even this.

I have yet to complete the book I promised him nine years ago. Honoring him in a form that removes the blank page makes the endeavor feel possible. Honoring him in a form issuing wholly from loss feels right. To eulogize my father using a method that at once alludes directly to him and reminds one of his absence, all the while describing my feeling of loss: this is why erasure interests me. It is an example of what words are for. ✳

REBECCA TAYLOR

VIRGINIA MOUNTAIN
SCREAM QUEEN

DISCUSSED: *The Setup, Meryl Streep's Daughter,*
The Girl Before the Opening Credits, No-Budget Horror Movies,
A Stipulation Regarding Nipples, A Dream Sequence,
Hopeful Non-Union Actors, The Preparation of Spiderella,
Evil Jesters, Different Nightmares

A movie can set up a lot in a few fast moments before the opening credits: this is whom to care for, this is whom to fear, this is who will love, who will hurt, who will die. The first moments of a movie can foreshadow the end, or they can tell you what came before.

A sixteen-year-old girl moves alone to New York City with the dream of becoming an actress. Her mother believes in dreams like these, so she lets her go. In New York City, the girl lands an agent who sends her on her first audition—to play the part of Meryl Streep's daughter. The role goes to Claire Danes, and this is the way it always goes. She reads for a dance movie—she is not a dancer. She reads for Juliet—she is too tall. The girl does not become an actress, but she learns how to lose an agent, and how many days of solitary silence it takes to forget the sound of her own voice. By her eighteenth birthday, she's back home in Virginia. She's a waitress living in the woods with her parents.

Here, in the Virginia woods, is where the opening credits start, where the names of the stars appear. But there are no big stars in this picture. The girl before the opening credits, whom by now you should care for, if she did her job—that girl is me. But I'm not a star, and I don't have top billing in this story. In this story, another name comes before mine, and it's the sort of name that appears before the title. I could have put it up top on this page to begin with, but I chose not to. I'm the one who gets to tell the rest of my story, and since this part is about moviemaking—and movies are made with tricks—I chose to deceive you. But I will reveal it now.

In the beginning, it's 2001, and I'm back home in Virginia, living with my parents and my fifteen-year-old sister in the house I grew up in. The house sits on a hill, surrounded by forest. It's the very end of the summer. You can't see the river through the trees, but you can hear it.

Here's a shot of me: a pale girl with long, brown hair.

Here's a shot of the house on the hill.

Here's a shot of the trees changing colors.

A title appears on the screen: *John Johnson's Virginia Mountain Scream Queen.*

Fade to black.

Fade in on my mother clipping an ad for me from the local newspaper: on Saturday, in a playground on the other side of the mountain, in the little factory town of Waynesboro, Darkstone Entertainment will hold an open audition for an "Independent Low-Budget Horror-Western."

When the day arrives, I put on my boots and my jeans and my denim jacket. I climb into my rusted-out Volvo wagon, and drive away from my mother and father and sister, away from our home in the woods. I drive twenty miles deeper into rural Virginia, up and over the mountain, to the Waynesboro playground. Beside the swing sets, I find a concert stage. Beside the concert stage, I find an audience of cowboys and Civil

War reenactors who introduce themselves as producers and investors. Among them is a young man with dark hair and green eyes, wearing a Hawaiian shirt and a vintage fedora—John Johnson, director and star.

John Johnson says he shot his first movie at the age of eight. In his twenty-two years, John Johnson tells me, he has made over fifty "no-budget" horror movies.

I tell John Johnson that I'm an actress from New York City.

John Johnson wants to know—can I ride horses?

I grew up with horses.

He hands me a Civil War–era dress. He asks me if I'll put it on for him.

I hold the dress up to my body, and John Johnson's casting director, Melissa, appears beside him. She whispers something in his ear, and I wonder if she's his girlfriend. She turns to me and asks me if I will follow her.

Melissa leads me to a spot behind a wall and turns her back to me. She tells me to take off my clothes and try on the dress. When I step out from behind the wall, I'm in costume.

I follow Melissa back to John Johnson, who is waiting by the stage. She tells him the dress is too tight in the bust. He looks me up and down, and assures me the dress can be altered. Then he gives me a script. He asks me onto the stage with him to read for the part of his love interest.

And I read with him. I take his direction. I read for him, and I put my heart into it. And when it's over, John Johnson smiles, and I climb down from the stage.

I change back into my own clothes, and I say good-bye to Melissa. I thank John Johnson and the cowboy producers and the Civil War reenactor investors. And I can feel John Johnson watching me as I walk away, across the playground to the parking lot. I drive back over the mountain to my parents' house in the woods, where I smile as I tell my mother that I think I did well, and she smiles as she tells me she has a pretty good feeling I will get this one.

The next day the phone rings. It's John Johnson calling to offer me the part of his love interest.

There's no up-front pay, he tells me, but there will be points on the back end.

I don't know what "points on the back end" means, but I decide this is the way it must be in Independent Low-Budget Horror-Westerns. I ask him—has anyone else signed on? Anyone that I might know of?

He tells me Conrad Brooks has a cameo, a veteran of the Ed Wood movies, an actor from *Plan 9 from Outer Space*.

I've never heard of Conrad Brooks or Ed Wood or *Plan 9 from Outer Space,* but I'm ready to believe that this means something.

Then John Johnson wants to know—how do I feel about nudity? How do I feel about my breasts in a sex scene?

And I know just what to say: I'll have to read the script first. I'll have to get back to you.

After we hang up, John Johnson emails me the script. I read it, and my mother reads it, and I read the script again. The movie is called *John Johnson's The Just.* It's a tale of love, betrayal, and vengeance in which a cowardly soldier (John Johnson), with the help of a phantom cowboy and an escaped slave, must stand up to a band of notorious gun-slinging outlaws.

My character's name is Liz, and she's a waitress in an Old West saloon. And to be her, to be Liz, I will need to love John Johnson's character, and I will need to be loved by John Johnson's character. I will need to suffer. I will need to cry. I will need to fight back.

I decide that I'm up for this.

My mother agrees. Just don't show your nipples, she warns me.

I pick up the phone. I call John Johnson back. I tell him: I accept the part. I will do the sex scene. I will not show my nipples.

John Johnson agrees to my stipulation—it must be that he does not want anyone else but me. John Johnson, maker of over fifty no-budget horror movies, has chosen me over all the other actresses who must have also auditioned on a Saturday in a playground in a little factory town in the Virginia mountain valley.

Two weeks later, I'm riding horses Western saddle. I'm wearing corsets and firing pistols. I'm an actress, and I've found my director.

*   *   *

Cut to one month later: I've moved out of my parents' house, and I'm living with John Johnson in his double-wide trailer at the foot of Afton Mountain. The iron mountain water stains my hair red, makes my skin smell like hard-boiled eggs. The trash man won't come up the rutted-out driveway, so John Johnson keeps the trash on the roof, where the bears can't reach it. I find all of this terribly romantic.

A montage: snow falls on the trash on the roof of the double-wide trailer. By day, I lounge on John Johnson's little red bunk bed while he edits me together in *John Johnson's The Just*. By night, I lie on John Johnson's couch, while he plays me five features, one television show, and forty-four scrappy video shorts, starring John Johnsons ranging in age from eight to twenty-two—and featuring all the screaming women who have come before me.

Then, one night while we're sleeping, there's a dream sequence—John Johnson's dream, not mine. In it, I'm naked in a hot tub. My breasts are the size of watermelons, and, like balloons, they're floating on top of the water.

I know this dream because John Johnson tells it to me the next day. He says he likes my much-smaller breasts the way they are—that he likes me the way I am—but his dream made him realize that if I had a boob job, I could take over the horror industry. I'm just a boob job away from becoming a scream queen.

John Johnson loves the horror industry, so I take this as a compliment.

The reason he loves horror, he says, is because all other genres can exist within it. There can be drama-horror, comedy-horror, fantasy-horror, action-horror.

There can be a love story within a horror story.

John Johnson's The Just, starring Mitch Toney, David Harscheid, Rebecca Taylor, David Simmons III, and John Johnson, premieres at a discount movie theater in Staunton, Virginia. The exclusive one-night engagement sells out to mothers, fathers, sisters, grandmothers, aunts, uncles, friends and friends of friends, parents of friends, ex-boyfriends and new girlfriends, fellow waitresses from restaurants, cowboy producers, and Civil War reenactor investors. I wear a long black lace dress and fire-engine red lipstick. John Johnson wears his fedora and his best Hawaiian shirt. My mother arrives with her hair curled. My father arrives in a tuxedo.

The theater goes dark, and since John Johnson does not watch his own movies, he slips out back to go for a walk, leaving the seat beside me empty.

John Johnson's The Just begins, and for the first time I see myself on the big screen, and for the first time I understand what it means that the movie has been shot on a home video camera. Night scenes are so dark that they're just disembodied voices over a black screen. David Simmons, the actor who plays the escaped slave, has no discernible facial features—he's only a faint outline of a man in a poncho and a wide, floppy hat.

And of all my many scenes, there is only one—the sex scene—where I find myself convincing, where I know that I am any good at all.

Two-shot: I kiss John Johnson's character.

Medium-shot: I unhook my corset—nipples hidden under my long brown hair.

Close-up: innocence. Longing. Love me. *Take me.*

The movie ends. John Johnson returns to receive his audience, and the lights come up on my mother, my father, my sister, my grandmothers, my aunts, my uncles, my friends, their friends, their parents, my ex-boyfriend and his new girlfriend, my fellow waitresses from the restaurant, the cowboy producers and Civil War reenactor investors. In the lobby of the discount movie theater, I am hugged by them all: congratulations, what an accomplishment, this is only the beginning.

I assist John Johnson with two short films whose titles he does not put his name before, because they are short. In *Darkness*, I'm an innocent young mother murdered by a demon. In *Cryptic*, I'm a ghost of a mute woman who's lost her lover. The shorts are good enough to be accepted into the first annual Blue Ridge-Southwest Virginia Vision Film Festival in Roanoke, Virginia, in the spring.

John Johnson decides he's ready to make another feature. He does not read, but he thinks he might like to make a Dracula movie that is true to the book. He has me read Bram Stoker's novel for him, and I decide I want to be the character Mina Murray.

Mina is a writer. She has "brains and foresight." She's seduced by darkness, but she overcomes it. I tell John Johnson that the book is amazing—epic, romantic, Gothic, and full of adventure. John Johnson tells me we will make the most faithful retelling of *Dracula* the world has ever seen, but we will set it in modern times, so the movie can be made for under two thousand dollars. He calls the movie *John Johnson's Alucard*—*Dracula* backward.

John Johnson tells me I am the perfect Mina, but that if we want to sell "our movie," it would help if I showed my left breast.

And I agree to show my left breast. Because I want so badly to be Mina. Because I am devoted to John Johnson, and John Johnson is devoted to making *John Johnson's Alucard,* a movie he is calling "our movie," and I want to sell "our movie."

Since "our movie" will have my left breast in it, I want the movie to be better than *John Johnson's The Just.* I want to help John Johnson make *John Johnson's Alucard* the very best a two-thousand-dollar movie can be. John Johnson thinks this is a good idea, and so after he casts himself as Quincy Morris, the American cowboy martyr, he makes me his new casting director, and I wrangle together one hundred-plus hopeful non-union actors who are willing to work for free.

But John Johnson's two-thousand-dollar budget doesn't include paying himself, either, so right when we're about to start shooting, we get evicted from his double-wide trailer. And since I am devoted to John Johnson, and my parents are devoted to me, they let us move into the basement of their house in the woods.

This is where we are when I turn nineteen, when production on *John Johnson's Alucard* begins and the actress playing Lucy Westenra discovers that she's pregnant. John Johnson is not confident that we will be able to finish our three-and-a-half-hour movie before her second trimester, so I must recast.

I'm having a very hard time finding a beautiful blond actress for John Johnson until my younger sister gives me the number of her friend Mariah, an eighteen-year-old waitress, dancer, and aspiring actress. So I invite Mariah to audition for Lucy, my character's best friend—John Johnson's character's love interest.

Mariah is perfect. She's even better than the original—beautiful and sexy, dimply and enthusiastic, and more than willing to work for free. I think she's really great, and John Johnson really loves her. She won't do nudity, but John Johnson agrees to this stipulation because he has no choice. There isn't anyone else.

Two weeks later, we're all playing our parts. We're making *John Johnson's Alucard* together.

A month later, my father gives John Johnson a tiny, windowless office, in a building he manages, as an effort to get him out of the basement. So John Johnson moves out of my parents' basement and into this office, and then he leaves me for Mariah.

But I am his Mina—I've exposed my un-augmented left breast—and there are countless hours of footage of Swannanoa, a Virginia mountain castle, already shot, and there are one hundred-plus hopeful actors I hired myself who have been working for free for months. So I finish our movie, and John Johnson rewards me for my dedication—he asks me to be his producer.

A producer finances, supervises, coordinates, and controls the execution of a story. A good producer does all of this while remaining as dedicated as possible to the creative vision of the director. John Johnson has Mariah now, but he wants me beside him—he wants me to control the execution of his vision. So I take the power John Johnson has given me—the only power I have left—and I learn how to wield it.

I move out of my parents' house and into my grandmother's house to be closer to the Darkstone office, and before John Johnson finishes editing *John Johnson's Alucard*, we begin planning our next project. I turn twenty spending my days and nights with John Johnson, watching every straight-to-video horror movie we can get our hands on, and I learn from these examples that if we want our movies to make money, we need to have a lot more sex, nudity, and gore. And we need a very sensational premise:

Four fedora-and-trench-coat-clad demon hunters are trapped in a haunted hospital with a gaggle of wannabe sorority girls pledging in their underwear.

John Johnson's Shadowhunters stars John Johnson as Hudson, the demon-hunting Byronic hero, and while Mariah does not have a part in this movie—she is not willing to be in a movie in her underwear—I do. I play Sera, a sullen sorority pledge whose looks are deceiving, who turns out to be much more than she appears.

As casting director and producer, it is my job to initiate John Johnson's nine other sorority girls, to prepare them for the winter shoot in the unheated, abandoned hospital. So in an empty room in my father's office building, beside the windowless office John Johnson sleeps in, I form a circle with the women. I tell them to strip. Then I help them choose the most flattering and character-appropriate bra-and-panty sets possible.

I do this for John Johnson, and he sells his first movie, to the shock-and-horror distributor Brain Damage Films. *John Johnson's Shadowhunters* lands on the shelves of Hollywood Video, Best Buy, and Movie Gallery. It eventually makes it onto Netflix, and even hits cable television—in Thailand.

The relative success of *John Johnson's Shadowhunters* helps John Johnson attach his first scream queen, Brinke Stevens (*The Slumber Party Massacre*), which helps me raise enough financing for John Johnson to remake one of his fifty no-budget horror titles—*John Johnson's Skeleton Key*, a comedy-horror movie (not to be confused with *The Skeleton Key*, starring Kate Hudson). This financing also makes it possible for John Johnson to hire another scream queen—Debbie Rochon, of Troma's *Citizen Toxie: Toxic Avenger 4*.

The premise: a down-on-his luck tabloid reporter, Howard (John Johnson), travels to the town of Nilbog in search of a two-headed, five-legged goat. There he does not find his goat, but he finds a town overrun with monsters.

A few outtakes from *John Johnson's Skeleton Key*:

Spiderella (Brinke Stevens) sits topless on a chair I have taken from the dining room of my parents' house, while I paint spiderwebs across her breasts. She is small and sweet and perky, as are her breasts, and John Johnson was wrong—I do not need a boob job to be a scream queen.

Late one night, on location, John Johnson asks me to get down on my knees to clean up the pig guts he's used to effect the disembowelment of another aspiring actress.

Here, on my knees, with my hands covered in gore, I realize how unhappy I am.

In 2005, at twenty-one, I leave John Johnson. I move back to New York City with the dream of rekindling my sixteen-year-old dream.

But in New York City, my Darkstone reel is unconvincing, and I'm unable to find another agent. I do not become a serious film actress. I become a cocktail waitress in a bowling alley in Port Authority Bus Terminal, a cashier in a dumpling shop in the Flatiron district, and a shot girl on East Fifty-Third Street and Second Avenue.

But then one afternoon while I'm crossing West Houston, something happens: I find myself, for the first time, enjoying the experience of walking alone down a New York street in springtime, and, for just a moment, I realize that I'm happy to be where I am.

Four days later, John Johnson visits New York. And again, *alone* and *lonely* become one and the same for me, and I do not know why I left Virginia to become a cocktail waitress, cashier, and shot girl.

A month later, I'm back for the premiere of the long-awaited *John Johnson's Alucard*, posing beside Mariah on the Darkstone green carpet outside the theater at Piedmont Virginia Community College, and before I know what's happening, I'm moving out of my apartment in New York City, and I'm moving back into my grandmother's house across from the Darkstone office. Before I know what's happening, I'm escorting John Johnson to his very first horror convention—Horrorfind Weekend in Maryland—where pale men in black T-shirts line up at the Darkstone Entertainment booth with Sharpies to collect our autographs.

One year. Three John Johnson movies. They all start with the letter *D*:

John Johnson's Deceptors—*Ghostbusters* meets *John Johnson's Shadowhunters* meets *John Johnson's Skeleton Key*. John Johnson plays a sex-crazed con man. I play a love-struck princess turned beast dog. Mariah agrees to do nudity, so John Johnson gives her two parts: a naked succubus without eyes and a naive victim of a sex-crazed con man.

John Johnson's Darken—*The Last Unicorn* meets *John Johnson's Deceptors* meets *Die Hard*. John Johnson revives his role of the romantic lead with an eighteen-year-old actress. I turn twenty-two, begrudgingly producing *John Johnson's Darken*, and John Johnson makes me a villain. Mariah's father plays a villain, too. Mariah plays a torture victim.

John Johnson's Democ—*Blade Runner* meets *John Johnson's Shadowhunters* meets *Trancers* meets an '80s computer game. John Johnson plays the lead—a zombie-hunting gangster playboy. But the part I want (the lounge singer who seduces John Johnson's character) requires nudity, and since I've decided I will no longer do nudity, I take a cameo, and Mariah choreographs a dance for the opening credits, and then she plays the heroine.

After wrapping *John Johnson's Democ*, Mariah's mom gives me a book—*The Princessa: Machiavelli for Women*—and I start taking meetings with another Virginia production company.

* * *

The summer John Johnson and I make our final movie together, I'm house-sitting for my parents while they're on vacation, so John Johnson and I begin prepping *John Johnson's The Jester*—a movie that can be shot entirely in the house my father built, which is as old as I am.

And so with my parents gone, I sleep in their bed, while the actor who picks his nose (whom John Johnson casts as my love interest) sleeps in my old bed, while John Johnson sleeps with Mariah in my sister's old bed, while extras sleep in sleeping bags in the basement, where John Johnson and I once slept, while my parents' half-feral cocker spaniel howls at the woods for my parents to come back. While my mother and father tour Venezuela, evil jesters catapult themselves from the treetops onto the roof of my childhood home, self-taught West Virginia stuntmen light my gravel driveway on fire, and women scream naked and bloody in the bathtub where my mother once bathed me.

When my parents return, four weeks later, the movie is shot and the horror is over.

A month before turning twenty-three, I move out of my grandmother's house and back into my home in the woods.

Here, in the Virginia woods, I use John Johnson's equipment to produce and direct a short film of my own called *Never Seen by Waking Eyes*. I do not act in this film—I give the lead to one of John Johnson's actresses. I do not have the words yet to write my story. Since I'm a moviemaker, I use images.

A girl is lost in the forest until she meets a man. She follows him through different dimensions, through different nightmares, until she finds herself standing alone in a spotlight, on a stage before an empty theater.

The girl looks out and sees a shadowy figure standing in front of the exit. She watches the figure disappear through the door, and she runs after it, off the stage, through the empty theater. She hesitates before pushing the door open and stepping out into the light.

Outside, the girl finds herself back in the forest, standing face to face with her old self. In the end, she sees who she was before she met the man. And she smiles. *

DARK FAMILY

DISCUSSED: *Familial Debauchery, Lowered Sensibilities,
The Dark Side of the '70s, Freudian Romance, Adolescent Rage,
Middle-Class Suburban Drama, Recurrent Incest,
The Mordant Reality of Hansel and Gretel, Nostalgia,
Repressed Childhood Desires, Fears That Do Not Vanish,
Soulless Retribution, Maternal Unrest, Dying Alone*

1.

This year marks the thirtieth anniversary of the publication of V. C. Andrews's *Flowers in the Attic*, the best-selling novel about incest, imprisoned children, and very, very bad parenting. Andrews went on to write six more books, each one beloved by millions of readers, mostly young women, and each a play on the same themes that made *Flowers* wonderful and unique: lust, violence, and pain. For two generations now, a private ritual of female adolescence has been reading Andrews's spine-creased paperbacks, often passed down from an older, wiser girl with the whispered promise of secret knowledge hidden between the covers.

But despite her popularity, almost nothing has been published on Andrews. While gallons of ink have been spilled over genre

Illustration by Tony Millionaire

novelists Philip K. Dick and Jim Thompson, the sum total of book-length Andrewsiana consists of one guide for the library market, one bibliographic checklist, and one mass-market trivia book. It's hard to imagine another writer in the same peculiar position.

You could argue that Andrews's books are so unusual and original that critics, scholars, and other "serious" readers don't know what to do with them. Though there's an obvious debt to the Brontë sisters, nineteenth-century sensation novels like *Lady Audley's Secret,* and Daphne du Maurier's Gothic fiction, at heart Andrews's novels have little in common with the genres they ought to fit into. They're too offbeat for romance, too slow to qualify as thrillers, too explicit for Gothic, and far too dark and complex for young adult. Many booksellers shelve them with horror, but Andrews's concerns with family, emotion, and relationships put her books firmly outside the genre. Although the supernatural makes brief appearances in Andrews's work, her largest topic is the all-too-natural tragedy of families gone wrong.

Ultimately, Andrews's novels constitute their own genre, in which secrets, lies, desire, and moral corruption all stem from—and are contained in—the family. In her world, parents starve their children, sister and brother become husband and wife, and grandparents punish grandchildren for being the "devil's spawn." No one is to be trusted, and few adults are who they claim to be. Most significantly, there are no happy endings. For all their teen-girl fantasy elements, the books are also gritty, raw, and extremely dirty. There is little cynical or formulaic about them. If anything, they are too raw, too revealing of the author's own obsessions—which, as we'll see, might be exactly why no one ever talks about them.

On the rare occasions when reviewers have been compelled, presumably by cruel editors, to write about the books, they concur: V. C. Andrews isn't just bad, she is beneath contempt. *"Flowers…* is deranged swill,"* a *Washington Post* reviewer opined in 1979. In a 1982 *New York Times* "Fiction in Brief" column that includes reviews of potboilers like Danielle Steel's *Crossings* and Shirley Conran's *Lace,* the most venomous is reserved for *My Sweet Audrina,* Andrews's strangest book and her only stand-alone novel.

The reviewer claims she's unable even to follow the story line, then asserts that she not only doesn't understand the book, she doesn't want to. "The story begins when the second Audrina, the narrator, is about 7 but since she isn't allowed to go to school and is regularly told she has no memory, who knows?" she writes. "Who cares is another question.... Damian and Ellsbeth become lovers again. Ellsbeth dies. Does a sensible reader really want to know more?"

More recently, in 2001, Zoe Williams, writing in the *Guardian*, dismisses Andrews's writing as stunted ramblings that read as if "done by computer, with a built-in Teetering On The Brink Of Womanhood template."

The passage of thirty years, and the devotion of millions of young women, hasn't helped Andrews's reception at all (although, to be fair, the devotion of millions of young women has rarely helped any artist's reputation much). In the first glow of *Flowers*'s success, when Andrews was at least mentioned in industry news reports, she was often cited in the same breath as up-and-coming horror writer Stephen King. But while King has gone on to respectability and full-page reviews in the *New York Times*, V. C. Andrews is still the same shunned "trash" novelist. And while horror, mystery, and science fiction have earned some respectability from a blurred high/low division in pop culture, Andrews's books are pretty much just where the *Times* reviewer left them in 1982. The sensible reader does not want to know more.

If we were less sensible, and *did* want to know more, what would we see? Maybe that Andrews picked up on something that was swirling around her, a dark side of the 1970s we still haven't looked at very clearly and whose shadows still cling to us. Maybe we would discover that her books actually contain a taloned commentary on the Freudian family romance, the process by which children escape their parents' erotic hold by fantasizing that they are the abandoned offspring of a noble family (or, in the case of *Flowers*, the cast-aside product of an incestuous marriage). Certainly we find in Andrews's books a more disturbing look at the secret lives of girls. In a 2004 article in this magazine, Amy Benfer writes of the gauzy pleasures of the *Sweet Valley High* novels, their pastel covers offering "the most satisfying form of pornography I had." When we look at Andrews, however, we see an astoundingly sinister view of girls' sexuality that yokes punishment and desire. Both *Sweet Valley High* and *Flowers* feature twins prominently—and it is hard not to see a dark joke in the name Andrews gives her twins, Dollanganger, as if they are the dark doppelgängers of every teen twin tale to come before, or after. But while the *Sweet Valley High* books reassure teen readers with creamy covers and tales of malls and school rivalries, the *Flowers* series offers up a saga of sin, terror, and revenge, the dark covers featuring a keyhole, beckoning us in. In reckoning with our pleasure in her books, then, we must examine our own drive to see our darkest desires and shame writ large again and again. We might even have to revisit our own personal tales of abuse, and our feeble attempts to lock trauma up and throw away the key. Most of all, if we weren't so sensible, we would see a full flowering of adolescent-girl rage.

2.

V. C. Andrews's books were an instant success, beginning with the publication of *Flowers*, in 1979. While most famous for her first series, Andrews also completed one stand-alone novel, *My Sweet Audrina* (1982), and the first two books of a series about the trials of the intertwined Casteel and Tatterton families. (After Andrews's death—around the time of the second book of the Casteel series—books continued to be written under the V. C. Andrews name by ghostwriter Andrew Neiderman.)

At the center of *Flowers* is the Dollanganger family, a beautiful, middle-class suburban clan whose blissful life is shattered when the beloved father is killed in a car accident. Our narrator, teenage Cathy, along with her three siblings—older brother Chris and a pair of younger twins, Cory and Carrie—accepts her mother's word that the only way they can survive is if she can win back the love of her wealthy father, who rejected her when she married. The family moves to the estranged father's ancestral estate, Foxworth Hall. The four children bunk in the attic while their mother attempts to reestablish her relationship with her father. At first the attic, which is spruced up with bedrooms, a bathroom, and desks, seems like a safe, if dreary, temporary resting place. As we go on, we learn that the initial estrangement occurred because Cathy and her siblings are the product of an incestuous union: their mother and their (late) father were half-uncle and niece. (In a later book it's proven they are, actually, even closer relations.) As the four children languish, we slowly learn that their grandfather doesn't even know they exist, and that their mother and grandmother have conspired to hide them until their grandfather's death.

From here, as the mother visits less and less often, virtually abandoning her children, the attic becomes a nightmare (or fantasy) of deprivation and desire. A string of hysterical events unfurls, including confrontations with the wicked grandmother, the violent consummation of Cathy and Chris's incestuous longings, the fatal poisoning of one of the twins, and the near murder of all the children by their unhinged mother. After four years the three remaining children finally escape Foxworth Hall by their own devices, pale and stunted from years without sunshine, fresh air, or companionship. The rest of the series details the children's lives as they become adults outside the attic and Cathy's rage-fueled obsession with exacting revenge on her mother and grandmother.

The writer and critic Douglas E. Winter, one of few to consider Andrews seriously and one of only a handful to interview her, describes the fantastical quality that's central to the book's appeal: "[The story] is animated by nightmarish passions of greed, cruelty, and incest, yet is told in romantic, fairy-tale tones, producing some of the most highly individualistic tales of terror of this generation." Andrews herself picks up on this note later in the interview, saying about her own writing process: "I didn't want a real horror, like a rapist or a murderer, but I wanted a fairy-tale horror."

Returning to Andrews's books as an adult, we find that they retain their fairy-tale quality. As with re-reading favorite children's books, the experience is like stepping into a dream. There's a sense of déjà vu, as that which has been forgotten—not just the books but the whole world of associations they carry—becomes real again. But given the luridness and eccentricity of the books, the feeling is far from a cozy one. It's a feeling many of us resist: do we want to venture into that world again? Do we want to admit how much we loved that world or, worse, how much our desires, in fact, constructed it?

To acknowledge Andrews's appeal, then, forces us to go to a place we visit in daydreams and poems but not in our normal, everyday, waking life—the semiconscious, half-remembered realm of children's stories, fantasy, and fairy tales. And as anyone who's read the unsanitized Grimms' tales knows, this is not the candy-colored vista where Disney movies were filmed. As adults we try to forget that we ever visited this sinister place—the place where Cinderella's stepsisters cut off their toes to fit into the glass slipper, where children were cooked and eaten in a gingerbread house, where Cathy Dollanganger was locked away in the towers of Foxworth Hall. But Andrews's books remind us that we've kept a hidden key to this world in our pocket all along. In other words, what makes us uncomfortable isn't the feeling that, when we open the pages of Andrews's books, we don't recognize anything. Instead, we're made uncomfortable because we recognize *everything*.

Freud wrote about this discomfort at remembering in his 1919 essay "The Uncanny." He focused on the unusual etymology of the German words *heimlich* and *unheimlich*, both of which carry at least two seemingly contradictory meanings: of *homely* and *familiar*, but also of *concealed, secret, kept from sight*. The uncanny sensation derives from encountering *not* what is strange or distant from our experience, but rather its opposite—that which is close to home, familiar, intimate, but has been rendered unfamiliar through repression, and so we cannot access the source of that familiarity. The uncanny draws a map to what has been repressed. We feel the sensation when we encounter a person, an event, a situation that harkens back to something in our childhood—something prior to prohibitions, order, prior even to language. Suddenly, something that should have remained hidden returns. We react with dread or even horror. This is one reason why horror narratives involving dolls, imaginary friends, or other childhood relics are so successful in scaring us—they remind us of our childhood wishes, fears, and fantasies, which are often more complex, and much crueler, than we like to remember.

But the uncanny was also a fundamental part of Andrews's initial appeal when we read her books as young adolescents. Encountering them at age twelve or thirteen, many of us were aware that something odd was going on, but it wasn't the strangeness of the unknown. It was a familiar darkness, held tight in our chests since reading Hansel and Gretel. Reading Andrews, the repressed desires of childhood and the attendant fears of punishment for those desires were reactivated. The themes of fractured innocence, the dangerous family romance, parental fury—they all come hurtling back, a fairy tale gone to gorgeous rot. As Andrews told Winter, the fears she writes about are those lodged in us as children, the ones that "never quite go away: the fear of being helpless, the fear of being trapped, the fear of being out of control."

In another essay, "The Relation of the Poet to Day-Dreaming," Freud points to the power of creative writers to indulge our hidden desires—desires that are only otherwise given play in daydreaming, because they are somehow shameful. Somehow, the creative writer gives us license, assuring us that we are merely reading *his or her* personal daydreams, not ours, so we should feel free to take pleasure in them. Freud writes, "How the writer accomplishes this is his innermost secret; the essential *ars poetica* lies in the technique of overcoming the feeling of repulsion in us." What makes Andrews so challenging, however, is that she makes us acknowledge what some of our daydreams were—and probably still are.

3.

Fundamental to Freud's notion of the uncanny is the desire to repeat without knowing why. Andrews's books both embody and indulge this desire. As repetitions shudder through her books, it's almost as if Andrews threw her obsessions—abused and sexualized children, parentless homes, rape, revenge—up in the air and let them fall down in different places and configure new meanings. The most common strand is parents who either abandon or terrorize or seduce their children, leading to incest, tragedy, and the drive for revenge. Other recurrences are miscarriages, broken bones, falls and accidents, physical disabilities resulting from childhood neglect or abuse, and an obsession with hair. Central to many of the plots—and telling in a series of books structured on repetitions—are two contradictory ideas: memory as both permanently traumatizing and utterly malleable.

These repetitions fashion a dense network of associations and meta-associations, and it's in *My Sweet Audrina* that Andrews's obsessions reach their limits. Instead of one very complicated heroine (as in *Flowers*'s tormented Cathy), we have a pair of polarized girls: the passive, trusting, easily confused Audrina and her whip-smart, cunning cousin/sister, Vera. What was united in Cathy in *Flowers* becomes two characters in *Audrina*—a good girl and a bad one. And coincidentally or not, Vera and Audrina embody two highly typical responses to childhood abuse, particularly sexual abuse: Audrina blacks out and forgets/ denies that the abuse ever happened, and even tends to deny that sex exists. But Vera, overwhelmed with rage, sexualizes everything. And in many ways, she's the more sympathetic and compelling character. Her mockery of the weak and pallid Audrina is eerily dead-on. Vera tells the truth and is reviled for it—but that doesn't make the truth any less true. Meanwhile, Audrina tries to deny her past, but it keeps coming back to swallow her up in its uncanny confusion.

The recurrent theme of sexual abuse reminds us that Andrews's books didn't exist in a vacuum. As much as we like to think the desires of teenage girls are timeless—puppies, horses, makeup—the 1970s and '80s were, as an after-school special might have put it, a *very special* time. Stories about children in peril proliferated in this era, and for good reason. Considering the sexual revolution, the prevalence of drugs, a weak economy that led both parents to work outside the home, and a sky-high divorce rate, it's not surprising that people were worried about the kids. Fears of the decay of the great American family hum through Andrews's books.

But there's also a more specific contemporary paranoia that finds expression in Andrews. Her tales of child abuse and incest hit American culture just as the first wave of survivors of real child abuse and incest were starting telling their stories publicly. Influenced by an admixture of the women's movement, new-age philosophies, and various self-help schools (and, maybe, *Flowers in the Attic*), survivors of abuse started coming out of the closet in the '70s, often into a world that didn't believe

them, or if it did, that preferred not to hear their stories. By the mid-
'80s these stories had gathered into a howl from an underworld that
mainstream America had to acknowledge. Those telling their tales of
abuse were increasingly joined by those who claimed they had recovered
deeply repressed memories of childhood atrocities. While many stood
in a thoughtful middle, there were two extremes to the phenomenon:
those who believed every formerly repressed story they heard, even elaborate tales of entire towns overrun with child-raping satanists, and those
who discounted the entire idea of recovered memories. Andrews was
at the forefront of this twilight world of the half-remembered and half-
imagined—and she knew it.

"It was an odd sort of coincidence that I would start writing about
child abuse right when it became very popular to write about it,"
Andrews said in 1985. "There are so many cries out there in the night,
so much protective secrecy in families; and so many skeletons in the
closets that no one wants to think about, much less discuss. I tap that
great unknown. I think my books have helped open a few doors that
were not only locked, but concealed behind cobwebs."

If her books tap into a child's rage at his or her abuser, they also
reflect the minefield of growing up in the '70s and '80s, when children
faced problems their parents had no idea how to deal with: *their* parents
hadn't been divorced, *they* hadn't gone to schools where kids sold dope
in the halls, *they* hadn't grown up with parents taking part in est train-
ings and other faddish self-help therapies. They'd had Margaret O'Brien
as a role model, not problem-child poster-girl Jodie Foster. Parents
didn't know how to soothe their troubled children, but somehow V.
C. Andrews did.

While Andrews's novels scream with the cry of the abused girl, they
also flicker with the uncomfortable feeling that our memories may also
be fictions, stoked by wishes and fantasies. This tension makes the books
less easy but more interesting. For all the sensitive books for young adults
about abuse, for all the thoughtful after-school specials, it is Andrews's
books that speak to the complexities of such trauma on lower, and
deeper, registers. The books bristle not only with survivors' horror, but
also with pleasure and desire. Abuse and incest are often glamorized,

and punishment is always eroticized. There's a strong sadomasochistic streak that speaks to power and its effects on the body with a rare understanding that Foucault couldn't have explicated better. While Andrews denied that she herself was a victim of abuse, she certainly had a keen understanding of its subtle operations within the family: the drive to repeat that which you swore you never would, the urge to love even those who have wronged you the most—and, above all, the twin drives to forget and not to forget, to say and not to say.

When *Flowers* heroine Cathy's grandmother forces Cathy's beautiful mother to strip and show her children the wounds from a savage beating ordered by her father, the scene is attenuated, giving the horror and delectation plenty of room to stretch out and linger: "My eyes bulged at the sight of those pitiful welts on the creamy tender flesh that our father had handled with so much love and gentleness. I floundered in a maelstrom of uncertainty, aching inside, not knowing who or what I was." Later, the mother slaps Christopher, the son who nearly swoons with mother-love for her, after which she draws him into a dreamy embrace. "Kiss, kiss, kiss, finger in his hair, stroke his cheek, draw his head against her soft, swelling breasts and let him drown in the sensuality of being cuddled close to that creamy flesh that must excite even a youth of his tender years." She then "cupped his face between her palms and kissed him full on [the] lips." Cathy watches, transfixed, and the text itself begins to break apart in erotic confusion: "And those diamonds, those emeralds [on her fingers] kept flashing, flashing... signal lights, meaning something. And I sat and watched, and wondered, and felt... felt, oh, I didn't know how I felt, except confused and bewildered, and very, very young. And the world all about us was wise, and old, so old."

In her book *The Unsayable* (2006), Lacanian psychoanalyst Annie Rogers writes about girls who've been abused, and the double drive both to speak about the abuse and to remain forever silent about it. "I wanted to tell... by not telling," one girl relates to Rogers. This double drive is exemplified both in the writing of *Flowers*—which, while it revels in the telling, is fictional—and even more so in the adult reaction to it. We love to read the stories of the children's punishment, and we loathe them. We revel in the incestuous scenes between Chris and Cathy, but we don't feel very good the next morning. The books are compulsively readable, but judging by the mountains of Andrews titles at thrift shops, they are often disposed of soon after reading. Whether we are victims or not, those of us between, say, twenty-five and forty-five grew up in strange times, and her books uncannily fulfill our childhood fantasies while enacting our childhood fears.

Today, when it comes to abuse, forgiveness is popularly seen as paramount to healing, and while this idea has much merit, people often confuse it with a much easier, and unhealthier, path: that of burying the truth entirely. Andrews's heroines, however, offer a different model, one in which the needs and desires of the victim are the beginning and the end. And the expression of rage, at least in the work of V. C. Andrews, is one of the victims' greatest needs.

4.

Angry women drive Andrews's books. In their world, blinding, murderous rage is an everyday emotion. But the fury of Cathy from the Dollanganger series stands out. Cathy forgets nothing, never forgives, and never apologizes. While her brother, Chris, despite his uncontrollable desire for his sister, generally functions as the book's moral authority, Cathy does what she likes and pleases herself (echoing *Wuthering Heights*'s Cathy). She wants *everything*. She turns on her treacherous mother before any of her siblings do. She desires everything her mother has, and when she spots her mother's young lover, she wants him, too. It's pure unchecked oedipal hunger—and all justified by her mother's cruelty and by the books' own contorted, overheated logic. After she successfully consummates the primal fantasy of stealing her mother's new husband (the ultimate father substitute), that's still not enough. She wants to kill her mother even more. *Jane Eyre* is clearly a model, but Cathy is far closer to that book's Bertha Mason, the forgotten Other locked in the attic, waiting for her chance to wreak revenge in fire. (Foxworth Hall does, eventually, burn down.) Like their heroine, the books themselves lose the power to differentiate between revenge and madness. The rage of her mother and grandmother, both of whom feel wronged, irrevocably plants the seed in Cathy herself, who vows revenge and whose fury will eventually know no bounds.

While Cathy has justification for her wrath, she has no moral structure to contain or channel it. At the same time, there's also something admirable, even enviable, about it. Unlike the "nice" methods of coping that young women are still routinely implored to use, Cathy never denies her rage or her sexuality (two major challenges for women of any age, let alone teenagers). Cathy is never "nice" or "good." Even her love for her younger siblings is fiercely protective, never "maternal" or sentimental. A million girl-books, like *Sweet Valley High*, foreground the good girl, with whom we should identify, and the bad girl, whom we resist while vicariously enjoying her badness. Andrews's books don't combine these two girls so much as create an entirely new paradigm: a girl who is "good" and sympathetic but also very, very angry.

Female rage—especially the rage of young girls—remains an uncomfortable topic in our culture. It's commonplace now to speak of male adolescent anger expressed outward with violence, and female adolescent anger expressed inward via eating disorders or Queen Bee–style social malice. But Andrews's books and their appeal speak to a much deeper, darker shriek of girl-fury, and—like the reviewers who claimed not to even understand what Andrews was writing about—we may find ourselves averting our eyes.

The books' persistent theme of anger and victimization born of mother-daughter rivalry, cruelty, and hatred is perhaps even more taboo than the sexual abuse the books gave an overt voice to. Fairy tales swarm with instances of parental cruelty to children, of course, but what we see in the *Flowers* series brings it one (developmental) step further—a terrible dread of female identification: *I hate my mother and most of all I fear I will become my mother.* Increasingly her mother's mirror image as she grows up, both in looks and in hot-blooded temperament, Cathy fixates on the idea—a not-unfamiliar feeling among girls and women, and the frequent subject of jokes and eye-rolling complaints. But the *Flowers* series shows that cultural punch line's darker edges: Cathy's mother, after all, seduced her own uncle and killed one of her own children. But she was also beautiful, wealthy, and powerful. Cathy's fear is also her fantasy. Cathy wants her mother's power over men, over her life—and especially over her own moral limitations, the petty mores that hold her back from taking everything she wants. It's hard not to see a biographical parallel: Andrews said that, after finding an interested publisher who urged her to be "more gutsy," she revised the book that would become *Flowers* by adding "unspeakable things my mother didn't want me to write about, which is exactly what I wanted to do in the first place." Andrews went on to dedicate the book to her mother, whom she claimed never read any of her books, or any books. "She thinks they're all lies anyway," Andrews said.

Then, behind Cathy's identification, and her anger, too, is a demand for female power in any form, even its most violent. It's a demand for self and a refusal of any notion of a sacrificing, compliant female; an embrace of career ambitions; a refusal of motherhood itself. "I never wanted to be an ordinary housewife," Andrews, who never married, said. "I had no intention of getting married till after thirty, but life kinda threw me a curve. I think if I had failed at writing, maybe I would be bitter now. I always wanted to be somebody exceptional, somebody different, who did something on her own."

When Cathy eventually becomes a mother, her children are, thankfully, male. But eventually her horror and anger at the prison of motherhood emerges. Moving into a new home with her brother-husband, Chris, she walks up to the attic, the symbolic place of maternal punishment, and finds two twin beds, "long enough for two small boys to grow into men." "Oh, my God!" thinks Cathy. "Who did this? I would never lock away my two sons.… Yet… yet, today I bought a picnic hamper… the very same kind of hamper the grandmother had used to bring us food." She lies in bed that night with Chris, wishing she could be optimistic like him. Of course, she cannot: "But… I am not like [Mamma]! I may look like her, but inside I am honorable! I am stronger, more determined. The best in me will win out in the end. I know it will. It has to sometimes… doesn't it?"

This is the flip side of rage—the examination of the qualities that one has in common with one's tormentor. Cathy experiences that terrible feeling when she sees the beds, a feeling that she's seen this before. She, like the reader, is lost in the fog of the uncanny and the unsayable, and trying not to look too closely at what she finds there.

5.

At the end of *Flowers,* the Dollanganger kids are out of the house, on the road, with some money in their pockets. *Heaven* ends on a similar hopeful note, and the series is overall much less dark than the other books. But *Audrina,* the most complicated and saddest of Andrews's books, ends on an odd, flat note. Our heroine has found out the truth about herself (or has she?), and she's stood up to her abusive father. But she's decided to stay in her grand family home, with the people who've manipulated her for the past ten years. It's unclear if this is out of concern for her mentally disabled sister, because she loves these people and wants to repair their relationships—or, chillingly, out of resignation. You can run, but you can never leave home—just ask Cathy, who at the end of the *Flowers* series dies in a replica of the same attic in which she began her story.

In fact, if you put the books together, you could fashion a single epic story, one in which the young woman from the big house may leave home but always returns to it in the end. Cathy the Noble Avenger is also Vera, the Evil Stepsister. But Cathy the Survivor is also Audrina, the sad, lonely, confused "good" girl who doesn't know the time of day, the year, or the truth about who she is. The girl for whom, in the words of the *New York Times* reviewer, "nothing else makes much sense"; the girl whose life unfolds, as Zoe Williams writes in the *Guardian,* like "the Brady Bunch describing a decade of orgiastic abuse"; the girl for whom, as the *Washington Post* has it, "[death] is the only way the child could remove [her]self from such a silly book." The final lines of *Audrina* offer a chilling shorthand of the life of a misused child: "I wanted to scream, scream—but I had no voice.... I was the... Audrina who had always put love and loyalty first. There was no place for me to run. Shrugging, feeling sad... I felt a certain kind of accepting peace as Arden put his arm around my shoulders.... Arden and I would begin again in Whitefern, and if this time we failed we'd begin a third time, a fourth...."

The book ends on that sad, telling ellipsis.

If these novels speak to repressed female rage, to the complexities of desire and pleasure, to an ambivalence toward prescribed roles, then what little we know of the author's own life story provides a plaintive echo. Injured in a fall at fifteen, Cleo Virginia Andrews (her initials reportedly inverted by her publisher because "V. C." sounded "more male") went on to develop crippling arthritis that kept her homebound for much of her life. Her mobility was further hindered by botched surgeries to fix the damage done by the fall. Completing a four-year correspondence course in art, she worked as a commercial artist and a portrait painter until she turned to writing, at the age of forty-eight, in 1972. With her mother, she moved from Virginia to Missouri and then Arizona to be near her brothers. But then she moved back to Virginia, where—as her readers will have guessed—she spent the rest of her life in a big house, alone with her mother.

For a woman who craved excitement, who claimed, "I really wanted to be an actress. I think it's very boring being one person," such a life must have cut to the bone. Like a Victorian woman in the attic, she counted on her pen to let loose her demons. "I will pray to God that those who should will hurt when they read what I have to say," Cathy asserts in *Flowers*'s prologue. "Certainly God in his infinite mercy will see that some understanding publisher will put my words in a book and help grind the knife that I hope to wield."

Only two interviews with Andrews are available: one from *People*, in 1980, apparently so full of either lies or revelations that Andrews vowed never to do another, and a second one (for Douglas E. Winters's 1985 book, *Faces of Fear*) in which she tries to set the story straight. In 1986, age unknown, the mysterious Cleo Virginia Andrews died of breast cancer.

Andrews's editor, Ann Patty, is quoted in the *New York Times* describing the writer as "a very romantic woman schooled on fairy tales and soap operas who has a little hint of Bette Davis lurking around." And in *Faces of Fear* she presents herself as a woman of great mystery: "I get older and younger as I want," she says. She hints of precognitive powers and great erudition and grand schemes for the future, including directing films based on her books.

But the *People* interview tells a different story, and a much sadder one: "At 56 [Andrews later claimed they were wrong about her age], she has spent most of her life as an invalid in her Portsmouth, Va. home....

Stiffened joints confine her to crutches and a wheelchair.... She is flattered by gentleman callers, but discourages any serious romance while waiting to see if an operation suggested by her doctors will allow her to walk freely again.... She taught herself to embroider and sew, and makes most of her mother's dresses...."

"I couldn't live without fantasy," Andrews told *People*. "I can lose all my problems and make things the way I want them to be. That's what you do when you write a book. You play God." ✲

BRIAN T. EDWARDS

WATCHING *SHREK*
IN TEHRAN

DISCUSSED: *Illegal Ogre as Repressed Id, Immoral Materials, Idiosyncratic Censorship Methods, Limited Bathroom Real Estate, Manifold Misreadings of Muslim Societies, Trench Coats, The Preferred Means of Destruction, Mistaken Notebooks, An Alien Logic of the Look, Flirting with Juliette Binoche*

DUB, DUB, AND REDUB

owntown Tehran, winter: impossible traffic, the energy of nine million Iranians making their way through congested streets, the white peaks of the Alborz Mountains disappearing shade by shade in the ever-increasing smog. The government's declared another pollution emergency, and the center city is closed to license plates ending in odd numbers. The students at the university, where I am teaching a seminar on American Studies, are complaining openly about the failures of their elected officials.

Nahal[1] and I are sitting in a café off Haft-e Tir Square. She is smart

---

1. Not her real name. All of the names have been changed, except for public figures.

Illustration by Tony Millionaire

and dynamic, a graduate student and freelance journalist who is quick to criticize the US government and the perfidy of CNN. When I mention that, a few days ago, I had overhead Friday prayers and was taken aback by the chanting of *Marg bar Amrika!* ("Death to America"), she retorts: "But you call us the Axis of Evil!"

Our conversation turns to the movie *Shrek*. Nahal loves *Shrek* so much that she's seen the first installment of the DreamWorks trilogy "at least thirty-six or thirty-seven times." Her obsession is, apparently, shared by many Iranians. The image of Shrek appears everywhere throughout Tehran: painted on the walls of DVD and electronics shops, featured in an elaborate mural in the children's play area of the food court at the Jaam-e Jam mall. Once, from a car, I passed a five-foot-tall Shrek mannequin on the sidewalk; like his fellow pedestrians, he wore a surgical face mask to protect him from the smog.

Nahal explains: "You know, it's not really the original *Shrek* that we love so much here. It's really the dubbing. It's really more the Iranian *Shrek* that interests us."

The Iranian film industry has a long and illustrious tradition of high-quality dubbings. In the post-Revolution era, and the ensuing rise of censorship, dubbing has evolved to become a form of underground art, as well as a meta-commentary on Iranians' attempt to adapt, and in some way lay claim to, the products of Western culture. A single American film like *Shrek* inspires multiple dubbed versions—some illegal, some not—causing Iranians to discuss and debate which of the many Farsi *Shrek*s is superior. In some versions (that have since been withdrawn from official circulation), various regional and ethnic accents are paired with the diverse characters of *Shrek*, the stereotypes associated with each accent adding an additional layer of humor for Iranians. In the more risqué bootlegs, obscene or off-topic conversations are transposed over *Shrek*'s fairy-tale shenanigans.

But still, I asked her, why *Shrek*, of all things? Was it the racially coded weirdness of *Shrek*'s cast of characters that somehow spoke to Iranians? Did Shrek himself symbolize the repressed id of people living in a sexually censorious society? Or was it simply the impossible lushness and the tactile pleasures of American CGI technology itself?

But Nahal found my questions beside the point. Because our *Shrek,* she told me, isn't an American film at all.

Perhaps the question I should have been asking was this: what does it mean that Americans and Iranians make such different things of each other's cinemas? I returned to Tehran last winter to try to make more sense of these cultural readings and misreadings, and in particular to try to better understand the debate in Iran over Iranian directors like Abbas Kiarostami, lionized in the United States but not generally admired in Iran. Kiarostami, the director of *Taste of Cherry* (1997), *The Wind Will Carry Us* (1999), and *Ten* (2002), is the reason that Iranian cinema is currently upheld—by critics in France and America and elsewhere around the world—as the greatest since the French new wave brought us Jean-Luc Godard, François Truffaut, Jean-Pierre Melville, and Eric Rohmer.

And yet, to many people within his own country, Kiarostami, as one Iranian film critic said to me, is considered "a crime against the cinema of the world."

THE IRANIAN HENRI LANGLOIS

I've arrived in Tehran at an auspicious time for filmgoers—February marks the beginning of the annual Fajr Film Festival, which includes multiple competitions (the national and international competitions as well as those for documentaries, shorts, Asian cinema, and "spiritual films"), plus retrospectives and screenings of classic films. But more important, the festival is the only time the censors allow all new Iranian films to be screened; only after the premieres will they determine what can be shown in wider release. The festival, thus, is a precious ten-day window of unrestricted viewing.

A colleague from home has connected me with an editor in Tehran who has in turn put me in touch with a young film critic named Mahmoud. He and I speak on the phone before we meet. He wants to take me to an unusual place. He says: "I think it will be very interesting for your research."

The next morning I find Mahmoud outside the Bahman Cinema wearing a Woody Allen trench coat.

"Let's walk," he says. "Ali is waiting for us."

Ali, Mahmoud tells me, has a sizable—and illegal—collection of classic Hollywood films, lobby cards, and posters—though that only begins to describe what I'd soon encounter. As to why such a collection would be considered illegal, apparently it is illegal for "nonofficial" people to own 35 mm films at all. Also, much of what Ali owns is considered "immoral" material. A poster of a semi-clad Marlene Dietrich in *The Garden of Allah* (1936), in other words, can get you into serious trouble.

"Ali is the Henri Langlois of Iran," says Mahmoud. This reference to the famed creator of the *Cinémathèque française* (the archive in which Langlois preserved miles of footage from destruction—and, later, from oblivion—during the Nazi occupation of Paris) is as much for Ali's daring as for his near obsessiveness. And Ali has taken risks, to be sure: twice he has been arrested and sent to jail. The last time he was arrested, in the early 1990s, the Islamic Republic confiscated a truckload of tins of film. Mahmoud estimates that three thousand canisters of film were lost; fortunately, Ali had many others hidden elsewhere.

As we walk through the grime of downtown Tehran, Mahmoud talks of his other film-critic friends who have been sent to jail. "The authorities accuse the critics of advertising Western values with their reviews," says Mahmoud. "These films have sex in them. They tell us, 'You are advertising sex.'"

According to Mahmoud, the censorship rules governing what's allowed onto Iranian screens are haphazard and idiosyncratic. One day, the Ministry of Culture will allow a film, but the next, the Supreme Council of Clergymen (an unofficial group that Mahmoud calls a "powerful, mafia-like organization") may reverse the ministry's finding and the picture will be banned.

I struggle to keep up with Mahmoud's quick pace. As if to underscore his indictment of the government's haphazard and eccentric censorship methods, Mahmoud leads me past an endless string of street vendors offering pirated DVD copies of banned movies. Back in the United States, it's nearly time for the Academy Awards. Here on the streets of Tehran, I buy copies of many of the contenders for $1.50—*The Curious Case of Benjamin Button, Slumdog Millionaire, Frost/Nixon, Revolutionary Road*.

We finally arrive at Ali's apartment. He invites us inside what seems less a home than a storage space—posters stacked against the wall of a cramped sitting room, lobby cards piled in a cluttered kitchen, bags and bags of film canisters arranged haphazardly in the hallway. Ali's bedroom is a crumbling crawl space lined with metal shelves. The majority of his bathroom is given over to film canisters, with only a tiny bit of real estate allowed for the toilet and the curtainless shower.

Ali is about sixty and wears a plaid shirt under a worn tweed jacket. He tells me that he started collecting early, and explains his clever methods of subterfuge. When Hollywood films were screened throughout Iran under the shah's regime, they were licensed for a brief run, after which they were returned to the studio's Iranian headquarters in Tehran. But rather than pay to ship the bulky prints back to the United States, the studios allowed the film stock to be destroyed in front of witnesses. (The preferred means of destruction was to take an ax to the reels.) Ali, who worked as a projectionist, substituted worthless copies of easily accessible Iranian films for the Hollywood pictures, then secreted away cans holding the more valuable films by United, Paramount, Disney, etc.

He keeps his collection—worth millions of dollars, according to Mahmoud—scattered in a number of locations south of downtown, in basement apartments and storage rooms. Ali pulls out catalogs showing prices being paid at Sotheby's for posters that he owns. "Here, look: ten thousand dollars."

Over the years, Ali has come to serve as a valuable resource for the film communities in Tehran, and as such occupies a strange place both above and below the government's radar. He tells me of the day in the early 1970s when he met director William Wyler, who had come to Iran for a screening of his film *Roman Holiday*. The Tehran branch of Paramount couldn't get its hands on a copy of the film in time, and someone thought to contact Ali. He supplied his copy for the screening. He continues to provide rare films for Iranian film students and scholars, and his screenings are reminiscent of the ones with which Langlois inspired the French new wave.

Mahmoud tells me: "Everybody knows Ali in Iran, but nobody knows where his archive is."

THE SUDSY GUN

The following day, Mahmoud introduces me to Kamran, a critic who Mahmoud claims knows Iranian cinema better than anyone.

The three of us meet at Jaam-e Jam mall; walking among the high-end stores and Western-style cafés, I feel as if we have blundered into another world. We sit in the basement café where we can smoke. Kamran asks me which film theorists I respect most—and then he grills me on their fine points better than my own graduate students in the United States can. But I'm most curious to learn what Kamran makes of Abbas Kiarostami.

Kiarostami, born in 1940, is the director of nearly forty films, one of which (*Taste of Cherry*) won the Palme d'or at Cannes in 1997, launching his international celebrity and bringing post-Revolution Iranian cinema into global focus. In Iran, he's seen as an art director whose films are far removed from politics or any sense of contemporaneity, inhabiting instead a more mythical and contemplative place. In *Taste of Cherry,* a man drives around Tehran looking for someone to help him commit suicide, stopping to chat with pedestrians and workers at construction sites, the dialogue becoming more and more metaphysical. In *The Wind Will Carry Us,* a fictional film crew visits a remote town to await the death of an ancient (ever unseen) woman, after which some sort of ceremony will take place. In *Where Is the Friend's Home?* (1987), an eight-year-old boy living in a village far removed from urban life attempts repeatedly to return a notebook he took home from school by mistake.

Kiarostami's reputation in Iran is surely affected by his popularity in the West, and by how French and American film critics extrapolate from his films assumptions about Iranian society. For some, Kiarostami's celebrity abroad is reason to cherish him more. For others, his international fame is a reason to be doubtful of him; his prominence reinforces their belief that he is just another pawn in the West's media game of demonizing Iran. Some even suspect that he may be capitalizing on it.

Such skepticism is hardly unfounded. When Deborah Solomon interviewed Kiarostami in 2007 for her weekly page in the *New York Times* magazine, eleven of the sixteen questions published were explicitly about politics, Islam, violence, and repression; two were implicitly political; only the final three left politics behind, but they were flippant and short. ("Do you always wear sunglasses?") What's still more striking is that Solomon herself pointed out that Kiarostami's filmmaking is hardly political: "It's odd that your films would be viewed as subversive, when they're more philosophical than political and abound with picturesque views of the countryside."

Few people I spoke to in Iran thought of Kiarostami as subversive, or as anything but an art-film director. Most thought he was overly feted in the West, to the neglect of other Iranian directors. And that of course makes him, unwittingly, a political director. Alas.

Joan Copjec, a professor at SUNY Buffalo and distinguished psychoanalytic film critic of a Lacanian bent, writes of Kiarostami and, by extension, about Iranian cinema itself:

> Iranian films are an exotic experience for audiences
> accustomed to Hollywood-dominated cinema. Not just
> for obvious reasons but because the obvious—the foreign
> locations and people, everything we actually see on screen—
> is produced by a different distribution of the visible and the
> invisible and an alien logic of the look.

Her take on Kiarostami crystallizes just how his films are seen in such a deeply political light in the West—and also how this vision is so alluring. These alien people with their alien logic have, she writes, "a different distribution of the visible and the invisible." This claim worries me, because what is unseen by Copjec—"the hejab covering women that obscures them from the sight of men to whom they are not related"—leads to a celebration of this "alien logic of the look." Despite her intention to champion Kiarostami's work, her gesture is an unwittingly exoticizing one. Thus, Kiarostami's becomes a cinema that anyone with orientalist urges—from the browsers of Anthropologie clothing catalogs to those addicted to the *New York Times*'s Sunday travel section to the fedayeen of Samuel Huntington's *The Clash of Civilizations and the Remaking of World Order*—can cherish.

And when Copjec goes on to posit Kiarostami's subtle "cinema of respectful reserve and restraint" and the way his camera seems to "separate itself from the action by inserting a distance between itself and the scene and refusing to venture forward into the private space of the characters," it is in the service of her argument that Iran is an "all-exterior world." Her Kiarostami is "uniquely interesting" because he finds an original way to reinsert interiority and privacy into a "world" that cannot have any, or cannot be depicted as having any, because of the all-encompassing hijab she sees covering it. And this allows her to forward Kiarostami's vision of Iranian culture against the manifold misreadings of Muslim societies by the US government (from the horrors at Abu Ghraib to the post-9/11 wiretappings), all of which, she suggests, are based on a misreading of Islamic society as based in a culture of "shame." To be sure, the Bush Administration's reliance on Raphael Patai's intellectually corrupt book of 1973, *The Arab Mind*—with its shaky distinction between "guilt cultures" and "shame cultures," where the former is associated with "advanced" societies and the latter with "primitive" Arab ones—led to some of the worst American excesses since 9/11. Patai's argument is racist, to be sure. But Iran, of course, is not Arab, though Copjec fails to make this distinction in "confront[ing] directly" Patai via her own conflated reading of "Muslim people."

Here is where Copjec's act of politicizing a nonpolitical filmmaker starts to become not only problematic but also misleading. To claim that a "woman must be secluded from the sight or touch of unrelated men" is a bit exaggerated when it comes to today's Iran, I've got to tell you. Sure, there are lots of women in Iran who believe in modesty—and men, too—which is a precept of Islam. But nor is it unusual to see, as I did one evening in a restaurant on Valiasr Avenue, an Iranian woman wearing a form-fitting white leather jacket—covering her arms and her hips, as Islamic code dictates—but also white leggings, tall boots, and a scarf that loops up and over blond highlighted hair and perfect makeup. And when I finally got myself invited to a North Tehran party, I saw miniskirts and backless tops on braless young women in their mid-twenties and thirties, to say nothing of the heavy flirting and the dirty dancing. Even among the non-elite and the working-class, female friends and students of mine often made a point of shaking my hand (against convention), lifting their head scarves to reveal their hair, and even showing me cell-phone photos of themselves uncovered. Let me just say this: Joan Copjec was describing an Iran I saw only before I got to Iran.

Yes, walk in downtown Tehran and there is the hijab, the chador, the coverage of much of a woman's body, though again it depends on where you look. And yes, a woman in a white leather jacket can seem provocative because of the contrast with what is mandated, what is common. But in their homes, Iranians are watching DVDs of Hollywood films, and downloads from websites everywhere, and Facebook pages and lively Iranian serials and comedies and, if they want to and have a satellite dish (which almost everyone does, even though they're technically not permitted), sexy music videos from Lebanon and unrestricted porn from the Persian Gulf. Everything is here, people like to say, just in the right place. You need to know where to look for it.

Read Copjec's essay out of context, in other words, and you may get the wrong idea about Iran and its cinema: "The look of desire around which Hollywood-dominated cinema is plotted had to be forsaken, along with the well-established system of relaying that look through an alternating pattern of shots and counter-shots and the telling insertion of psychologically motivated close-ups." There is a sophisticated psychoanalytic argument about shame in Copjec's essay, but it doesn't square with what one sees in mainstream Iranian films that don't make it to the festival circuit, or in daily life in Iran. Kiarostami works too well for the argument, in other words, and the argument works too well for Kiarostami.

Kamran refers to a witty critique made by Khosro Dehghan, an Iranian film critic and screenwriter, to explain what is wrong with Kiarostami: "Remember the gun made out of soap in Woody Allen's *Take the Money and Run*? That's what Kiarostami's films are like. Eventually it will rain and the gun will melt away."

The only conclusion I can make, I realize, may seem obvious, even if it runs counter to the logics by which both Copjec and the fearful clerics—and indeed the champions of US cultural diplomacy—operate. As films like *Shrek* and *Taste of Cherry* make their way across the ocean to new interpretive communities, they not only accrue different political meanings but they become different things. The Iranian *Shrek* and the American Kiarostami do not represent, in their new homes, what they represent in the film worlds where they originated. In fact, the American Kiarostami is just as American as the Farsi-dubbed *Shrek* is Iranian. In each location, they become convenient foreign elements against which domestic film production can more clearly distinguish itself as domestic.

When American State Department officials imagine that the export of Hollywood film and American pop music can be a simple weapon in the battle for "hearts and minds" of other cultures (as so many of the champions of so-called "cultural diplomacy" do these days), they are suffering from a Cold War hangover. When Iranian clerics wring their hands that Hollywood movies will corrupt Iranian youth just by their captivating presence and attempt to squeeze them out of circulation, they are looking only at the flashy posters. Neither is seeing the ways these foreign products signify within a much richer cultural context and resonate in ways that their producers could hardly have predicted.

DROPS OF WATER

In June 2009, President Ahmadinejad is reelected in the first round of voting, beating three opponents—including Mir Houssein Mousavi (the major challenger)—by a margin significantly larger than expected and foreclosing the anticipated runoff. The opposition claims widespread voting irregularities. People take to the streets in protest and, based on the evidence of cell-phone videos uploaded from the streets of Tehran, are beaten back viciously. To many, the government's brutal repression of the protest signals the demise of democracy in Iran. From my home in Chicago, I watch YouTube videos of what looks like a counterrevolution building on the streets.

Mahmoud forwards a major op-ed published on June 20 in the *Guardian*. Titled "I Speak for Mousavi. And Iran," the piece is written by Mohsen Makhmalbaf, another key filmmaker of the Iranian New Wave. Makhmalbaf, then fifty-two years old, is a generation younger than Kiarostami and had a markedly different trajectory. Born poor in South Tehran, raised within a religious and political family, Makhmalbaf was connected directly to the Revolutionary project. As he taught him-self the art of cinema, his own films moved from moral tales to political critiques of fascism in its many forms to more-speculative explorations of the complexities of the Iranian condition, such as *The Cyclist* (1987) and *Gabbeh* (1996), his most famous films.

In his *Guardian* op-ed, Makhmalbaf claims to be the spokesman of the defeated Mousavi. "I have been given the responsibility of telling the world what is happening in Iran," he writes. Since the flawed election—many Iranians wanted not simply a recount but an annulment of the results—the notable examples of Iranian democracy had, in the film-maker's words, "vanished." Makhmalbaf mourns the Islamic Republic's visibly violent attempts to quash coordinated opposition among the people. Ahmadinejad's reelection, however, had promoted a resur-gence of "togetherness": "All the armed forces in Iran are only enough to repress one city, not the whole country. The people are like drops of water coming together in a sea."

But in his op-ed and in a subsequent interview in *Foreign Policy*, Makhmalbaf does not call for the end of the Islamic Republic itself—rather, he calls for a rejection of the results that named Ahmadinejad president, the Guardian Council that certified them, and the position of the Supreme Leader that is tantamount to "dictatorship." Makhmalbaf argues that an Iran that is a "democratic Islamic country" could be a model for other "Islamic countries." And not everyone who demands the annulment of the election results wants to end the entire system of government created in the wake of the 1979 revolution. Listen care-fully for the differences, and attend to the way in which many of us in the West collapse those two positions as if they were the same. It is an important distinction.

Makhmalbaf was one of several important Iranian directors who made public statements in support of the protesters: other important directors such as Jafar Panahi, Asghar Farhadi, and Bahman Ghobadi did so as well. The latter did so from inside Iran, which Mahmoud rightly saw as yet more daring—the critique from within always has more force for Iranians wary of outsiders' frequently tone-deaf calls for Iranian "lib-eration." (Makhmalbaf moved to Paris in 2005 after the first election of

Ahmadinejad; Panahi was arrested in Tehran in July of 2009 and had his passport revoked shortly thereafter.)

I ask Mahmoud what people are saying about Kiarostami. "Kiarostami is not in Iran right now. He is making a new film in Italy," he replies. "If you want to know how people think of him see the latest poll in my blog. His films are absent from the top ten films."

Mahmoud writes back a few days later to say: "Kiarostami now is flirting with Miss Juliette Binoche in the countrysides of Italy and making love stories among the poetic landscapes!"

He wants to make sure I understand. "We know that always there have been artists who believed in the constancy of their art in any political and social condition," he writes. "To them the key to the truth is to believe in 'if there is art, changes and improvements will be unavoidable.' It's why Kiarostami always quotes from Sohrab Sepehri [the poet], because he was one of the true believers in this concept. But I don't know if Kiarostami belongs to the same league or if he is only a coward!"

Meanwhile, in Chicago, I pull out the alternate versions of *Shrek* in Farsi that I collected with Nahal and my students at the University of Tehran and watch them again, looking for clues. I recall how the Alborz Mountains appear and disappear at the edge of the city when the smog overwhelms the sky. How, like those mountains, what is seen and unseen in Tehran is always there, you just need to know where to look. ★

RACHEL KAADZI GHANSAH

IF HE HOLLERS
LET HIM GO

DISCUSSED: *Ohio's Rolling Farmland, Hippies in Tie-Dye,
Paul Laurence Dunbar, Oprah, A Simpler Way of Life,
Seventy-Year-Old Comparative Literature Professors in Birkenstocks,
Negritude, Thurgood Marshall, Black Activism, Patrice Lumumba,
Dick Gregory, Mark Twain's Pudd'nhead Wilson, Hemp Stores,
Reuben Sandwiches, Dusk in Yellow Springs*

Although the city of Dayton is small and has been hit hard by the decline of industry, in Xenia and Yellow Springs the land is green, fecund, and alive, even in the relentless heat of summer. Xenia is three miles from where the first private black college, Wilberforce, opened, in 1856, to meet the educational needs of the growing population of freed blacks that crossed the Ohio River. Yellow Springs, a stop on the Underground Railroad, was initially established as a utopian community in 1825. In 1852, Horace Mann founded Antioch College and served as its president. During the '50s and '60s, Antioch and Yellow Springs were hamlets of anti-McCarthyism and antiwar and civil rights activism. Today there are a lot of hippies and there's even more tie-dye. Between the villages, you can drive over rolling hills and pastures and

Illustration by Tony Millionaire

not see another car for miles, and only far off on the horizon will you be able to spot a farmhouse.

I spent a week in this part of Ohio, and during my stay I was invited to do all sorts of things with people of all kinds—rich and poor, white and black. I was invited to go flying, dig for worms at midnight, and plant raspberry bushes. My request to drive a tractor was turned down, not because I don't know how to drive but because the tractor had been put away. In Ohio, there is space for people to do what they want. There is a lot of land, plenty of it. This is where enslaved people ran to, certain that they had finally evaded capture. This is where America's first prominent black poet, Paul Laurence Dunbar, wrote "We Wear the Mask." And somewhere in the midst of it all is Dave Chappelle's home.

From above, everything seems smaller and less complicated—or at the very least things are put into perspective. From a plane at thirty-five thousand feet it was much easier for me to understand why Dave Chappelle quit his hit TV show, *Chappelle's Show*, and said goodbye to all that, and didn't stop until he got home to Yellow Springs, Ohio. When news of his decision to cease filming the third season of the show first made headlines, there were many spectacular rumors. He had quit the show without any warning. He had unceremoniously ditched its cocreator, his good friend Neal Brennan, leaving him stranded. Chappelle was now addicted to crack. He had lost his mind. The most insane speculation I saw was posted on a friend's Facebook page at 3 am. A website had alleged that a powerful cabal of black leaders—Oprah Winfrey, Bill Cosby, and others—were so offended by Chappelle's use of the *n*-word that they had him intimidated and banned. The controversial "Niggar Family" sketch, where viewers were introduced to an Ozzie and Harriet–like 1950s suburban, white, upper-class family named "the Niggars," was said to have set them off. The weirdest thing was that people actually went for such stories. *Chappelle's brief moment in television had been that incendiary.* It didn't matter that Chappelle himself had told Oprah on national television that he had quit wholly of his own accord.

Chappelle didn't seem to understand that these rumors of drugs and insanity, though paternalistic, were just the result of disbelief and curiosity. Like Salinger's retreat from fame, Chappelle's departure demanded an explanation: how could any human being have the willpower, the chutzpah, the determination to refuse the amount of money rumored to be Chappelle's next paycheck: fifty million dollars. Say it with me now. Fifty. Million. Dollars. When the dust settled, and Chappelle had done interviews with Oprah and James Lipton in an attempt to recover his image and tell his story, two things became immediately apparent: Dave Chappelle is without a doubt his generation's smartest comic, and the hole he left in comedy is so great that even ten years later very few people can accept the reason he later gave for leaving fame and fortune behind: he wanted to find a simpler way of life.

You know you must be doing something right if old people like you.
—Dave Chappelle

Dave Chappelle was in his teens when he first appeared on the comedy-club circuit. He was twenty-three when he and his friend Neal Brennan wrote *Half Baked*, a now-classic stoner flick about four hapless friends who try to enter the drug-dealing game so they can get bail money for their friend Kenny, who has landed in jail after inadvertently killing a cop's horse. They were young and had no expectations except to have fun and be funny. They certainly had no idea *Chappelle's Show*, another collaboration, would become the most talked-about show on television. But early into the show's first season, critics at the *New York Times* would take notice of Chappelle's "kind of laid-back indignation" and his "refusal to believe that ignoring racial differences will make anyone's life better." What Brennan and Chappelle were doing every week was so unusual that the *Times* declared that "it almost looks like a renaissance for African-American humor on television."

Chappelle's comedy found fans in many worlds. At a recent barbecue in Philadelphia, a friend of the host dutifully but disinterestedly interrogated me about my life, and got excited only when my mother let it slip that I was working on a piece about Dave Chappelle. "Aw, man. I miss that guy," he said. "He was my friend. I really felt like he was my friend."

I hear this a lot, usually from white people, and usually from white people without many black friends—like this seventy-year-old comparative literature professor in Birkenstocks. Part of what made the show so ingenious was that Chappelle's racial invective found friends in strange places. With a regularly broadcasted television show, Chappelle was finally able to display what writer and activist Kevin Powell described in an *Esquire* profile as a "unique capacity to stand out and blend in, to cross boundaries and set up roadblocks." Almost overnight, Chappelle became America's black friend. He was a polyglot. He told Powell that, growing up, he used to "hang out with the Jewish kids, black kids, and Vietnamese immigrants," and it was apparent that Chappelle had used these experiences to become America's consul and translator for all things racial. More than any comic of his generation, he lanced the boil of how race works and also prodded at how nuanced race had become. "Sometimes convention and what's funny butt heads," Chappelle confessed to *Entertainment Weekly* in 2004, "and when [they do], we just err on the side of what's funny."

Besides race, three things make Dave Chappelle's comedy innovative and universal: wit, self-deprecation, and toilet humor. This is the same triumvirate that makes Philip Roth's writing so original. Woody Allen's movies, too. Chappelle had a keen sense of the archetypal nature of race, and understood just as acutely how people work on a very basic level. In a *Chappelle's Show* sketch about the reality show *Trading Spouses*, a black man sits on a toilet in a white family's house and flips through a copy of *People* magazine while taking a dump. He looks up: "Who the fuck is Renée Zellwedger?" In another sketch, a stodgy, Waspy white man (Chappelle in whiteface) lies in bed with an attractive black woman in classy lingerie. He wants her. But he wants to make love with his pajamas on.

Chappelle did such a good job of truth-telling, on every subject, that nobody knew what to do when he just stopped talking. In no way did his quitting conform to our understanding of the comic's one obligation: to be funny. To talk to us. To entertain us. To make us laugh. We aren't used to taking no for an answer, to being rejected, especially not by the people who are supposed to make us smile. Especially not by black men who are supposed to make us smile. And yet Chappelle did just that. And so, like everyone, I wondered what had happened. What had happened, and, more so, what had brought Chappelle to—and kept him in—Yellow Springs? At a stand-up appearance in Sacramento in 2004, a frustrated Chappelle lashed out at his hecklers from the stage, yelling, "You people are stupid!" So what was it about this small college town—where hippies slipped me bags of Girl Scout cookies, where Tibetan jewelry stores and fair-trade coffee shops dotted the main street, and where kindly white ladies crossed the street to tell me my wild hair was giving them life— that made it more satisfying than celebrity or fame?

Even before Chappelle himself, politely but firmly, turned down my interview request, I had begun to suspect that the keys to everything he was doing politically and culturally—block parties with Erykah Badu, videos with Mos Def and De La Soul, and campaigning for young black candidates like Kevin Powell, who stressed social responsibility—represented interests deeply informed by his parents. His mother is a historian and his father was a dean of community services and a professor of music. Edward Countryman, the American historian, has pointed out some worthwhile context: "Until John Hope Franklin joined the University of Chicago in 1964, no black person held a senior rank in a major history department that encouraged research and trained doctoral students." But Chappelle, like Kanye West, grew up in a home where black activism and black leftist thought were the languages of the household. No wonder, then, that both Chappelle and West have wrestled so bitterly and publicly with their sense of responsibility to and also their failure to meet those same obligations. "It's a dilemma," Chappelle told Kevin Powell. "It's something that is unique to us. White people, white artists, are allowed to be individuals. But we always have this greater struggle that we at least have to keep in mind somewhere." Chappelle's throwback kind of celebrity and his many concerns about "social responsibility" are faintly reminiscent of the work that his mother, Professor

Yvonne Seon, did in the '60s and '70s as a scholar of the Negritude movement.

In 1939, the poet Aimé Césaire would return to his island homeland of Martinique, in the Caribbean, after spending years in Europe. The move would prompt his book-length piece of prose poetry, which André Breton would call a masterpiece: *Cahier d'un retour au pays natal* (*Notebook of a Return to the Native Land*). Césaire, a gifted writer, was sent to Europe as a young man to study in the center of the French-speaking world. Once there, he reunited with his childhood friend Léon Damas and a young poet and future Senegalese president named Léopold Sédar Senghor. Together, as black men in France, they attempted to educate themselves in a culture where the word *negre* was inherently a pejorative. To cope while living under the double bind of colonialism and racism, they created "Negritude," literally a "Blackness" movement.

Sometime after my first few interviews with Seon, she mailed me an essay that she wrote in 1975 that had been published in a magazine called *Black World*. The issue features Muhammad Ali on the cover, and in her essay Seon describes Negritude as being more of a sensibility than a literary movement that is fixed in the past. To me, more than anything, it voices the dilemma her son would experience decades later:

> When one speaks of Negritude, one may be speaking of either of two quite different things. In its narrow definition, Negritude is a literary movement of the late 1930's. In this restricted sense, it represents the use by Black French-speaking poets, of the techniques of French Impressionism to break away from French culture and to give creative expression to an inner, African self that had been hidden away. But the broader, more important meaning of Negritude has to do with a process isolated and identified by these poets. It is the process by which Black people, who have been cut off from and made to learn to know themselves again, come to accept themselves, and begin to believe in (i.e. to value) themselves.

Seon was born in Washington, DC. Her father was a fair-skinned man who was adopted by a black woman. Although he self-identified as black, by all accounts he looked Greek. He was also blind. On the day Martin Luther King Jr. was shot, Chappelle's grandfather was on a city bus and overheard rumblings of a beat-down about to happen to a white fellow on his bus. That guy's gonna be in trouble, he thought. He did not realize that *he* was the white man being threatened. This anecdote about his grandfather would inspire Chappelle's "Clayton Bigsby" sketch—the unforgettable short mockumentary about a blind white supremacist who does not know he is black.

Beginning in 1944, Seon's mother worked as an administrative assistant for the NAACP. Seon tells me about early memories of sitting outside of NAACP meetings and waving hello to the organization's chief counsel, Thurgood Marshall, who was working on the cases that would dismantle the Jim Crow laws. In the '50s, when Africa began to hammer off its colonial shackles, her family found itself in the front lines as black American allies.

"My mother was very much one of the people who was paying attention to what was going on in Africa; she knew the ambassadors, we went to the celebrations of independence. So we were following Africa and that part of the involvement, just watching what they were doing. We were aware of the avant-garde, the people who were questing for liberation in Africa."

Seon was twenty-two when she met Patrice Lumumba, the young, energetic prime minister of the Congo, at a society mixer. That same afternoon, he offered her a job. She went home and asked her parents for permission, and they came back and talked with Lumumba. It was agreed she would fly to the Congo and help Lumumba, who, unlike Ghana's president, Kwame Nkrumah, didn't have a college degree or much of a background in government. Instead, Lumumba was a beer-selling postmaster who had crushed one of the most dehumanizing, despotic colonial regimes with pure rhetoric and was now learning how to establish a new nation. She made plans to leave in the winter, but on December 1, 1960, Patrice Lumumba was arrested. "The hardest part was not knowing," she says. In the weeks to come they found out:

Lumumba had been murdered, most likely by American and Belgian operatives; Lumumba's pan-Africanism, his vision of a unified Congo, and his utter lack of patience had alarmed the West so much that they had had him killed. (Belgium apologized in 2002 for its "moral responsibility" in the murder.)

But here is the part you should remember if you want to understand Dave Chappelle's unbridled wit and compulsion to be free: a young Yvonne Seon still decided to take off for the Congo, not knowing what to expect, but knowing that her contact there—a man who was being mourned by Malcolm X and Che Guevara, whose death incited outraged protests all around the world— had been murdered. She needed to fulfill her promise to the dead man and his hope for a "history of dignity" for African people. "We were very much aware that if America was going to have its independence, our independence was tied to the independence of the African countries. And I personally believed at the time that African Americans would not be able to get civil rights until Africa had won its independence, that the two things were interrelated." Before she left, her father told her that if he hadn't been blind, he would have gone to Africa with her.

When she returned to the States two years later, Seon attended graduate school and met her husband, William David Chappelle (who died in 1998), in those times of great hope and unrest. In the late '60s, they came to Yellow Springs to visit friends for the weekend, and, besotted with the town's counterculture, diversity, and leftist vibe, her husband didn't want to leave. When Chappelle was two, his parents divorced, and his father returned to Yellow Springs to teach at Antioch while his mother stayed in Washington, DC, with the children. Dave Chappelle has said of his childhood, "We were like the broke Huxtables. There were books around the house; everybody was educated to a college level. We used to have a picture of Malcolm X in Ghana. Last Poets records. We were poor but we were cultured."

When they reached the age where he and his siblings could start "running the streets," his mother sent them to Yellow Springs to live with their father. Chappelle returned when he was fourteen. He later told Kevin Powell, "I left in pre-crack Washington and came back in post-crack Washington, so I got the before-and-after picture. It was literally jolting, like, what the fuck happened? My freshman year of high school, over five hundred kids my age were murdered."

In addition to the typical growing pains that accompany adolescence, Chappelle found himself having to navigate what he described to James Lipton as being "a very segregated city, especially at that time. Statistically speaking to this day—statistically speaking—there's not one poor white person in Washington." DC was a far cry from Yellow Springs, and he struggled to adjust to the culture shock. It was his mother who gave him a copy of a magazine with Bill Cosby on the cover. Chappelle felt instantaneously connected to the comic. When he finished reading, he says, "I put it down. And it was like: I'mma be a comedian. And, man, I'm telling you, I could see it so clearly, so clearly, man—this is it. I was so excited I told my family, 'I have an announcement to make: I'm gonna be a comedian.'"

Because he was fourteen and his mother took him to gigs around the city, other comics called him "the kid." He remembers telling his grandmother once before he went onstage, "You might hear me say some things that you might not want to hear your grandson say... And she said, 'Just relax and do that shit.' I was like, Wow. I had never heard her curse!"

Over lunch in Ohio, Seon tells me, with the same optimism as every other time we've talked, about the years she spent in Kinshasa. Her stories are populated with dangers she still seems impervious to: Évariste Kimba, a prime minister who soon succeeded Lumumba, was also executed, and the Congo was at the start of a long period of war. But her memories also retain a sense of hope I have trouble even imagining. "You know," she says, "I've never gone back to the Congo, because it is difficult, you know, to look back at a place that was so full of possibilities and see what has happened. That is always hard to see, isn't it?"

There is a strange moment in James Lipton's interview with Chappelle where the comedian discusses his decision not to attend college. "I was the first person in my family not to go to college, that had not been a slave." The audience laughs. I can never tell if they realize that he is serious.

In his fantastic profile of Muhammad Ali, Hunter S. Thompson writes that "the Champ, after all, had once hurled his Olympic gold medal into the Ohio River, in a fit of pique at some alleged racial insult in Louisville." The medal was a symbol of a white world that Ali "was already learning to treat with a very calculated measure of public disrespect." Like most people of the post–civil rights generation, I think that Chappelle, whose family had long been free, educated, leftist, and radical, had hoped that his success would not need to follow that same militant path. Despite the fact that four in ten white Americans do not have any black friends, and, more pressingly, that all too many workplaces are integrated only in theory, I think Chappelle hoped that he could bring Yellow Springs' open-mindedness to the world. For a while he did, but then he became aware that his brand of humor was not without a history and was forced to acknowledge its context. Next came conferences with suits at Comedy Central about his use of the *n*-word and his being chastised in the press, and finally he was humiliated and called insane. Like Thompson once wrote of Ali, Chappelle was put through "one of the meanest and most shameful ordeals any prominent American has ever endured." Without knowing his history, Dave Chappelle's decision to figuratively toss his gold medal into the Ohio River does seem like a bizarre, illogical act that abbreviated a successful career on its ascent. But was it illogical? Hardly. Revolutionary? Possibly. To turn his back on Hollywood, to walk away from the spotlight because it was turning him into a man he didn't want to be—a man without dignity—was a move that was, in a way, Chappelle's birthright, his own unwieldy kind of Negritude.

There's no friends like the old friends.

—James Joyce

"I wasn't crazy but it is incredibly stressful," Dave Chappelle explained to Oprah on *The Oprah Winfrey Show* in 2006. With his mother sitting in the front row, he was trying to explain why ten months years earlier— without explanation to his wife, to Brennan, or to his bosses at Comedy Central—he had quit his show.

"I would go to work on the show and I felt awful every day," he said. "I felt like some kind of prostitute or something. If I feel so bad, why keep on showing up to this place? I'm going to Africa." Five years have passed since that interview, and Brennan has gone on to write for President Obama at the White House Correspondents' Dinner and to work with comedians like Amy Schumer and Chris Rock. Brennan repeats to me how much he respects Dave, but he tells me that being "trashed" by Chappelle on *Oprah* still bothers him. In 2011, he told a reporter: "You know, for a black artist that's beloved to go on TV and say he was victimized by a white corporate structure, that is like white-people nectar, it's like white liberal nectar, like, 'Oh my god, this young black man has been victimized.' Dave did real well from the show, you know. There was a huge benefit to Dave. So the idea that somehow he was victimized... My experience was he wasn't victimized and that it was a matter of pressure and needing to eject from the pressure."

Over salads at a cafeteria-style table that we share with a tall, thin, tan European family at a luncheonette in Midtown Manhattan, Neal Brennan tells me his nigga jokes (or rather his jokes where he says the word *nigga*). Two weeks earlier, in New Orleans, I had hung out in the whitewashed wings of the Civic Theatre and watched Brennan direct his first Comedy Central one-hour special. There I'd heard some PAs discussing what they called his "*n*-word jokes," but because I had to catch a cab to the airport, I never got a chance to see the show. In New York, sitting a few feet from Brennan, I tried to prepare myself for the inevitable, but each time I thought about it my hands had instinctively cocked and curled into fists under the table.

Brennan says *Chappelle's Show* told two stories: "What it was like to be a dude, and what it was like to be a black dude." He grew up in the Philadelphia suburbs and is a former altar boy, the youngest of ten kids in a large Irish Catholic family. He is very thin and he has what himself calls a "roguish charm." Brennan is really, really funny and quick. He wears a uniform of jeans, sneakers, and a T-shirt. He has large ears and wide eyes and spiky hair that is often gelled to a point, cockatoo-style. As we talk, I realize that I recognize many of his expressions from the show. Brennan tells me that as a writer he knows how to shape and structure a joke. He directs the jab. "My job and life are basically just saying, 'Hey, say this.' Say, 'Doctor says I needs a backiotomy.'"

Brennan met Chappelle when they were both eighteen. Everyone else in the New York comedy scene was in their late twenties. "Comedy," he shrugs and sighs deeply, "is incredibly racially integrated. Probably the most diverse workplace there is, and it's not clannish—there is a table at the Comedy Cellar where we all go, and you can look around some nights and it is Mexican, white, Jewish, black. You are friends based on your comedy ability, not based on your age or something. Like race is almost irrelevant." Brennan studied film at NYU during the day, and at night he stood outside and worked as the annoying guy who yells, "Hey! Come inside and check out the comedy show!" Chappelle had moved to New York to do stand-up and was working in Washington Square Park, learning from a street comic named Charlie Barnett.

Neal and Dave had similar sensibilities: they liked the same movies (Spike Lee Joints), the same music (hip-hop), the same TV shows (*Family Ties*). It was kismet. "Chappelle had been on all of these pilots and had been paired with all of the wrong writers, wrong actors; like no thought to chemistry. Just: 'He's a hot writer and you're a hot stand-up,'" Brennan says. *Entertainment Weekly* would say of Chappelle's first sitcom: "The worst thing about *Buddies* is that it makes racism boring."

Years passed, and Brennan left New York to live in Los Angeles and write comedy for Nickelodeon, but he stayed in touch with Chappelle. Their film, *Half Baked*, was totally unexpected and came about quickly. In fact, they had only a month to outline it. "We pitched it. Universal sold it in, like, March, and we were shooting it in July. Which is crazy. Really crazy. But we didn't know anything because we were, like, twenty-three."

From the moment they arrived on the set, Brennan says he knew that something was off about the production. "First of all, it should have looked more like *Kids* and *Trainspotting*. So we get there and Dave turns to me and asks, 'Is this how you pictured the set?' And I go, 'Nope.' And he goes, 'Me neither.'" Neal shrugs again. "But again, twenty-three. And there is just nothing you can do. I'm not a fan of the movie. Dave's not a fan of the movie." Directed by Tamra Davis, *Half Baked* was released in 1998, the same weekend as *Titanic*, and flopped. Brennan and Chappelle stopped talking for a while. These silences are themes in their friendship. I ask him why. "I guess not wanting to acknowledge responsibility, negative association, you want to leave the scene of the crime. Like having a child die and the parents want to get a divorce."

It would be the first defeat in a series of many. After *Half Baked*, Dave bought his "Fuck you, Hollywood" farm, sixty-five acres of land in Ohio. He was living there and having a tough time professionally. *Killin' Them Softly*, his one-hour special, came out in 1999. Brennan is blunt about it: "No one cared. But *Killin' Them Softy* is a great one-hour special.

"Dave called his manager the Monday after it aired," Brennan says, "and [his manager] goes, 'Sorry, man, the phone's not ringing.'" That is how it was. It cemented a sense within Brennan and Chappelle that show business is built upon what's hot and what's not, and, worse, that show business is random, anti-intellectual, and often pretty far behind. "We were the underdogs. We were left for dead and came from behind and did CPR on ourselves." He pauses and peers over the heads of the tow-headed European family sitting next to us. "To give you a sense of things, this is how little respect Dave was getting: we pitched *Chappelle's Show* to one station and they literally looked at us like we were lepers. Like, because Chris Rock had just gone off the air, they were like, 'Chris Rock is everything and you're nothing, Dave.' Then we walk up Fifth Avenue and pitch it to Comedy Central. They buy it. And it becomes the show. And now *Chappelle's Show* has sold three million copies on DVD." (It remains the world's top-selling TV-to-DVD series.)

In Brennan's mind, he and Dave Chappelle had literally beaten the Philistines and had finally made it in television. But, as Chappelle told Oprah, this was not at all true. When Brennan discusses the demise of the show, he discusses it as a conflict about renegotiating the terms of the third season. Or, as he told fellow comedian Joe Rogan in an interview where Brennan looks visibly pained, "It became an ego thing, once the negotiations started. It was the worst period of my life… but as Lorne Michaels once said, 'Comedians don't like admitting they have help.'" Brennan says that at the height of the contretemps, they both said awful things to each other. When Chappelle discusses his exit, he does not deny that things went haywire, but he attributes it mostly to his discomfort with the material, the politics of the show, and the climate on the set. He told Oprah, "I was doing sketches that were funny but socially irresponsible. It was encouraged. I felt I was deliberately being encouraged and I was overwhelmed."

I ask an older friend who is black and a theorist of sorts what he thinks about *Chappelle's Show*. I get an answer that surprises me with its vitriol: "Chappelle was at the end of the one-hundred-and-fifty-year minstrel cycle and fifty years after the height of the civil rights movement and ten years after the beginning of Southern hip-hop and in the midst of the most coonish aspects of dirty South hip-hop. He wrung the last bits of potential energy out of taboos that had been in guarded reserve that show niggas as violent, unintelligent, unlettered beasts. And he portrayed niggas that way (while maintaining an ironic distance from those caricatures). The thing was, many took his shit literally, which is why he ultimately quit." I go back and watch "The Mad Real World" sketch, a spoof of the MTV reality show. In the sketch a white man moves into a house full of black roommates and, in the ensuing weeks, his father is stabbed while visiting, his blond girlfriend is turned out by two guys, and the living room is regularly transformed into a makeshift nightclub. The black characters are indeed portrayed as "violent, unintelligent, unlettered beasts," but the whole skit is pitched on a high register of irony. When I ask Brennan how he dealt with backlash about the show's use of the *n*-word and its edgy racial humor, he objects. "As much as people say that about *Chappelle's Show*, no one ever got pissed. People ask, 'Were you worried?' and it's like, no, because it was all founded on real, empirical observations and lived lives. Like, that 'Real World' sketch was a discussion we had been having for a decade about black people on *The Real World*. The guy who pulled the blanket off the girl was Dave's best friend. So we knew what that shit was like.

"Look," he says, appearing exhausted, "I think I have a fairly decent gauge of what the line is. It is not perfect, but, like, I say the *n*-word eight times in my stand-up. And it works. People can tell if you mean it. And the other thing is *I* never say it, I'm always paraphrasing someone. And… I open up by shitting on white people. And pedigree. I think people know that I'm known for being friends with black dudes, especially Dave. And

I talk about that, I talk about being called it. I talk about the first time I was called the *n*-word. I get called the *n*-word every day. I can show you texts."

Scrolling through his phone without looking up, he tells me, "So it is a weird thing where you expect me to inhale something and not exhale. And people are like, 'You can't say that.' But I get called it every day. Constantly, for twenty years."

Later on, Brennan brings up an idea first posited by the psychologist Beverly Tatum about the ways we tend to segregate ourselves as we get older and grow apart from our friends of different races. Neal tells me, "It's like when black kids sit at the lunch table with only black kids, and the white kids sit with white kids. I think it is just like, 'Well, they look like family.' It is just some animal shit. It is safety." When I read Tatum's book, she says something that sticks with me: that so often the difficultly in discussing race is about working around the divide of that which we do not know. As I listen to Brennan talk, I think about how he is right, that comedy is different. Comedians live for the joke and the joke alone. White writers have long written jokes for black comics with great success (my favorites being Ed. Weinberger for Bill Cosby and Louis C.K. for Chris Rock), but at the same time none of this goodwill can negate the possibility that Chappelle experienced what his mother had written about twenty years before: the desire to "learn to know himself again." And that for all the post–civil rights progress we have made, it is possible that you could be best friends with someone of a different race without being able to enter worlds and spaces that they can, or in the way that they do.

After two hours of remarkably easy conversation, I can tell it is time for the moment I've been clenching my fist about. Maybe he had needed to feel me out. Neal Brennan, who definitely embodies the best of the easy wit of *Chappelle's Show*, goes for it.

"The joke in my act is: 'It is so bad I call myself it when no one's around.' It will be lunchtime and I'm like, Nigga, you need to eat. And I'm like, Who are you talking to?"

My hand unclenches. His *n*-word joke reminded me of the weird moments when I've been around young white men who identify with hip-hop culture and who, for some strange reason, despite their stated best intentions, need to access that word as proof that they are accepted or acknowledged by the community they are involved with. They do not realize the hubris and dominance inherent in the act of wanting to use that word. Brennan's joke is a joke on those guys, but it is also, inadvertently, a joke on himself. I think he knows this. Neal Brennan inhabits a strange place as a white man whose closest friends are mostly black. But what, if anything, does that mean? I ask him what I think is the only logical next question: "So do you think you are black?"

"No!" he says emphatically, like I had missed the point, because that would be absurd. "I also think that is a silly thing. Like I've never spoken Ebonics."

"Do you think that you're a racist?" I ask, but not because I think Brennan is any more racist than any other white person, especially if racism is viewed as a system of white privilege and unearned benefits. I ask this because part of knowing where the line is is knowing where you situate yourself along it or against it.

"Uh, I think that everybody is racist. It is a natural human condition. It's tribal."

Another evening, Brennan and I talk about what the ride of success felt like. He remembers hanging out at a club in Arizona where he and Chappelle were approached by a white fan who was loose with his use of the word *nigger* and who praised Chappelle for making it so funny. "It was awful," Brennan recalls.

The thing is, I like Neal Brennan. And I got the joke, I think. But when he first told it to me, there was an awkward silence that I think both Brennan and I noticed. The cafeteria seemed to swell with noise. And for a brief moment, my head clouded, and there was nothing I could think of to say, so to get out of the silence, I did what was expected: I laughed. When I got home, this troubled me deeply.

You can't say anything real when it comes to race. That's why Bill Cosby's in such trouble for saying black folks have got to take responsibility for their own lives. I spoke at my high school last week and I told them, "You've got

to focus. Stop blaming white people for your problems... Learn to play bas-
ketball, tell jokes, or sell crack. That's the only way I've seen people get out."

—Dave Chappelle

Last time I was down South I walked into this restaurant, and this white
waitress came up to me and said: "We don't serve colored people here."
I said: "That's all right, I don't eat colored people. Bring me a whole
fried chicken."

—Dick Gregory, *Nigger*

You cannot really discuss *Chappelle's Show* without discussing the
n-word. One also cannot discuss the *n*-word without discussing Dick
Gregory. Neal Brennan and Dave Chappelle weren't even born yet when
Dick Gregory bounded onto the American comedy scene and asked to
stand flat-footed or to sit down and be spoken to like a man. Yvonne Seon
tells me that when Dick Gregory campaigned for president in 1968, "we
all had our eyes on him." Dick Gregory is a larger-than-life sort of man.
To reach him, you have to get past his wife of fifty years, Miss Lillian.
"You were lucky," Gregory tells me. "She is tough. She once told the president I'd have to call him back."

Although things have slowed down from the days when he commanded a weekly rate of something just shy of fifteen thousand bucks,
when the only peers in his earning bracket were Woody Allen, Mort Sahl,
and Lenny Bruce, Dick Gregory is still on the move. All of his activity
is made even more remarkable by the fact that he is now eighty. He still
runs and does regular juice fasts, and his long white beard makes him
look like a Methuselah among men. And maybe he is. Richard Pryor
once said: "Dick was the greatest, and he was the first. Somebody had
to break down that door. He was the one."

Before Dick Gregory, there were no elegant black men in comedy.
The generation before Dick Gregory's grew up on Stepin Fetchit, the
stage name of a black actor named Lincoln Perry and one of America's
most famous black personalities for more than twenty years. These days

it is difficult to find clips of Stepin Fetchit and the existing films are rarely shown. Stepin Fetchit acts like a shuffling, befuddled fool, and because of this many of Perry's films have been deemed offensive. Little remains to show his enormous influence on- and off-camera: he was the first black A-list actor, a millionaire during the Great Depression; he owned a fleet of limos and sports cars and he employed a retinue of Asian maids and butlers. He carried guns, he wrote essays for black newspapers, he was handsome, he was a Hollywood outlaw—but none of that mattered on-screen. On-screen he stooped his neck, and dropped his bottom lip, and acted as shiftless and stupid as possible. Stepin Fetchit is the id figure, in characterization only, that sits on Chappelle's shoulder in one of his skits and demands that Chappelle make himself happy and order chicken during a flight. It is not the chicken that is the problem, it is the familiarity of the characterization. That whether Chappelle liked it or not, whether Dick Gregory liked it or not, this was the precedent.

"When the Playboy Club brought me in," Dick Gregory recalls, "up until then you could sing, you could dance, but you could not stand flat-footed and talk and just tell jokes, because the people upstairs didn't want folks to know just how intelligent black folks were. [The Playboy Club] brought me in, though, and it opened up the floodgates. Now," he says, "Will Smith's movies alone have made three billion dollars." Dick Gregory's gig at the Playboy Club started in 1961, and three years later he would write his memoir, entitled *Nigger*. This is the part of his dedication to his mother that is often quoted:

> Dear Momma—Wherever you are, if you ever hear the word "nigger" again, remember they are advertising my book.

When I suggest to Gregory that he used his comedy as a weapon, he shouts, "What?" so loud I get scared. "How could comedy be a weapon? Comedy has got to be funny. Comedy can't be no damn weapon. Comedy is just disappointment within a friendly relation." Chappelle, he says, was very good at it. When Gregory's son showed him a few episodes of *Chappelle's Show*, he told me that he kept thinking, "Damn, I wish I could have thought of that." Then Gregory volunteers to tell me the names of the three greatest comedians of all time, and in a proud and awesomely fraternal way, he says, in order: "Lenny Bruce, Richard Pryor, and Mark Twain."

"Yes," I say. "But isn't it difficult to be that profane and that profound, in droves, especially as Twain in *Pudd'nhead Wilson*?"

"Did you say *Pudd'nhead Wilson*?" Gregory shouts.

"Yes," I say, scared again that I've said the wrong thing.

"*Pudd'nhead Wilson*! Brilliant stuff! I could kiss you! Mmhm," he says. "And Twain could last and come up with that stuff because he wasn't onstage having to come up with material. But listen," he says, waiting a beat. "Nobody said comedy was easy."

Dick Gregory admires Mark Twain's audacity as a white man to discuss race in America. He hates the idea of concealing the word *nigger* behind euphemisms like "the *n*-word," and he seems to think it should be a shared burden. "Before Twain, no white people would ever write about lynchings. So his column was 'There were two people lynched last weekend and then we found out they were just "niggers."'" And then he did the whole article about how the good Christian church people were there. And the white women brought their babies and children were selling Kool-Aid and lemonade, like, 'So what? They were just niggers!' That was the first time that anyone in history wrote anything like that; nothing about those gatherings had ever been written about lynching! That had never been done before! And like that, that is comedy!" When I ask Estee Adoram, the lovely, legendary, no-nonsense booker at New York's best comedy club, the Comedy Cellar, what sort of person becomes a stand-up comic, the first thing she says is "A very brave person. A person willing to be laughed at."

When I read about Twain saying the word *nigger*, in the exact same way Neal Brennan did, it does not raise the hairs on my neck. I do not think we want censored comics. But I'm given pause. Estee tells me she can sense when there is "an unfunny bitterness behind the joke." The fun of humor is the way it pushes at the boundaries. The joke is indeed a tricky thing. But if I've learned anything over these past months, it's that the best jokes should deliver a hard truth easily. It is the difference between asking girls in the crowd how their butt-holes look—a roast my sister and I endured one night at a comedy club—and mastering the subtlety of the uniquely American art form of stand-up comedy. Dick Gregory has a joke for me:

> So I'm standing at the airport and I see this white lady talking to her daughter. Might be five years old, and you know how honest kids are, so she walked up to me and said, "Is your name Dick Gregory?" And I said, "Yes." And she said, "My mamma says you have a tail." And I said, "Yes, and you tell her my tail is in my front."

Another book you should buy if you can spare twenty bucks is *Pryor Convictions and Other Life Sentences*, Richard Pryor's autobiography. In it, he tells of a dinner party thrown in his honor by Bobby Darin. Pryor is seated across from Groucho Marx, who told him "that he'd seen me on *The Merv Griffin Show* a few weeks earlier, when I'd guested with Jerry Lewis."

> It hadn't been one of my better moments—Jerry and I had gotten laughs by spitting on each other, and Groucho, it turned out, had a few things to say about that.
> "Young man, you're a comic?" he asked.
> "Yes," I nodded. "Yes, I am."
> "So how do you want to end up? Have you thought about that? Do you want a career you're proud of? Or do you want to end up a spitting wad like Jerry Lewis?"
> The man was right... I could feel the stirrings of an identity crisis. It was coming on like the beginning of an acid trip. Groucho's comments spoke to me. "Wake up, Richard. Yes, you are an ignorant jerk, pimping your talent like a cheap whore. But you don't have to stay that way. You have a brain. Use it."

The next sentence? "The thing was, I didn't have to."
The thing about Chappelle is that he wanted to use it, and he knew

how. There is no doubt that *Chappelle's Show* is his finest work, but the block party that he put on and filmed in Bed-Stuy in 2004 is also a revealing production in the sense that we get to see the comedian almost at rest, listening to the music he enjoys with his celebrity friends. I was there, both in the crowd and backstage, and there was a remarkable amount of solidarity, love, and exuberance even in the drizzly September rain. The kind that I can't forget. Watching a triumphant Lauryn Hill resplendent in cream slacks and a Yankees cap, reunited with her bandmates from the Fugees. Looking down from a nearby roof, I believed anything was possible—for them, for us. Chappelle was the kind of celebrity who wanted to reach out to fans who looked like him, and it was clear that as much as he aspired to universality, he realized that "the bottom line was, white people own everything, and where can a black person go and be himself or say something that's familiar to him and not have to explain or apologize?" So sometimes it was very nice to have, as the comic himself said, "Five thousand black people chillin' in the rain," like a Pan-African Congress right off of Putnam Avenue.

When I ask Yvonne Seon what she thinks about the *n*-word and how easily it is used these days in hip-hop culture, she says, "There has always been a tendency to try and rehab a word that has been used as an epithet for you. It's a way of claiming something that hurt you, hoping that you can say, 'Now this word won't hurt me anymore.' It's a part of the attempted healing. When James Brown sang, 'I'm black and I'm proud,' that is an example of how he tried to rehabilitate that word. Because there was a time when I was growing up when you didn't call anybody black unless you wanted to get knocked into next week. There was too much shame involved."

"Do you think—" I start.

And she laughs and cuts me off with a question. "Do I think, like, 'I'm black and I'm proud,' 'I'm a nigga and I am proud!' could exist?" We both laugh at the absurdity, and also the very real possibility, of that song. "Hm," she says. "I have trouble with the word *nigga*. I associate that word with lynching, violence, and hate, and I don't associate the word *black* with that. But I do associate the word *nigga* with that history. So it's not a term that I could ever use easily or encourage the use of. There have been articles written about teaching this history, and we've discussed them in my black studies class, but what usually happens is that the class eventually decides that they're going to be part of the movement against the word *nigger*. Once they understand what the history is and what the word means, they stop using it and they encourage their friends to stop using it."

"It is about choices," I say, feeling guilty for a lot of reasons before she demurely stops me.

"Yes, it always is," she says, "about choices."

Just being a Negro doesn't qualify you to understand the race situation any more than being sick makes you an expert on medicine.
—Dick Gregory

Tamra Davis, the director of *Half Baked*, is feeding her children, so she can't say out loud the last lines of the movie she directed. These are lines she had to fight for, and, along with Brennan and Chappelle, she had to try to convince fifteen studio executives that they deserved to be in the movie. She tries to talk around the lines, but finally she whispers, "I love weed, *love it*! Probably always will! But not as much as I love pussy!" She giggles. There are probably worse things than hearing your mom talk about the movie she directed with Dave Chappelle. Tamra Davis is nonchalantly cool, despite having the distinction of having directed the early movies of Adam Sandler (*Happy Gilmore*) and Chris Rock (*CB4*). She grew up in California and has been around comedy all her life. Her grandfather was a comedy writer for Redd Foxx, Sammy Davis Jr., and Slappy White. She understands comedy instinctually, and knows that the difference between a writer and a comic is the energy and love a comic must bring to the stage, to the audience.

Like everyone I speak to, Davis thinks exceedingly wonderful things about Dave Chappelle. The man has a hagiography; I hear it from everyone: from Neal Brennan to a former executive of Comedy Central, who tells me, "I have so, so much respect for Dave. He is a great guy." For all the bridges he has supposedly burned, Dave Chappelle is beloved. Tamra Davis is the most direct. "I just really think his voice is an important voice to be heard. I've spent my life working with young people who all of a sudden get launched into an incredible position of celebrity and fame and it's very, very difficult to handle. And people handle it in different ways. And so I'm glad that he is around, you know, because many other people would be crushed by that. Having to have that inner dialogue in your head, knowing that everybody is talking about you. It's a very difficult thing to have to navigate."

What separated Dave Chappelle not just from Neal Brennan but also his fans is that he was suddenly vaulted into the awkward position of being the world's most famous interlocutor in a conversation about race—the one conversation no one likes having. Yes, it is hard to look back. But it's easy to understand why Chappelle was done with being misread, tired of explaining, finished talking. As Brennan, and then everyone else, told me: the man turned down fifty million dollars. You will never get him to speak with you.

Beware, my body and my soul, beware above all of crossing your arms and assuming the sterile attitude of the spectator, for life is not a spectacle, a sea of griefs is not a proscenium, and a man who wails is not a dancing bear.

—Aimé Césaire, *Notebook of a Return to the Native Land*

When a chance came to visit Yellow Springs, I had no expectation that Chappelle would be there. But I wanted to see it. In Yellow Springs, I met Yvonne Seon. We had a good time. We discussed my wedding, we discussed Michelle Alexander's *The New Jim Crow*, and she introduced me to her family. It was a lovely day. Idyllic, even. On my way out of town, I felt tired, so I stopped for some coffee at a local coffee shop. As I was paying, I saw a few guys out back in the garden, talking, and then I saw Dave Chappelle, in a weird white tank top that strained to contain his muscles. No longer lean. Well-defended.

So at a cash register in Yellow Springs I stood and watched as the person I had so badly wanted to talk to walked toward me. But when he said hello, I made a decision that—until my plane ride home—I kicked myself for. Moving on pure instinct, I simply said hello, turned and finished paying my bill, and left.

Did I mention that the light is beautiful at dusk in Yellow Springs? The people walk the streets, going to the grocery store or looking at the theater listings. There is a café that was once a house on the Underground Railroad and that now serves delicious Reuben sandwiches and plays disco music. People say hello in passing, kids with Afros zip by on scooters. It is small-town America, but with hemp stores. I didn't want to leave, because it seems like an easy place to live. Not without its problems, but a place with a quiet understanding that conversation is the minimum for living in a better world. You know, simple things.

At a memorial for his father a few years back, standing next to his mother at the podium at Antioch College, Dave Chappelle ended his speech by thanking the community of Yellow Springs. "So," he said, "thank you to you all for giving my father a context where he could just exist and be a good dude, because to be a good dude, as many good dudes have shown you before, is just not a comfortable thing to be. It's a very hard thing to aspire to. And so thanks for honoring him, because sometimes it is a lonely, quiet road when you make a decision to try to transcend your own demons or be good or whatever he was trying to do here."

In my car's rearview mirror, it doesn't seem strange to me at all that I am watching America's funniest comic standing in a small town, smoking cigarettes and shooting the shit with his friends. Like everyone else on the street, one friend is white, the other is black—the only difference being that they are with Dave. But here Dave is just Dave. Totally uninterrupted, unheckled, free to be himself, free to have a family, and land, and time to recover. Time to be complicated, time to be a confessed fan of fame who one day decided that it was important to learn to be himself again. Chappelle took a drag on his cigarette, and laughed, and it was apparent that he was doing what he said he wanted most in life: having fun and being funny. So, for better or for worse, I took this to be my answer. ✳

KENT RUSSELL

MITHRADATES OF FOND DU LAC

DISCUSSED: *Unwinding at Applebee's, The Poison King,*
A Litany of Physiological Horror, Love Potion,
The Problem with Antivenom, Tinned Bunk, Peer Reviews,
The Miami Serpentarium, Off-Market Uses for Rose Pruners,
The Temperament of the Skin-Shabby, Recessive Steps

n the way were still more beers, the night being young in Fond du Lac, Wisconsin, and Tim's blood stanching where the cobra had bitten him. He wanded a good finger over the restaurant's menu pictures and told me, "If it was you, dude, you'd be dead in this Applebee's."

If it was anyone else on this earth, they'd be dead. The African water cobra that had tagged him two hours earlier is so rare a specimen that no antivenom for it currently exists. Yet cobra bite and lagers notwithstanding, Tim looked fresh; he was well on his way to becoming the first documented survivor of that snake's bite.

"Which reminds me," he said from across the table, taking out his phone so I could snap a picture of his bloody hand. "For posterity. After tonight, every book is fucking wrong."

Photo by Tim Friede

It was on my account that he had done this, willfully accepted the bite. Even though we'd only shaken hands that bright winter afternoon in the salted parking lot of a Days Inn. Tim Friede, the man from the internet who claimed to have made himself immune to the planet's deadliest serpents. I'd come to test his mettle, to goad him into an unprecedented ordeal: five venomous snakebites in forty-eight hours.

Around us, young people were getting unwound in a hurry. The hour was fast approaching when the restaurant would flip off the APPLE portion of its lighted sign, clear out the tables and chairs, turn the edited jams to eleven, and allow for boner grinding on the floor space. Our server returned with the beers, and Tim looked up at her with his serious blue eyes, smiling, and said, "You never did card me. You have to guess." She demurred. He continued: "I could be your dad."

While Tim fumbled for an in with her, I considered the swollen hand he propped next to his head. Two streams of blood had rilled down and around his wristbone, reading like an open quote. He was a dad's age, forty-four years old, but he appeared both strangely boyish and grizzled. He had an eager smile of small, square teeth. His hair was a platinum buzz. The skin over his face was bare and very taut; it looked sand-scoured, warm to the touch. Scar tissue and protuberant veins crosshatched his thin forearms, which he now covered by rolling down the sleeves of two dingy long-sleeve T-shirts. His neck was seamed from python teeth.

The snake that had done his twilight envenoming was *Naja annulata*, about six feet long and as thick as elbow pipe. She was banded in gold and black, a design not unlike that of the Miller Genuine Draft cans we'd bought and then housed on our way to Tim's makeshift laboratory. When we walked in, the snake was shrugging smoothly along the walls of her four-by-two plastic tank. She was vermiform mercury. And she greeted us with a hiss, a sourceless, sort of circular sizzle, what one would hear if one suddenly found oneself in the center of a hot skillet. Kissing-distance past my reflection in the glass, the cobra induced a nightmare inertia of attraction and revulsion. She had not spirals but eclipses for eyes.

"I love watching death like this," Tim had said, leaning in, startling me. "Some nights I watch them all night, like fish. Mesmerizing."

The cobra was one of a $1,500 pair he'd just shipped in, Tim preferring to spend much of what he earns—working the 10 pm–to–6 am line shift at Oshkosh Truck—on his snakes. The thing nosed under an overturned Tupperware container while I checked her CV on my phone. Her venom was a touch more potent than arsenic trisulfide. Tim unlatched the front of her tank, reached in, and was perforated before he knew it. The cobra flew at him with her mouth open and body lank, like a harpoon trailing rope.

"Ho ho, that's just beautiful," Tim said, withdrawing his hand. There were two broken fangs stapled into his ring finger.

He picked up a beer with his other hand, cracked it expertly with his pointer. I glanced around at all the other caged ampersands—mambas, vipers, rattlesnakes—and I smiled. Rosy constellations of Tim's blood pipped onto the linoleum, shining brighter than the old dead ones.

A little while ago, I was searching the web for the man who best embodied the dictum "That which does not kill me makes me stronger." I was looking for someone who thought he'd succeeded in fortifying his inborn weaknesses, who believed he had bunged the holes left by God. I discovered Tim among the self-immunizers. They're this community of a couple dozen white, Western males who systematically shoot up increasing doses of exotic venoms so as to inure their immune systems to the effects. Many of these men handle venomous snakes for business or pleasure, so there's a practical benefit to their regimen. A few prefer instead to work their way from snakes to scorpions to spiders, voiding creatures' power over them. Most seem to be autodidacts of the sort whose minds recoil at the notion of a limitation deliberately accepted— something I sympathized with, being myself an unfinished, trial creature. On their message boards, Tim talked the biggest medicine.

Their practice of self-immunization has a great old name: mithridatism. It comes from Mithradates VI of Pontus, a.k.a. "the Poison King." In his lifetime, Mithradates was the last independent monarch to stand against Rome. He tried to unite Hellenic and Black Sea cultures into a neo-Alexandrian empire that could resist the Western one. For a moment, he was successful. Rome was forced to march against and to attempt to occupy the Middle East because of him. The Roman Senate declared him imperial enemy number one. A ruthless general was dispatched to search and destroy. Mithradates went uncaptured, hiding out in the craggy steppes.

Machiavelli deemed him a hero. Racine wrote him a tragedy. A fourteen-year-old Mozart composed an opera about him. A. E. Housman eulogized what was most remarkable about Mithradates:

> They put arsenic in his meat
> And stared aghast to watch him eat;
> They poured strychnine in his cup
> And shook to see him drink it up.

Like any despot, Mithradates inverted humanity's basic psychic task and made insecurity less, not more, tolerable. He trusted no one, and in anticipation of conspiracy and betrayal, he bricked up his body into an impenetrable fortress. Each morning he took a personal cure-all tablet that included things like cinnamon, castor musk from beaver anuses, tannin, garlic, bits of poisonous skinks and salamanders, curdled milk, arsenic, rhubarb from the Volga, toxic honey, Saint John's wort, the poison blood of pontic ducks, opium, and snake venom. His piecemeal inoculation worked so well that, when finally cornered, Mithradates was unable to poison himself. According to Appian's *Roman History*, he begged his guard to murder him, saying, "Although I have kept watch and ward against all the poisons that one takes with his food, I have not provided against that domestic poison, always the most dangerous to kings, the treachery of army, children, and friends."

The official recipe for his *mithridatium* was lost. But from Nero onward, every Roman emperor ingested a version of the Poison King's antidote. Some had thirty-six ingredients, others as many as one hundred and eighty-four. Charlemagne took it daily, as did Henry VIII and Elizabeth I. The Renaissance poor had their generic versions. Oliver Cromwell found it cleared his skin. London physicians prescribed it until 1786. You could buy it in Rome as recently as 1984. It was believed to kill the helplessness in your constitution. It's the longest-lived panacea.

Tim is adopted. A cop raised him. Asked about his childhood, he offered: "I grew up fighting in the streets of inner-city Milwaukee." He once tried to reach out to his biological parents after one of his children was born dead, strangled by the umbilical cord. "I thought it might be some kind of genetic thing," he told me. "But I never found out. I couldn't get an answer out of them as to why they didn't want me."

What he'd wanted for himself was to be a Marine, a Special Forces agent, but he broke his ankle in a car accident two months before basic training. He took a year off, reenrolled in basic, re-broke the ankle. He could never be Special Forces if he couldn't jump out of a plane, so he did the next best thing and became a high-rise window washer.

Ten years of window washing put him up to injecting snake venom. "Why?" He explained, "Because when you wake up feeling no pain, then you'll know you're dead." He began by injecting a dilution of one part Egyptian cobra venom and ten thousand parts saline solution into his thigh, every week for a year. Then he upped the potency to one to one hundred, including in the mix Cape and monocled cobra venoms. From his journal of that time:

> 9-17-02
> Small rise in fever, but started to eat and drink. No painkillers yet, but I'm barely hanging on. No one was allowed near me.

> 9-18 to 9-23-02
> To sick to take notes, just don't care.

> 9-24-02
> This is the first day of puss release, thank God. 3:00 p.m., puss release with great pressure. Urine is clear, no painkillers, no antivenom, no hospital. 6:00 p.m., had second puss release. Couldn't walk, needed to crawl.

He was left with a six-inch-by-six-inch scar on his leg and an immune system with twice as many venom-specific antibodies as most people have regular ones. He's since repeated the procedure with mamba and rattlesnake venoms. He takes booster shots every couple of weeks, and he has begun immunizing against the inland taipan, the deadliest terrestrial snake. "There's no standardized guide to this shit. Everybody's different. I sort of wrote the handbook on self-immunization," Tim said, referring to a self-published PDF available on his website for twelve dollars.

"I'm separated from my wife of fifteen years because of this. I didn't change oil or cut grass or really be a husband or father. I was researching venom twenty hours a day. I had a thirteen-hundred-dollar mortgage. One day I came home and my wife had taken the kids, and she had left." With her, he's maintained a kind of relationship; it's his kids, Tim admitted, that he's lost touch with. "My wife was supportive, but I never needed her. Oh, she'd said, 'The snakes or me' before I lost our house. I was sleeping in a tent. My two kids are fifteen and six. But self-immunization is my entire life."

Snake venom is this cocktail of ribonucleases, nucleotides, amino acid oxidases, and so on that, once injected into prey through hollow fangs, immediately goes to work disrupting cellular function. It breaks down tissue proteins, attacks muscles and nerves, dissolves intercellular material, and causes metabolic collapse. The stuff is usually classified as either neurotoxic (if it attacks the nervous system) or hemotoxic (if it goes for blood components), because even though most induce both neuro- and hemotoxic symptoms, each venom tends to induce more of one kind than the other. Meaning, the damage a venom does is species-specific. Snakebite is thus like lovesickness in that each time you're wrecked special and anew.

But there *are* generalities within the two categories. For instance: a potent, primarily neurotoxic venom will effect a quick death. Immediately after the bite, though, comes a lightness of being. Then an acute sense of hearing, almost painfully acute. Chest and stomach cramps next. Sore jaw. Tongue like a bed of needles. Inflamed eyes; lids closing involuntarily. The soles of your feet feel as if they're on coals. Numb throat. Blurred vision. Then every fiber explodes in pain. From head to toe you are under a barrage of agonizing spasms. Head, neck, eyes, chest, limbs, teeth—searing, aching. The pain feels like a filament burning brightest before it pops. Then your vision splits. Everything splits. Then your muscle contractions are disabled. Your body paralyzes gradually and methodically, as though someone were going from room to room, turning out your lights. Your central nervous system is not able to tell your diaphragm to breathe. You fall down the tiers of a sleep that feels just and due, a reward.

In North America, only a few snakes—corals, elapids, and Mojave rattlers—are neurotoxic like the old-world killers, the cobras and mambas. The vast majority of venomous snakes here—the copperheads, the water moccasins, and the rattlers—are hemotoxic. Though their bites are less likely to kill, their venom, even if survived, often causes chunks of tissue or whole limbs to fall away. It dissolves you. But first you feel a flame bud and lick at the wound. Your skin tickles, pricks, and burns, as if in the process of crisping. Your lymph nodes distend and your neck balloons into a froggish sac. The venom is going from door to cellular door, pillaging. Blood from ruptured vessels escapes into your tissues. Your afflicted limb swells, hemorrhages, and enlarges to monstrosity. You sweat and go dumb. Your blood pressure plummets like a barometer before a storm. You see double, go into shock, and barf up everything. It then feels as if red-hot tongs have plunged inside you, to seek out the root of the pain. This is a living death. You witness yourself becoming a corpse piece by piece. You are barely able to piss, and what does come out is ruby red. You twitch and convulse. Your respiratory system is no longer strong enough to pump the bilge from your lungs. The foam you cough up is pink. And hours to days later, cardinal threads fall from your gums and eyes until, beaten by suffering and anguish, you lose your sense of reality. A chill of death invades your being. Your blood is thin as water. If you die, you die of a bleeding heart.

None of the above, I should say, is Tim susceptible to. He's been treated with enough neuro- and hemotoxic venoms that his Swiss-army immune system will respond to a single bite by loosing the requisite antibodies to ghost through his blood, disengaging toxins like keys in locks. He'll swell up, but he'll be OK—if there's *one* bite. It's *multiple* bites that might overwhelm him. Still, he's worked hard to do this: reconcile himself to the old, grand foe.

Sifted flurries began to fall on the drive from the restaurant to the place Tim's rented since separating from his wife. We took my rental car because his rusted-out Intrepid had no heat. Try as we did, we could not figure out how to change the Club Life satellite radio station.

"Here's one for you," Tim said, doing an economical frug in his unbelted seat. "*Venus* and *venom* come from the same root—*love,* in Latin. *Venenum. Venom* used to mean 'love potion,' but over time came to mean 'poison.'"

I skidded us off the highway onto a lightless dirt road. I flipped on the brights and blinked several times to see if there was in fact more past the windshield than unspooling mud and velvet nada. The sputtering heater worked intensely when it worked. The rattle from the backseat meant the diamondback was up.

"Somebody's getting hot to trot," Tim said. He'd picked up the snake from a friend around the way. She was going to be the last one to bite him this weekend.

"What I'm saying is—" I began, and then stopped, having forgotten what I was saying.

"Snakes and love," Tim said. "Love and snakes."

"You fell in love with these beasts because why?" I asked. "They aren't pets. A snake doesn't know what a damn relationship is. The thing doesn't know your ass from Adam."

"No, no," he said. "With snakes it's cut-and-dried. They're like, 'I want to kill you, and you'll have to survive. I'm a badass motherfucker, and you need to be a bigger badass motherfucker.' And I'm like, 'You're going to kill me every single time, and I love you.' It's the best relationship I've ever had."

We jounced past huge barns pushed back from the road. They were hung with one high, bright light, and I felt drawn to each even as I thought of anglerfish and their bioluminescent lures. "But, bro," I said, "how can you still love them once you've become immune to them? You've inured yourself to their serpentine wiles. Now what? It's like—like the difference between being in love and then being in a committed marriage."

"That's a good analogy," Tim said around the Marlboro he was lighting. The diamondback bumped her head along the seams of her plastic Bed Bath & Beyond container. She was not in time with the 4/4 radio beat. "But the snake is ten times the woman for me than the women are. Besides, this shit right here has to be a one-man show. You can't depend on that snake-woman, because she don't give a shit. She just wants to eat and shit and kill you in defense."

Tim told me which unpaved byway to look out for, and we rode on in silence but for the electronica/serpent mashup. With his swollen right hand he handled his cigarette ineptly, inserting and then removing it from his mouth the way an intern might a thermometer.

"But how great is it to be a human and do that? Beat that?" he said, and turned to point in the backseat. "To be one of the only people in history to beat you?" And this is where I did not ask: is it really evil that tempts? Or is the temptation more about thinking you've found a shortcut to utopia? I was actually very curious about what Tim would answer. Because, to me, the desire to divinize oneself has always been the most tempting thing in the world.

"Yuh-oh," Tim said into the backseat.

I heard the rattling afresh, and then Tim muttered something, and then the plastic lid on the case snapped shut.

"The venom," Tim said, "it gives me something I need. If I had the time and the money, I'd become immune to everything."

I pulled the car around hay bales and dead tractors and parked next to an unfinished guesthouse on the edge of a llama farm. Somewhere in the night, a windmill lamented oil. We put the beers and the whiskey in the cold-storage shed and went on inside.

A fox pelt and an ankle trap were nailed to the wall of Tim's foyer. There was no furniture. On the floor in the living room/kitchenette lay a sheetless full-size mattress. Drifts of books on animal tracking and mixed–martial arts. Whey protein and fifteen-pound weights on top of a fridge that didn't work. A bran of roaches and plaster flakes, all over. Many delicate bones were laid out to dry on paper towels by the sink.

Tim put the rattlesnake case on his mattress. In the light I could see she was gravid with babies. Her poison head tracked me but not Tim as he approached a stereo and cued a skipping CD of Scandinavian heavy metal. We lisped beers and poured Gentleman Jack into them.

I crunched across the floor and picked up an old textbook on venom. I flipped to the middle where there were color photos of hemotoxic snakebite gore: carmine fissures and scabby limbs. Tim walked over, pulled a bookmark from the later pages, and unfolded it. It was a letter addressed to him from the textbook's author. "Dr. Findlay Russell told me that I'd never be able to survive pure venom," he said, handing me the letter. Then he told me about antivenom.

Antivenom is no new thing. We've produced it for well over a century. Back then, producing it was a simple if crude, painstaking, and resource-intensive process; it remains so today. Take an animal—usually a horse or a sheep because of their blood volume, but a shark works, too—and inject it with small but increasing amounts of milked venom over the course of several months. The animal develops antibodies in its blood. The animal's blood is then extracted and purified and made into a serum. The serum is injected into a victim of snakebite, and the purified antibodies ride in on hyperimmune plasma like cavalry over a hill. It works similarly to a vaccine, except the immunity it confers is short-lived. The antibodies are on loan, and their introduction doesn't spur the production of one's own immune cells.

The problem, Tim continued, is that even with antivenom available throughout much of the world, 125,000 people still manage to die from snakebites every year, most of them in Asia and Africa. This is because antivenom is a very particular drug. It must be stored at a constant temperature not exceeding 46 degrees Fahrenheit. It must be administered by a doctor under controlled conditions. And, in most cases, it must come from the species of snake that did the biting. This all presupposes things like reliable electricity, clean needles, expertise, and the money needed for five to twenty-five vials of antivenom, which in our country cost about fifteen-hundred dollars each.

"The cure is in the snake," Tim said. "People are stepping on the cure. The cure is in me. And I want to develop a vaccine from it. I want to be the first person in medical history to develop a vaccine with no degree." Tim walked into the other room and waved at me with his bitten hand. It looked like a cheap prosthetic, the fingers curled and fused. When I shifted my weight to follow, the diamondback coiled into her S-shaped strike posture, rattling.

This other room was carpeted and clean. Tim had hung it with streamers of shed skin belonging to every snake that had ever bitten him. Inside a curio cabinet against the far wall were antique snakebite kits, tinned bunk that had never saved one life: chloroform, chlorinated lime, carbolic acid, injections of ammonia and strychnine, tinctures of devil's dung, potassium permanganate, which was rubbed into sliced-open fang punctures as late as the 1950s. Kits like these were popular especially in Australia in the late nineteenth and early twentieth centuries. There they were hawked by traveling showmen who performed sideshow acts with deadly species. These men received so many defensive bites in which only trace amounts of venom were injected that, unbeknownst to them, they built up immunity. They thought they were being saved by the nostrums they'd cooked up in the bush and applied after every bite. They sold them, people bought them, they still died.

Tim showed me a photograph of one such showman, Thomas Wanless. In the photo, he's crouched in a dirt patch with a tiger snake clamped onto his forearm. Tim's marginalia read, "NO ONE HAS TALKED TO ME MORE THAN THIS."

Around us were turrets of books stacked on homemade shelves: *God: The Failed Hypothesis*, old leatherbound volumes of Darwin, *Calculus for the Practical Man*, *The Immune Self*, evolutionary biology, a history of self-experimentation entitled *Who Goes First?* I pointed out one called *The Beginner's Guide to Winning the Nobel Prize*.

He said: "I mean, if I do it, I do it."

Tim does not have a college degree. He does not have any formal training in medicine. "As much as school could help me, it's such a crock of fucking shit," he said. More than anything, he wants a university to agree to study him, to find out exactly what's going on in his body, how it might be reproduced in an easily injectable form, maybe even under-write the funding for the vaccine production agreement he has with Aldevron, an antibody research outfit.

But universities don't and won't, because of liability issues. They can't in any way be affiliated with a layman whose only test subject is himself. (When the History Channel asked to feature him on an impressively ridiculous segment a few years ago, his one stipulation—that the network arrange for the University of Wisconsin to study him—was not met.) "If they backed this, and then I died, or I somehow led to other people's deaths? Well, what's that gonna cost them?"

Tim won't personally help anyone who wants to start self-immunizing. "Liability. All you gotta do is make one calculation wrong, and then my shit's done, too," he said. What he does to himself isn't technically illegal. Even the Food and Drug Administration has given him the OK. It's just that this is not how objective research is supposed to be done.

"Bullshit," Tim said. "Mice, rats, sheep, equines—but no humans? There's no other recourse. Only humans know what a thing feels like.

"Whatever, though." He picked up a framed picture, a former friend who had become the director of a reptile zoo and had gone on something of a smear campaign against self-immunization.[1] The glass was webbed from the center out, suggesting a punch. "They may got seventeen degrees, but the one thing they don't got is their hand in the cage. I just don't see why they have to cockblock me on this."

Why would anyone try to stop you? I honestly wondered. "Jealousy. They're jealous of my ability to not get killed. And they hate me because I'm proving the books wrong. I'm proving *them* wrong. But that's the history of self-experimentation and immunology."[2]

---

1. This friend wrote: "There is no scientific evidence (published in a peer-reviewed journal) to back up self-immunization. [Bill] Haast is one example and therefore anecdotal... You can still suffer severe tissue damage or death before your antibodies have time to do you any good. That's why it's called an immune response. Therefore, the benefit of such 'immunity' is slim to none."

2. Some highlights: in 1803, Friedrich Wilhelm Adam Sertürner isolated the active ingredient in opium, dubbed it "morphine," and with three of his friends tried out ninety milligrams,

So, having given up on academia, Tim petitioned the government of Sudan for money. He took out a two-thousand-dollar loan to fly there this coming summer.

"Sudan," I said.

He told me a Sudanese immigrant he works with on the production line is going to introduce him to the minister of social affairs. Was supposed to have already, actually, when she was visiting Kentucky. But Tim's coworker's rental car broke down on the drive from Wisconsin. "Now, instead, I'm going to stay in Sudan for a week, get bit by mambas to buy confidence."

"That is crazy," I said.

"This is crazy? You just took a flu shot last week."

"I've actually never had a flu shot."

"What I have to have is a short nap on a long couch," Tim said. I went to fix us a couple more boilermakers.

When I returned, Tim took me on a tour of what he called his "peer reviews." They were printed-out Hotmails from scientists and one Nobel laureate. He'd framed some. Others he'd taped to the wood paneling. They were all polite and vague. "You are probably one of a few people who have immunity against snake venoms"; "I appreciate the studies done on you and there is no criticism." Each was a printout of the whole screen, not just the text, so there were a lot of perimeter ads for penis-enhancement pills and *Wedding Crashers*.

"This is as bad as it gets, with a good ending," Tim said, cheers-ing with a hand that was rooted with dried blood. Already the swelling was ebbing. "Write this down: if you can't do it yourself, well, then, what the fuck good are you?"

---

or ten times today's recommended limit. In 1892, Max von Pettenkofer drank cholera bacteria and showed no ill effects. In 1921, Werner Forssmann threaded a catheter through his arm and into his heart, to see if such an intrusion would be fatal. (It wasn't.) In 1954, John Paul Stapp strapped himself into a rocket sled that nearly reached the speed of sound before making an abrupt stop. Because of him, we have seat belts. In 1984, Barry Marshall swallowed a petri dish of *Helicobacter pylori* to prove that bacteria could live in our caustic stomachs. Marshall and Forssmann each received the Nobel Prize.

*   *   *

No man has lived through a wider variety of venomous snakebites—if not more bites, period—than Bill Haast. "I've been bit more than one hundred seventy times and maybe almost died twenty or twenty-five times," he said in a 2007 interview, four years before his death, from natural causes. "I don't count the little bites."

In his personal museum, Tim keeps a photo of himself with Haast, the most renowned modern mithridatist. ("I had to fill his gap," Tim said of the man.) Haast started self-immunizing in 1948, when he injected one part Cape cobra venom and one thousand parts saline solution into his left forearm with a number 25 hypodermic needle. He took a booster every three months and eventually upped his dosage to a drop of raw venom. Then he added Indian and king cobra venoms to the mix. No one could say what might happen to his liver and kidneys. One zoologist wrote to tell him that he wouldn't "give a plugged nickel" for Haast's life in three years. But there were no harmful side effects, no severe reactions except for some boils caused by Haast's refusal to use sterile solutions. By the time he was ninety-five years old, he was injecting himself weekly with a brew of venoms from thirty-two snakes and lizards. "I could become a poster boy for the benefits of venom," he told the *Miami Herald*. "If I live to be one hundred, I'll really make the point." He lived to be one hundred.

After stints as an engine tester, a bootlegger, and a cashier in a prohibition chophouse, Haast operated the Miami Serpentarium, from 1946 to 1984. There, he charged the curious to watch him milk venom from cobras, kraits, rattlesnakes, all of the dread host. He didn't have a high-school diploma, but he donned a white lab coat when doing extractions. Using no protective equipment, he handled up to a hundred snakes every day of the week. On Sundays he'd release a fourteen-foot king cobra onto the front lawn and spar with it, feint and duck its strikes until he'd grabbed its head and subdued it. (It often bolted for the audience, there not being any issues of liability in those salad days, and he'd have to yank it back to him by its fist-thick tail.)

The Serpentarium was the culmination of a boyhood dream: to encourage venom research by making it easy for scientists, especially those in the United States, to obtain all sorts of snake venoms from a reliable and knowledgeable source. "This venom has got to be useful," Haast said to his tearful second wife after he was laid up in the hospital by another bite. "It can't affect every nerve in the body like this and not be useful. It must be. Someday, someone will find a use for it."

Haast tried. He was leading a promising study on the effects of neurotoxic venom on polio when Jonas Salk discovered a vaccine. In the '70s, Haast and a Miami physician were using a venom-based serum called PROven to treat more than six thousand people suffering from multiple sclerosis, when the FDA shut them down, citing improper testing.

Scientists and academics did not much love him. "It is hard to evaluate the significance of Haast's work because so little has been published," wrote one of his customers, a leading venom researcher. "He has certainly demonstrated that a human being can recover from a hell of a lot of snakebites." But the self-immunizers Haast begot cherish his work, most of all his long-out-of-print biography. (Tim referred to it as "my Bible.") In it, Haast is described as "a sometimes unapproachable and stubborn man" who "doesn't waste motions or time," who "hopes and plans for the best but expects the worst and is ready to accept it." He was "strongly individualistic with an almost innate sense of pride. He could never bring himself to ask anybody for anything, least of all to beg or plead."

Haast was made an honorary citizen of Venezuela after he flew deep into its jungle and saved a snakebitten boy's life with a transfused pint of his hyperimmune blood. In all, he donated blood to twenty-one victims of snakebite; all of them survived. A letter from one, the director of the Des Moines zoo, read, "Each morning when the sun comes up, I think of you."

He ate meat on even-numbered days and seldom consumed refined sugar. He was fit and nimble till the end, and unusually youthful-looking. He claimed never to have been sick a day in his life, to have known neither the flu nor the common cold. He didn't even take aspirin. And he lives on as the self-immunizers' alpha, the apotheosis of how a man wins hard liberty and authors his destiny.

Haast's own hands, though, were gnarly. An eastern diamondback bite curled his left hand into a claw. A Malaysian pit viper ossified his right index finger. A cottonmouth bit the tip of his pinkie, which then turned black, lost feeling, and had to be clipped off the bone by his third wife, Nancy, who used rose pruners to do so. Nancy is writing Haast's updated biography, his first wife having left him before the Serpentarium opened, and his second having departed, saying, "I can't stand it. I can't stand it. I love you, Bill. I love you. But I can't stand it anymore."

It wasn't a full-blown hangover I had, more like a subcutaneous chafe. I could feel another sour me ruffling against seams that would've split had there been one more drink last night. By noon I was on my way back to Tim's lab.

What little snow there was had stuck, the day swaddled in clouds. The lab was in the old industrial rind along the south shore of Lake Winnebago, in a disintegrating crematorium. Tim was waiting for me amid piles of rubble outside. He had on the same dirty shirts and loose jeans. An open Pabst was in his hand. He introduced me to his best friend, Corey, who works with him at Oshkosh Truck. Corey is brown-haired and haunted. His wide-set eyes seemed clear on their surface but marred below, like resurfaced ice, and he wore both a black T-shirt and a trapezoidal mustache. He handed me a beer.

Inside, half a million dollars' worth of crossbred reticulated pythons spooled in rows and rows of tanks. They belonged to Tim's friend Gavin, who runs a tattoo parlor while mongrelizing new colors and patterns of snake on the side. Their bodies were taffied muscle, and they moved slowly if at all. The musk in here was hearthy, like wood chips and spoor; sedative, until one got wind of the antiseptic tang of chemicals used to clean up after a thousand digestive systems turning hard-to-swallow prey into boneless shit. This was where Tim slept after his wife left him.

We went upstairs. Under low pipes and cobwebs were many old sofas, and two plastic tubs with an alligator in each. "These were a gift to Gavin, from this guy, before he went to prison," Tim said. I asked what was going to happen when they outgrew the tubs. He pointed to a picket coop of unsound construction.

In the opposite corner, a doughy man in Sunday shoes was using both hands to rustle sheets of dead skin off a beaded lizard. Tim led us on past, and we entered the lab proper, a climate-controlled shed with room enough for eight tanks. Tim pays Gavin three thousand dollars a year in rent; cheap, compared to the five thousand he spends on the rats stacked everywhere in plastic drawers.

The lizard man's wife clutched a baby to her breast and followed us in. When she crossed the threshold, the newly interned western diamond-back roused herself, admonishing, and the wife decided to watch from the other side of the shack's one window.

Then a guy named Dan arrived with Tim's Mojave rattlesnake. The Mojave was smallish and decorated with tan chevrons. Here now, the most dangerous species on the North American continent.[3] This Dan placed on the floor, to kneel and poke at with a boldness I thought unwarranted.

Dan resembled nothing so much as a debased tax accountant. Five-five, wire-frame glasses, a dome Bic'd clean, but no front teeth. He regularly fed quarter-sized plugs of Skoal through the slot in his mouth. "She's a sweetie," he said, swimming his finger in front of the rattlesnake's furrowed brow. She lifted her front third off the ground. "She'll sit on the hook juuuust fine." Tim was crouching behind the Mojave, talking to me, when she turned and struck at his thigh. "Got only denim," Tim assured us.

Dan went to get everybody more drinks. Tim decided to take out the pregnant diamondback and practice with a new set of snake grippers ordered specially from Georgia. When he unlatched the box, the snake flowed straight up and out, a djinn from its lamp. She was *ornery*. On the linoleum, she seemed almost overwhelmed by the forest of legs she could snatch at. Tim tried one of the bigger grippers, speared her behind the head, but the diamondback wormed easily out from under it. She writhed and lunged about like a downed but sentient power line. Using a smaller gauge, Tim pegged her, picked her up, and held her out to us spectators as she yawned, her pink gullet bracketed by fangs that

---

3. In July 2012, a Mojave bit a six-year-old California boy, who needed forty-two vials of antivenom to stay alive.

winked drops of venom. Everyone in that room was, deep down, an introverted misanthrope who had never quite lost his adolescent fascination with the death act, snake on rat, who maybe still gazed upon it with a sort of jealousy.

Dan returned with an armload of Steel Reserves and another woman. "I asked you if there was gonna be pussy," he said to Tim. "All I found… was this." Her name was Megan. She was a slim woman with a bulb nose and inky hair kept bundled in a red kerchief. Lacy with tattoos, she exuded a pheromonal benevolence. She was Corey's fiancée, and the night janitor at Oshkosh Truck. But before that, when she was jobless and adrift, Tim had loaned her money, provided her with a place to stay, and put her in charge of his rats. His wife once briefly kicked him out after she found Megan's colors mixed in with his in the wash.

During quiet moments the night before, he had brought Megan up. "Do I want to see her and hug her and kiss her?" he'd asked at the Applebee's, apropos of a text message from her. "Of course I do! Do I want her to hold my hand and support me? Yes!" But he waved it all away and explained that love had been the downfall of his immunizer heroes. His mentor "fell off and got foggy" because of a woman. Bill Haast burned through two wives before he found someone who accepted her role in his ecosystem. "Megan knows that tremendously well," he'd said. "As far as what I need or don't need." What he didn't need was a woman worrying about him, about the risks he accepted voluntarily, begging him to stop. That it might be her who is consigned to the anguish he's inoculated against had not crossed Tim's mind. "I'm not some vulnerable idiot," he went on. "I know what I'm doing. Meg is horribly special. But I guess what it comes down to is I have to cut a few people out of my life to save a million."

He slid open the water cobra tank. He withdrew both snakes without incident. They entwined around his right hand in a Gordian knot, and he said to Dan, "There are always girls here." He propped his smartphone on the windowsill to record a video of the bite. One cobra, having recently shed, looked like she was mailed in good green glass. Tim put her back. He wanted a heavily venomous bite, and snakes are more temperamental when they're shedding.

The other one was skin-shabby. Tim gripped it by its neck and rubbed it around his left arm, trying to encourage a bite. It remained flaccid and pliant as he brushed it first down and then back up, muttering, "Come *on*," apologizing that "it's not usually like this, I swear." This was practice for his trip to Sudan, where he'd have to stand and deliver in front of strangers. He pushed the rope of the snake for two more minutes before dropping it to his side and sighing. "Performance anxiety."

It would have to be the black mamba, then. We took a beery recess while Tim mentally prepped. The black mamba is *the* snake, according to him. The fastest on the planet. Terrifically aggressive. Unwelcome in zoos. Well over ten feet long, and the gray green of guns, B-52s, all your finer life-taking instruments. The "black" comes from its mouth, which it opens when threatening, and which isn't pink but obsidian. Without antivenom, the mortality rate of a "wet" black bite is absolute. Two drops—that's all it takes.

"Let's, ah, let's just see," Tim said, badly missing the garbage can with his tossed empty. He watched as I started then stopped taking this down in my spiral ledger. I looked at him expectantly. "Brotherman, there's no black mamba on earth with venom enough to kill me." He made an expansive gesture with a new beer in hand. He embraced my spotlight. "I control them," he said. "I control death."

A freight train trundled across the far bank of windows, and the sun didn't set so much as slowly back away. Tim drank his beer to foam and said, "We go." He slipped his hands inside welding gloves. He opened the tank and hooked the mamba. He threw down one and then the other glove before taking the snake behind her head. She vined herself up his other arm, tonguing his ardor. She unhinged her abysmal mouth. "She's opened up!" somebody went. I thought I could hear a faint but continuous B flat.

Tim held his palm away from his hip as though reaching for another's hand. The mamba's gorgon eyes shined with an intense bigotry of purpose. Her exhalations seemed to jelly the air. Tim pursed his lips, tensed, and lowered the open mouth to his forearm. Then the snake *nipped* him. She nipped him twice, in quick succession, fangs through skin making the same small popping noises as air holes forked in microwave-safe shrink-wrap. Tim's arm immediately petrified.

"That might've been the worst one ever," he said, carefully unwinding the mamba and dropping her into her tank. He noted the bites on a *Sports Illustrated* bikini calendar and had me take a picture of them. People cleared out of the lab. He watched Megan go feed the rats through the shed's window.

"I'll never be that lucky," he said to Corey.

"Man, shut the fuck up," Corey responded. He talked thickly, as though there were a hand around his throat. "You ain't even divorced yet."

Six inches away from Tim, at eye level, a monocled cobra hammered the door of its tank, again and again, wishing to interject. "What I'm going to do is go for married chicks," he said, rotating his forearm, which was now a bloody delta.

"Oh, at Oshkosh Truck, it's mad easy," Corey said. "I've already had a couple."

Tim leaned forward and jabbed at Corey with his bitten arm. "Ay," he said, fixing his eyes. His smile unfastened his face, and for just one instant he looked ancient. "When you getting married, dog?"

They both forced laughter. "If it was gonna happen with you, it would've happened a long time ago," Corey said.

Tim's false laugh pushed Corey's out of the room. Dan came back in, accidentally defusing the situation. He was exponentially drunker, with a giant lizard held to one shoulder. He petted it and said in mommy talk, "He's just a big baaayyy-bee," whereupon the beast lifted its tail and sprayed a rich fecal foam across the laboratory floor.

"How about that Mojave?" I enticed. Tim was by then checking his Facebook messages on his phone. "Hey, should I bring the wife over?" he wanted to know.

From downstairs Megan shouted, "Noooooo! She fuckin' hates me!" She ran up into the lab, a tottering smile on her face, and reminded Tim to take a picture of the swelling that was pushing past his elbow.

"Nah," Tim said, eyes on his phone. "The wife isn't coming over, because she says she's baking. Bitch's *baking*? Bitch, you don't *bake*."

Megan sidled up to review the photo, her birdy hand alighting on his shoulder blade. She stepped on Tim's foot not accidentally but as though flooring him.

"Nine-by-nine-inch swelling," Tim said. "Now I just need a penis bite. A solid nine all around." He didn't betray the awful pain he was feeling, his nerves vised tighter and tighter by his own expanding self. A little later, good and drunk and sitting Indian-style, we watched the uncaged Mojave thread itself into a spring of stored energy, the position of last resort. Tim did some sleight of hand and collared it. "No dinner and a movie necessary with this one," he said, and plugged the Mojave into his forearm. It rattled excitedly as it drained itself. Tim's face gaped into an ecstatic rictus.

When he pulled the snake off, tartarous venom mizzled onto me. "There's the money shot," Dan went. This was Tim's fourth deadly snake-bite in twenty-four hours' time. I scrawled, "To sin is to cheat with order." Tim saw me writing and said through a grimace, "All right, hold on now, we still got the diamondback tomorrow."

After that, things got convivial, if hazy. Beers were drunk at a ferocious pace. A gun was brought out, maybe? Tim and Megan went off into the dark somewhere. With the winking meekness of a moonlighting vigilante, Dan explained how he forewent his usual rules and restrictions when selling cobras to undesirables. I poured up large-bore whiskey shots and rather hoped for pandemonium. When the couple returned, it was agreed that the afterparty would move to Tim's place.

I stopped at a gas station to get us some Millers and Tombstone frozen pizzas. When I finally blundered into Tim's farmland shanty, I found him supine on his mattress with his inflated arms in the air. His wrists zagged at right angles, and his hands hung plump. He looked as though he'd been long planted with his own wilted grave posies. Only Corey and Megan remained; they stood against the wall, looking down at him.

"Who else is impressed by this swell?" Tim asked, a lit cigarette balancing on his lower lip. His face barely chinned above his engorged neck. He was not able to turn to anyone. The holes in him had been squeezed shut.

"This is the sickest I've ever seen him," Megan said.

"That's what she said," Tim quipped in response to his own question.

Megan asked him to take off his shirts before he swelled up too much. I put a pizza in the oven. Corey's face contracted into a pitying squinch. What was he going to do, call 911 and tell the Fond du Lac paramedics to bring three kinds of foreign antivenom?

"Shit's too soft," Tim said when I brought a slice to his mouth. After swallowing, he went, "There's room enough for you on here, sailor," and pointed to the other side of the mattress with his eyes. My face went blank. "I suppose you're too good for the floor, too?" he asked.

Corey excused himself, saying that, after all, he's got three kids and a Packers game tomorrow. Megan threw a blanket over Tim, who looked to me. The swelling was creeping still farther, and the blue in his wet eyes seemed unnaturally bright. I slipped into my coat.

You can love a snake, but the snake's got no way of showing it loves you back. Selective pressures have made it so; the creature lacks the faculties. It probably never had them to begin with. Lucky thing, its existence was never a problem it had to solve—whereas a man like Tim was born a freak of nature, being within it and yet transcending it. He was tasked with finding principles of action and decision-making to replace the principles of instincts. He had to develop a frame of orientation that granted him both a consistent picture of the universe and a basis for consistent living. Thus did he choose to build himself up: his creation is one that does not care and will never cease. Seen this way, self-immunization not only makes sense, it's the only logical response to his world.

"I am gloved in fire," he said.

Last one out, I flicked off the light and took the beers with me.

The next day came and went. I sent Tim a couple of texts from my hotel room while four inches of snow fell. I wanted to see a fifth bite. When he didn't respond, I began to consider the attendant legal problems. It'd all been his idea, I argued, freely chosen. I was just there, observing.

Late in the evening, I stopped by. I found Tim huddled over a portable electric heater, only the one light on. Inflamed under his same clothes, he appeared soft but also rigid, like something that had been stuffed and mounted. He'd been lying in bed since I left. "Just staring at the ceiling," he said. "I came close to crying, and there were a couple uncool moments when my eyes started closing on their own."

"Do you think you could still pull it off?" I asked.

"If I didn't have to work tomorrow. Or if you thought you could throw some money my way."

I patted myself down, shrugged, and said that was against the rules. Tim's right arm had been cocked Napoleonically, but now he absentmindedly pumped it with his other hand, loosening his elbow. "What you have to understand," he said, "is you have to become the snake. The snake—they call it a 'recessive' step when you lose something through evolution. But the snake *improved* itself by getting rid of legs, extra lungs, everything."

He asked me to pass him the fifth of Jack Daniel's hidden among the bottles of generic painkillers on his countertop. He unscrewed the cap using only his palm. "Had you ever even *seen* a venomous snake before this?"

I had. One Christmas morning, in an overgrown strip of backyard. I was stalking trash, shooting it with the compressed-air rifle I'd just unwrapped. I stepped softly through rusted bike frames and skirted the Braille of hamster graves. I was about to set sights on a bleach bottle when my body froze. That's a cliché, but it's absolutely true: I was arrested by the cold and tingling sensation of the familiar gone strange. I suddenly knew I was in the presence of a ghost.

Amid the litter at my feet was the candy tilde of a coral snake. How long had it been there? Was it offering to bite *me*? I considered what that might be like, getting digested from the inside out by a creature that could never comprehend in me a full human being. I felt the urge to put my life in its hands, to see just what the outcome would be. I bent to the snake in the grass.

I had no doubt that Tim would take a fifth bite if I coaxed him. But there'd be time enough for that. After all, Tim's been doing this here, alone, for quite a while, and he'll be doing it for a long time to come. "Not to sound arrogant—and I hate to say it—but I don't think anyone'll ever be able to go through what I go through," he said. "Or want to. Not in a million years."

I looked down and ruffled through the ink-bloated pages of my pocket ledger. It was just shy of full. A self that is its own antidote—there's something to be hellaciously proud of. The cheap paper hissed with crinkly sibilance as I flipped to its cardboard backing. With that, I was gone. ✶

COLIN ASHER

BUT NEVER A LOVELY
SO REAL

DISCUSSED: *Zealots Turned Grifters, The Dream of Making a
Living Writing Journalism, Chicory Coffee, Angry Husbands,
Nickel-Ante Gamblers, The New Anvil, An Occasion for a Tux,
Life Between the H Bomb and the A, Hacking, Life Advice*

Nelson Algren was the son of a no-luck working stiff
and the grandson of a religious zealot turned grifter,
and he was a type of loser we can't stomach in this
country. Algren made his living as a writer for forty
years, occasionally to great acclaim. At the height of
his career, wealth, leisure, and the lasting respect of his peers were on
offer, but Algren shrugged at those prospects and kept going his own
way. For Algren, the decision was as much a question of constitution as
it was of rational choice, and he paid for it dearly. America has always
been able to countenance beggars, short-con men, and nine-to-fivers
who just can't get ahead, but we've never known what to do with the
type of person who could have been really big but chose not to make
the concessions required.

Photo by Robert McCullough, courtesy of the Library of Congress

Algren wrote eleven books in his lifetime: one polemical, amateurish, and overwritten; five brilliant; one bitter, satirical, and unfocused; and four very good; more or less in that order.[1] From the publication of his first book, in 1935, until his death, in 1981, every word Algren wrote was guided by the belief that writing can be literature only if intended as a challenge to authority. He didn't compromise that position when Hollywood called, or the FBI, or Joseph McCarthy, junior senator from Wisconsin, or even for the sake of his own sanity after he decided that his life's work had been in vain. Which may be why all of his books were out of print when he died, alone in the bathroom of a $375-a-month Long Island rental, at the age of seventy-two. Only a few friends, no family, and a single black-clad fan were present at his funeral to hear Joe Pintauro, a young writer of short acquaintance, read seven lines of Algren's poetry as a pressboard coffin was lowered into the ground:

> Again that hour when taxis start
>   deadheading home
> Before the trolley-buses start
>   to run
> And snow dreams in a lace of mist
>   drift down
> When from asylum, barrack, cell
>   and cheap hotel
> All those whose lives were lived by
>   someone else

1. I can imagine a challenge to the number of Algren's books I've chosen to count, to say nothing of my assessments. I am including every book completed while he was living. Two of them, *Nonconformity: Writing on Writing* and *The Devil's Stocking*, were published after his death but completed before he died. I am not counting two posthumous collections of his writing, *The Texas Stories* and *Entrapment*; the collection he edited (*Nelson Algren's Own Book of Lonesome Monsters*); or *Conversations with Nelson Algren*, a book-length autobiographical interview that was published in 1957. I am also not counting *America Eats*, a gastronomical book he wrote on assignment for the Works Progress Administration. It was not published during his lifetime, and he didn't want it to be.

Come once again with palms
outstretched to claim
What rightly never was their own[2]

Algren was born Nelson Algren Abraham in Detroit in 1909, where his father, Gersom Abraham, worked at the Packard plant. Gersom was a plodding, uneducated, inarticulate man who married young, regretted leaving the family dirt farm in Indiana, and felt most at ease with mechanical objects. "Other men wished to be forever drunken," Algren once wrote. "He wished to be forever fixing." Gersom made a living as a mechanic, mostly, but had a regular habit of hitting his superiors without warning, for reasons he never could verbalize. At one point he opened a garage, and ran it with so little guile that his teenage son, Nelson, felt obliged to tell him that when he sold parts he should mark up their price. Gersom declined the advice, and eventually lost everything to repossession or foreclosure.

The family moved to Chicago in 1913, and settled in a South Side Protestant neighborhood, where Algren had a sandlot sort of childhood. He delivered the *Abendpost* with a pushcart, and picked up discarded corks and bottles for pocket change. When the White Sox were in the World Series, Algren began calling himself "Swede," after Swede Risberg—the Swede walked pigeon-toed and so did Algren. In 1921, the family moved to the Near Northwest Side and Algren, then twelve, began sneaking into the local pool hall. When gamblers connected to Capone opened the Hunting House Dancing Academy on the same block as his father's garage, Algren talked his way past the doorman and went upstairs, where he learned to gamble and watched police officers collect bribes. By seventeen he had ditched his childhood friends and had begun exploring Prohibition-era Chicago, knocking on the unmarked doors of speakeasies and offering the phrase "Joe sent me."[3]

---

2. From "Tricks Out of Times Long-Gone."

3. I owe a debt to Bettina Drew for her excellent biography, *Nelson Algren: A Life on the Wild Side.* Since it was published, in 1989, little has been added to the record that significantly contradicts

In September 1927, Algren began attending the University of Illinois at Urbana-Champaign. His parents couldn't pay, or understand why he wanted more schooling, but his older sister Bernice could. She had married into a small amount of money, and offered to help finance his four years at Urbana. To cover living expenses, Algren worked for the university, hustled pool, and set pins in a bowling alley. Later he claimed that he spent his free time in Chicago's slums and never socialized on campus. In his sophomore year Algren decided to become a sociologist, and then resigned himself to journalism because he couldn't afford a master's degree. He graduated the next year, possessed by the very American dream of making a living writing respectable, sociologically informed journalism.

Never mind the bleak 1931 economy, Algren believed he was going to have an easy time finding work. He borrowed money for an interview suit, passed a test administered by the Illinois Press Association that qualified him as a reporter or editor, and set off hitchhiking through the Midwest clutching a card certifying he was a newspaper man. He stopped in Minneapolis, where he lived in a whorehouse and then the YMCA, and wrote headlines for the *Minneapolis Journal*. He was there for a few weeks before asking for his check and learning there wouldn't be one. The paper had been doing him a favor, he was told, by allowing him to gain experience. Defeated and broke, he hitched back to Chicago and the home his parents had just mortgaged. He was depressed and directionless, and when his family pressed him to find work, he headed south.

Among the tens of thousands of hobos hitching and hopping freight that summer in search of work they never did find, at least one wore a suit bought with borrowed money. Algren still thought he could find work with a newspaper, and applied to every one he found as he drifted through Illinois, down the Mississippi, and through east Texas. His tramping ended in New Orleans, where he slept under the stars, on

its assertions. The essays "Nelson Algren's Last Year: 'Algren in Exile'" and "The First Annual Nelson Algren Memorial Poker Game" offered additional insight into Algren's character and are well worth a read, as are "Nelson Algren: The Iron Sanctuary" by Maxwell Geismar, and "A Voyeur's View of the Wild Side: Nelson Algren and His Reviewers" by Lawrence Lipton.

park benches or in alleys, and lived off chicory coffee and bananas given to him by a local mission.

By the end of the summer, Algren submitted. He pawned the suitcase but kept the suit, which may have been the thing that attracted the Luthers. The Luthers were a pair of confidence men who shared a pseudonym and needed a legit-looking patsy. One was a Texan with a steel plate in his skull, a remnant of a World War I injury; the other was a Floridian, long on get-rich-quick schemes and short on work ethic. Algren met them while working door-to-door sales on commission and rarely earning enough to eat. He was young, pretty, and poor enough to demean himself: exactly what the Luthers were looking for.

The new trio printed counterfeit certificates for free hairstyling that they distributed, for a small gratuity, to every New Orleans housewife who answered when they heard a knock. The scam earned one of the Luthers a beating from a group of angry husbands. After that, the trio fled the city for the Rio Grande Valley, where they picked fruit for seventy-five cents a shift, until the day the steel-skulled Luther returned to the picking shed holding a pistol and informed the other two that they were going to rob a supermarket called the Jitney Jungle. Algren and the Florida Luther ran again, and stopped next in Harlingen, Texas, where Luther convinced a Sinclair agent to lease them an abandoned gas station on a road no one drove. Algren signed the papers, took responsibility for the station, and bought gas with money provided by a friend from Chicago. As a sideline, he shucked and canned black-eyed peas, received on credit from local farmers. Luther disappeared and then returned only long enough to siphon gas and vanish again, leaving Algren to answer to the farmers and account for their debts to Sinclair; he nearly starved.

"Well, here you get to be a writer when there's absolutely nothing else you can do," Algren told the *Paris Review* in 1955. Harlingen was the place where he realized there was nothing else he could do. Hungry, alone, and having just been hustled, he limped home. He was picked up for vagrancy in El Paso, and walked out of the drunk tank through the cell's unlocked door.

When Algren returned to Chicago, by way of a thousand small towns, he possessed nothing but a few angry letters written on the road and a new dedication to writing. His vagabondage had divorced him of his middle-class pretensions. He had tried to play by the rules and hadn't made good, and maybe, he reasoned, the same was true of the people he had met in Chicago's slums, New Orleans's whorehouses, and Texas's hobo jungles. He had witnessed enough predation during his year on the road to last a lifetime. All of it troubled him, but none more than the violence committed under the guise of authority: the police who beat train jumpers for reward money, or locked Algren up for being broke in the wrong town. From that point forward, no matter his sporadic moments of fame, Algren identified himself with society's losers. Even near the height of his influence, in 1953, he described a writer's proper stance toward the status quo by writing: "If you feel you belong to things as they are, you won't hold up anyone in the alley no matter how hungry you may get. And you won't write anything that anyone will read a second time either."

In Chicago, Algren lived with his parents and associated himself with a group of young writers. He produced a consistent string of rejects before Larry Lipton, a friend and fellow author, suggested that he rework one of his Texas letters into a piece of short fiction. The result, "So Help Me," is a retelling of Luther's plan to rob the Jitney Jungle that results in the death of Algren's fictional counterpart. The piece was accepted by *Story* magazine around the time Algren joined the Chicago chapter of the John Reed Club, which was part of a national network connected to the Communist Party. Richard Wright was also a member. He and Algren became close; six years later, Algren would give Wright the title for his most famous book, *Native Son*.

Algren received a letter from Vanguard Press in late 1933, asking whether he was working on a novel. Not knowing how to respond and too excited to play it cool, he hitchhiked to New York City and presented himself to James Henle, Vanguard's president. At twenty four, Algren assessed himself as a promising new commodity and demanded what he imagined to be a professional rate. A hundred dollars, he figured, would be enough to get him back to Texas and pay for room, board, rolling tobacco, and liquor for four months, at the end of which he would have a book. Henle gladly gave him what he asked for.

Algren headed south from New York City, traveling rough and paying close attention to the men he hoboed with. By the time his freight passed the spires of a college building in a small southwestern Texas town called Alpine, he had the main character of his first novel. The book was written, for the most part, on the campus of Sul Ross State Teachers College, which Algren accessed by presenting his commission letter from Vanguard Press to the college's president. He wrote frantically for four months, occasionally holding court for students, and then, because part of the story took place in Chicago, he headed home. Along the way he spent a few weeks in jail, and nearly died after being trapped inside a refrigerated train car.[4]

The book produced as a result of Algren's hoboing, incarceration, and return to Chicago's left-wing literary circles was a polemical mediocrity. Two of the four sections of *Somebody in Boots* were introduced by quotations from the *Communist Manifesto*. The main character, Cass McKay, a petty criminal who desires only a tattoo and the love of a woman named Norah, experiences or witnesses violence and exploitation so severe they supplant the plot. In the introduction to a paperback reissue of *Somebody*, published thirty years after the original, Algren himself assessed the book as "an uneven novel written by an uneven man in the most uneven of American times."

Somebody in Boots was Algren's big chance, but when he stepped into the ring he swung and he missed. It was released in March 1935, and a year later it had sold only 762 copies. Algren hadn't found a straight job, and after his publishing failure it seemed he wouldn't be able to make it as a writer. He had nowhere to go, and no idea what to do next, and so resigned himself to nothingness. In the apartment of a girlfriend whose name has been forgotten, Algren removed the gas line from the back of a stove, placed it in his mouth, and breathed methane. The girlfriend

---

4. On the evening of January 25, 1934, before leaving Alpine, Algren entered Sul Ross, wrote for fifteen minutes, and then placed a cover on the typewriter he was using and walked out the door with it. Later that night, after being arrested a few miles outside of town, he made the pitiable confession: "I wanted a typewriter very bad because I am a writer by profession, I've never owned a typewriter of my own." He was in jail almost a month and was freed very near his deadline.

discovered Algren nearly but not quite dead, and handed him over to Larry Lipton and Richard Wright, who looked after him for months. Eventually they had him committed to a hospital, which discharged him to his parents' apartment. He spent the remainder of his life denying his suicide attempt.

Seven years passed between the publication of Algren's first book and his second, and during those years he grew into himself and became the stubborn, hilarious, fiercely loyal, brilliant, pugnacious, and fickle person he would be until his death. He met a woman named Amanda Kontowicz at a party thrown by Richard Wright, and they began living together in desperate poverty.[5] Algren stole food so they could eat, and he and Amanda sometimes lived for days on milk, potatoes, and onions.

When she could find work, Amanda cleaned houses. Algren stacked boxes in a warehouse and then worked in a health club, where he hosed off businessmen as they completed their workouts. During those years he cultivated friendships with literary types, and also nickel-ante gamblers, criminals, and his peers, the undistinguished poor. Eventually Wright secured a job for Algren with the Works Progress Administration, first as a writer and then as an editor. After hours he went bowling with Studs Terkel and Howard Rushmore, and drank and caroused with a gang of small-time criminals who called themselves the Fallonites.

Writing came in fits and starts. Algren founded and edited the *New Anvil*, a journal of "proletariat" literature, with his friend Jack Conroy, and published poetry, once in *Esquire*. He placed a few short stories. For material, he corresponded with inmates in Illinois prisons, haunted lineups at Chicago police stations, and observed criminal trials. In 1939 he created a pretext for leaving Amanda so he would have more time to write, and by '40 he was living in a flat without a telephone, near the heart of Chicago's Polish triangle. Emboldened by Wright's success

---

5. Over the course of more than two decades, Kontowicz and Algren would break up three times and marry twice. Amanda was a remarkable woman, but, no matter her virtues, Algren treated her through the decades in the careless way he treated most women. He needed affection, and longed for stability in an abstract way that reality never could measure up to. Each time he moved in with a woman he quickly became indifferent, listless, and absentee, longing to be able to write through the night and gamble for days without answering to anyone.

with *Native Son*, he had begun a new book. When he wasn't writing, he played cards in backroom games, spoke with the residents of the transient hotels lining South State Street, and visited the psychiatric institution at Lincoln.

That year marked the beginning of a stretch during which Algren would produce his greatest works. He wrote five books in quick succession: *Never Come Morning, The Neon Wilderness, The Man with the Golden Arm, Chicago: City on the Make,* and *Nonconformity.* With each one he advanced and expanded upon his conviction that the role of the artist is to challenge authority. He pressed that refrain throughout his life, at every opportunity he found. The formulation that best captures his intention and method is: "The hard necessity of bringing the judge on the bench down into the dock has been the peculiar responsibility of the writer in all ages of man." After his first book, Algren never traded in the idea that the poor are purely victims. Sometimes the accused were guilty, he believed, sometimes innocent, either way their perspective deserved consideration.

His publisher didn't like it, but Algren took his time writing *Never Come Morning,* the book that redeemed him. He delayed for artistic reasons and because both his sister and his father died before his deadline. By 1941 he had completed his manuscript; it was published the next year.

Never Come Morning contains a complete world bounded by the limits of Chicago's Polish triangle and populated by characters who resist simple categorization. The book's protagonists, Bruno "Lefty" Bicek and his love interest, Steffi Rostenkowski, are young, poor, self-serving, and ignorant of the world beyond the few blocks they grew up on. But neither is a caricature. Steffi, Algren wrote, is "one of those women of the very poor who feign helplessness to camouflage indolence. She had been called upon, as a child, following her father's death, for so many duties, the family's circumstances being so precarious, that she had early learned evasion." Bruno Bicek is a sandlot baseball player and sometimes-boxer who lives with his widowed mother and desires fame in the uncomplicated way a child longs for birthday presents. Bicek is a tough guy, to be feared—that's the word he puts around—but his self-image is never certain:

Bruno Bicek from Potomac Street had his own cunning,
he'd argue all day, with anyone, about anything, in daylight,
and always end up feeling he'd won, that he'd been right all
along. He'd refute himself, in daylight, for the mere sake of an
argument.
    But at night, alone, he refuted no one, denied nothing.
He saw himself close up and clearly then, too clear for any
argument. As clear, as close up, as the wolf's head in the
empty window.
    That was the trouble with daylight.

Rough as he claims to be, Lefty is a coward when it counts. One
night, Bicek's gang follows him and Steffi to a shed where they plan to
have sex. The gang waits outside while Bruno and Steffi drink and make
love, and when the deed is done they connive to rape Steffi. At first Bicek
protests, then he pleads, then he tries to negotiate, offering the gang's
leader, Kodadek, a better position on their baseball team the following
year. "Next summer we'll both be dead," Kodadek says, dismissing him.
Rather than lowering himself in his friends' estimation by admitting
that he loves Steffi, Bicek abandons her. He leaves the scene and returns
drunk. Among Steffi's attackers he spots a stranger, a Greek, and beats
him to death because he doesn't know what else to do, because he was
too cowardly to defend Steffi or fight the man fair.

By turns brutal, terrified, disenfranchised, and murderous, Bicek is
a far more nuanced and challenging protagonist than any Algren had
created before; and he is evidence that Algren had, in the seven years separating his first two books, decided that bearing honest witness was a more
effective means of challenging authority than protest was. The world of
Somebody in Boots had been a high-contrast, good-and-evil place, populated by two-dimensional characters who existed to advance Algren's
thesis. But the world of *Never Come Morning* is a finely rendered, gray-
hued, fatalistic place populated by angry, hungry young people whose
lives are governed by rules that are clear, though impossible to abide by.
Not one of them is innocent. They prey foremost upon each other, but
also upon the wider world, and they acknowledge responsibility for their

actions and pay for them. The reader might empathize with or fear them, but they are above pity, victimhood, or stereotype.

With this book Algren got his due. The *New York Times* called *Never Come Morning* a "brilliant book and an unusual book," and Malcolm Cowley declared Algren "not by instinct a novelist. He is a poet of the Chicago slums, and he might be [Carl] Sandburg's successor."

Never Come Morning went into a second and then a third printing. Algren had made a name for himself, but though he was finally confident in his ability to make a living as a writer, he couldn't bank on his potential yet; he was broke again almost immediately. By that summer he was in East St. Louis, hanging around with the Fallonites and working as a welder, a trade he was not skilled in. He returned to Chicago after a few months and took a position with the Venereal Disease Control Project, working alongside Jack Conroy. Together they scoured the city's brothels and transient hotels, looking for people who had contracted syphilis. Algren, of course, took notes. He supplemented his income by writing reviews for *Poetry* and the *Chicago Sun-Times*.

Algren and Amanda became a couple again, and then he was drafted into World War II. His induction form was stamped "Special Assignment," most likely because the FBI had been investigating him, at J. Edgar Hoover's personal request, for the past two years. Algren was under suspicion of being a leftist agitator, and was never trusted to be anything more important than a litter-bearer as his unit traveled to Fort Bragg, then liberated France, the Netherlands, and Krefeld, Germany. He returned to Chicago in late 1945, rented a two-room flat on Wabansia at Bosworth for ten dollars a month, and began writing. Doubleday approached him, and off the lingering prestige of *Never Come Morning* Algren was promised sixty dollars a week to write a collection of stories and a war novel.

The Neon Wilderness, the resultant collection of short fiction, was published in 1947 to good sales and better reviews; its prestige would only grow with time. Six years after its publication, Maxwell Geismar judged the collection "perhaps one of the best we had in the 1940s." In the introduction to the '86 edition, Tom Carson declared it the book that established Algren as "one of the few literary originals of his time."

His second success turned Algren into a public figure. Jack Conroy interviewed him on TV, then a new medium, and local cognoscenti groups like the Friends of Literature began calling. His profile was such that when Simone de Beauvoir passed through town that year, friends provided his number and told her to call.[6] He was, for the first time, in demand, well paid, and confident enough to begin shaping a few hundred pages of notes into his greatest work, *The Man with the Golden Arm*. Through 1947 and '48 Algren worked out of his Wabansia flat and split his social time the way he always had. He spent nights with a group of morphine addicts, going to jazz clubs. His days, when he wasn't writing, were spent with the intellectual set, sometimes onstage giving speeches that railed against the Taft-Hartley Act, Joseph McCarthy's House Un-American Activities Committee, and the Hollywood blacklist.

Golden Arm, which was published in September 1949, opens slowly, revealing itself a sliver at a time in the personae of its characters: Frankie Machine, a veteran with the "*right* kind" of army discharge "*and* the Purple Heart," who returned from the war with a piece of shrapnel in his liver and a morphine addiction. In his puddle-size world, he's a big fish, though his only bankable skill is his ability to deal cards, which he does in a backroom game run by Zero Schwiefka. "That's me—the kid with the golden arm," Frankie brags. Sparrow Saltskin, "a kid from nowhere," steers suckers into Frankie's card game, and fills the daytime hours shoplifting and stealing dogs. Record Head Bednar, the police captain, a man "filled with the guilt of others," picks up either of them anytime the neighborhood's equilibrium requires it. Sophie, Frankie's wife, whom everyone calls "Zosh," sequesters herself in the couple's room, trapped by a psychosomatic injury and the idea that infirmity will keep Frankie from leaving her. Violet, Zosh's only friend, cuckolds her husband with Sparrow, and justifies his thieving ways by declaring, "Lies are just a poor man's pennies."

If *Golden Arm* had a purpose, it was to challenge the idea, then

---

6. There is no way to avoid mentioning that Algren and de Beauvoir became lovers, but I don't have space to do their relationship justice so I won't try. They had a long-distance love affair that lasted many years; readers interested in the details can find many in the books *The Mandarins, America Day by Day*, and *A Transatlantic Love Affair: Letters to Nelson Algren*.

congealing into ideology, that an individual's social value is related to his or her wealth. Its message is that lives lived in the twilight hours, after swing shifts, in the shadows of newly erected towers, or beneath the tracks of the El, are as passionate, as meaningful, as funny and pointless, and as much a part of the American story as any. In *Golden Arm*, the war has ended and transformed the country. Postwar affluence has brought the world to Division Street in the form of billboards and handbills, television and neon signs, and an ethos that wrote the also-rans out of the script. Algren's characters feel themselves diminished by everything new. Even the presence of a Division Street bar that serves mixed drinks is a dark portent.

In earlier books, Algren's criminals were proud, angry, dangerous young people. Now they are older, and know they are a threat to no one but themselves. They don't have words to name the ways their world has changed, and in place of rage they have self-pity. "I never get nowheres but I pay my own fare all the way," Frankie Machine boasts pathetically. The characters that populate *Golden Arm* live in closet-size rooms tucked inside weekly rate hotels; most work, drink in a dark bar called the Tug & Maul, and then retreat to Frankie's card game, where they glance at each other, speak vaguely, and hide from the thing haunting them:

> The great, secret and special American guilt of owning nothing, nothing at all, in the one land where ownership and virtue are one. Guilt that lay crouched behind every billboard which gave each man his commandments; for each man here had failed the billboards all down the line. No Ford in this one's future nor any place all his own. Had failed before the radio commercials, by the streetcar plugs and by the standards of every self-respecting magazine.

For my money, no book more elegantly describes the world of men and women whom the boom years were designed to pass by. In the decades after *Golden Arm*, the country obsessed over the behaviors and fates of women and men like Algren's characters—and dedicated millions to altering them through wars on poverty and drugs—but in

1949 Algren was nearly alone in reminding the country that having an upper class requires having a lower class. For the skill and elegance of its prose, its compassion, and its prescience, I'd rank *Golden Arm* among the very best books written in the twentieth century. Before Algren's fall from favor and the onset of his obscurity, many people agreed with that assessment. The book received glowing reviews from *Time*, the *New York Times Book Review*, the *Chicago Sun-Times* and *Tribune*, even the *New Yorker*. Doubleday nominated it for the Pulitzer, and Hemingway, who had declared Algren the second-best American writer (after Faulkner) when *Never Come Morning* was published, wrote a promotional quote that went too far for Doubleday's taste but pleased Algren so much he taped it to his fridge:

> Into a world of letters where we have the fading Faulkner
> and that overgrown Lil Abner Thomas Wolfe casts a shorter
> shadow every day, Algren comes like a corvette or even a big
> destroyer… Mr. Algren can hit with both hands and move
> around and he will kill you if you are not awfully careful…
> Mr. Algren, boy, are you good.

A. J. Liebling, a writer for the *New Yorker*, followed Algren around Chicago for a story, and Art Shay, a young photographer, spent months taking pictures for a *Life* magazine cover story. Irving Lazar, a Hollywood agent, called to offer Algren work writing dialogue for ten times what he made writing books. John Garfield, then a leading Hollywood man, wanted to play Frankie Machine on the big screen, and he had a producer lined up. In March 1950, Algren won the first National Book Award. It was presented to him in New York City, by Eleanor Roosevelt, in a ceremony that required Algren to don a tuxedo for the first time in his life. Writing in the introduction to a fiftieth-anniversary edition of *Golden Arm*, Dan Simon, publisher of Seven Stories Press, describes a picture of Algren from that night. "He is biting down on a cigar and grinning to himself like a hard-boiled Mona Lisa, unmistakably a man who has taken on the world and won, and even more surprisingly, a man who had expected to win all along."

And that was the acme: not of Algren's talent, but of his career. The fall came fast and the landing was hard. That fact may lead you to associate this story with the now-common artistic sin-and-redemption cliché, the type that requires its talented star to succeed only so his moral failings—maybe women, maybe drugs, usually both—can unravel his career and chasten him, so that once his talent returns him to prominence he will be grayer, wiser, and much more humble. But that's not how this story goes. Algren had his vices—he never did see a dollar that wouldn't look better at the center of a poker table—but it was virtue that unwound his life.

Before *Golden Arm* was published, Algren had a profile, but not much of one outside Chicago. In the years after, anyone interested would have been able to dredge up dozens of facts that unequivocally disqualified him from being a leading cultural figure in 1950s America. In '48 alone, he stumped for Henry A. Wallace, the Progressive Party nominee for president, helped run the Chicago Committee for the Hollywood Ten, and signed an open letter to Soviet artists decrying "the exploiters who hope to convert America into a Fourth Reich." When he got to Hollywood in 1950, he kept company with men like Albert Maltz, who would soon be sentenced to jail for his role in the Hollywood Ten affair. More damningly, Algren had been a communist for years.[7] Worse still, he didn't regret anything he had done and didn't intend to change his persona or his politics.

Over the next few years, Algren paid for his intransigence in ways large and small. The FBI trailed him in Hollywood. Art Shay laid out the *Life* cover story and waited by the presses for the finished product; the story never ran. Algren sold the film rights to *Golden Arm*, and shortly afterward his Hollywood agent went underground to avoid jail.

---

7. There is dispute about whether he ever joined the Communist Party. It is unquestionably true that he considered himself a communist for a period of years, and spent considerable time at meetings of the John Reed Club. The FBI claimed Algren had been a card-carrying member of the Communist Party. Algren himself denied this, but never took the matter to trial, maybe to avoid perjuring himself. The truth of whether or not he signed a card and paid dues seems lost to history. I state here that he was a communist because he referred to himself that way ("I went into the Communist movement," he says in *Conversations with Nelson Algren*), and because I am inclined to think well of anyone who joined the Communist Party during the Great Depression and left when they got a sense of Stalin, and I think well of Algren.

John Garfield, also under investigation for his leftist sympathies, died of a heart attack at thirty-nine. Before his death, he sold the rights to *Golden Arm* to Otto Preminger, who used the book to get Frank Sinatra his only Academy Award nomination for a lead role. The deal was more than a little questionable, and Algren's biographer estimates Algren was cheated out of about $42,000 (about $360,000 today), which was far more than he had ever earned writing a book. Algren later claimed that he spent half the amount Garfield paid him for film rights and a complete script suing Preminger for control of his story. Algren had bought a small house with his proceeds, and by the end of the Hollywood debacle he had lost it to legal fees.

But it was his diminished ability to publish that cut closest to the bone. In the three years after *Golden Arm*, Algren wrote two short books, both nonfiction, both brilliant, unique, and unflinching in their critique of the country's changing ethos. The first, *Chicago: City on the Make*, is a book-length prose poem that relays Chicago's history through the lens of criminality. It may be among the most beautiful and brutally honest love letters ever written. The book opens with the theft of land from the Pottawatomie Indians, and ends in 1951, when "we do as we're told, praise poison, bless the F.B.I., yearn wistfully for just one small chance to prove ourselves more abject than anyone yet for expenses to Washington and return." Surprisingly, *City on the Make* received critical praise— "The finest thing on the city since [Carl] Sandburg's *Chicago Poems*," the *Chicago Sun-Times* decided—but, unsurprisingly, it didn't go beyond a second printing of five thousand copies.

The idea for Algren's next book came in the summer of 1952, over drinks with a *Chicago Daily News* editor who asked Algren to write an essay for the paper's book section. That winter Algren delivered a two-thousand-word anti-McCarthy essay that ran under the headline GREAT WRITING BOGGED DOWN IN FEAR, SAYS NOVELIST ALGREN. The essay ran fifteen months before Edward Murrow made his famous pass at McCarthy, and Algren's was almost the only discordant voice. To his surprise, and his editor's, the essay struck a chord. The *Nation* reprinted it, and progressive clergy members in two states introduced it into their sermons.

The essay had been extracted from a short book Algren had been writing on and off for more than a year, and in response to the attention it received, Doubleday asserted its contractual right to publish it. That was in January 1953. In March, Algren was denied a passport. In April, two informants told the FBI he had been a communist in the '30s; another came forward in June. Algren delivered his manuscript to Doubleday the same month. The book was to be published with an introduction by Max Geismar, who had assisted with the editing. Privately, Geismar wrote to Algren, "This will be one of the first books they will burn: congratulations." In September, after delaying and then giving Algren the silent treatment, Doubleday refused to publish the book. Algren sent the completed manuscript to his agent for placement elsewhere, and it disappeared. Either his agent lost it, it was lost in the mail, or it was taken en route by the FBI—its fate has never been clear.

In 1956, Algren gave the carbons from the manuscript to Van Allen Bradley, the *Daily News* editor who had commissioned the essay that spawned the initial book deal, over somber drinks at Ricardo's. After Algren's death, Bradley delivered the carbons to Algren's archive, where Bettina Drew, Algren's biographer, found them. Algren's lost manuscript was finally published, in 1996, by Seven Stories Press, as *Nonconformity: Writing on Writing*. In it, Algren argues that anyone can write, but literature can be created only by people who do not see themselves as part of "things as they are." It had always been possible for the casual reader to think of Algren as a stylist whose characters were a matter of convenience or an attempt to entice a voyeuristic public. In *Nonconformity*, Algren set the record straight.

The book is grounded in its historic moment—"Between the pretense and the piety. Between the H Bomb and the A"—but timeless in its vision. For Algren, writing is not a trade or a hobby. It is a calling that requires practitioners to give more of themselves emotionally than they can afford, and demands they tell the truest stories they possibly can, the kind that make the teller partner to the actions of their subjects and create complicity in the telling. Everything else is just words on a page. In exchange for these sacrifices he guarantees no reward. Instead he promises commercial failure and the risk of emotional collapse, yet keeps faith with his vision and claims the other side asks more. They demand conformity.

Algren believed in the equality of ideas—not that all ideas are equal, but that the value of an idea bears no relation to the social status of the person who formulated it. That belief shapes the narrative of *Nonconformity*. Algren develops and challenges his argument using his own voice and the voices of dozens of others—Dostoevsky, Fitzgerald, Carpentier, Dooley, de Beauvoir, and Durocher among them[8]—before arriving finally at the conclusion that the only vantage from which to write about America is the vantage of the impoverished. "Our myths are so many, our vision so dim, our self-deception so deep and our smugness so gross that scarcely any way now remains of reporting the American Century except from behind the billboards," he wrote. That was a unique vision in 1953, and it still is; its suppression weakened our literary tradition.

Because he needed the money, Algren accepted a contract from Doubleday to rewrite *Somebody in Boots*. After stalling for three years, he went to work, not rewriting it but writing a new book that shared just enough scenes with *Somebody* to meet his contractual obligations. It was the first time he had written purely for the need of a check, and he judged himself harshly for the compromise. While working on his manuscript, he wrote to Millen Brand, a writer and friend, and declared that all the writers of the '30s "gave up, quit cold, snitched, begged off, sold out, copped out, denied all, and ran." He included himself in the category: "[Kenneth Fearing] is hacking, Ben Appel is hacking, I'm hacking too. Nobody stayed."

Hacking or not, Algren abided by his own rules. The book was expertly written and comical, but, as in *Somebody in Boots*, the main character was a drifter who didn't pretend at the American Dream. Doubleday returned the manuscript for rewrites, fearing that its publication would result in obscenity charges. Algren rewrote it, and Doubleday refused to publish it. The book went to Farrar, Straus and Cudahy, which

---

8. Two writers, a world champion boxer, a fictitious bartender, a philosopher/writer, and an infielder, respectively.

published it as *A Walk on the Wild Side* in May 1956. This time the critics savaged Algren, not for the quality of the writing but for the book's content. The vision that had made him a sensation in 1950 made him a pariah in 1956. "What he wants to say is that we live in a society whose bums and tramps are better men than the preachers and the politicians and the otherwise respectables," Norman Podhoretz wrote in the *New Yorker*. Exactly right; but Podhoretz didn't mean it as a compliment. In the *Reporter*, Leslie Fiedler declared Algren "a museum piece—the last of the proletarian writers."

By September of 1956, Algren was so depressed by his reviews and his publishing prospects that his friends Neal Rowland and Dave Peltz had him institutionalized. He checked himself out two days later, and that December he walked across a partially frozen lagoon near the house he was about to lose in Gary, Indiana. He fell through the ice and was rescued by a group of working men who threw him a rope and dragged him to shore. He denied it had been a suicide attempt, but few of his friends were convinced.

History might have been kinder to Algren if he had died in 1956. Dead, he would have been a good candidate for rediscovery in the late 1960s or early '70s, after the political pendulum had swung back the other way. He could have been framed as a heroic figure whose career—and life— had been cut short by McCarthy and the stifling conformity of 1950s America. You can almost see the modern-classics reissues being printed, and hear the PhD theses being typed. But he didn't die, never quite went away, and refused to be championed.

About a year after he fell through the ice, Algren moved to a third-floor walkup at 1958 West Evergreen, in Chicago, near where he had lived when he wrote *Never Come Morning*, and a stone's throw from where he'd grown up. He stayed in the apartment eighteen years, and for those years he ground out a steady-ish income giving speeches; selling reprint, foreign translation, and movie rights; and writing book reviews, magazine features, and three books.

From time to time the rehabilitation of his career seemed to be on offer, but he was never willing to cede the ground necessary to make that a possibility, and he was too vulnerable to admit he was interested. In 1965, the Iowa Writers' Workshop offered him fourteen thousand dollars to teach, a significant increase over its previous offers. He accepted because he needed the money, but taught on his own terms. He critiqued papers at the bar, or over a card table, and told his students that living life was the only way to become a writer. The next year he received and accepted a spate of lecturing offers, something he referred to as "Going on the Ho Chi Minh Trail," because creating literature in '66, as he saw it, required speaking out against the Vietnam War. Onstage Algren played a recording of Hemingway reading "Saturday Night at the Whorehouse in Billings, Montana," and then inveighed against the war. The Tet Offensive was still two years away; the first large national protests wouldn't happen for three.

In his thirties Algren had been beautiful. He had looked like a boy from the poor side of the working class, all grown up and pretending to be an intellectual who was pretending to be a tough guy. He was trim, and had the gently angular features of a European mutt; a dramatic widow's peak centered attention on eyes that were kind but two clicks shy of forthright. But as he aged, as Chicago and the country grew wealthier and more refined, Algren became more disheveled and idiosyncratic, as if in defiance of the times. He grew a gut and took to wearing polyester pants, often unzipped. If he spilled gravy on his tie, he dashed salt on it as well. And when a young fan sought him out to discuss literature and receive learned counsel, Algren met him at a bar, and the only advice he provided the young man in earnest was that he should visit the animal house at the Lincoln Park Zoo, and a girl named Candy who worked the corner of Kedzie and Sixteenth.

Much of Algren's later work is brilliant, but he was never again a sensation and didn't aspire to be one. He socialized with people he liked at the expense of people who could advance his career, and stopped taking himself seriously, at least outwardly. He began calling himself a journalist, and a "loser," like Melville, and swore he'd never write another big book. When asked, he framed his new life the way his father would have framed his, if he had ever felt the need to explain himself. "If I could get by without writing, I'd be very happy," he told an interviewer. "I write for financial reasons. I don't figure I'm changing the world... I'm satisfied with this trade, which I do very easily—and because there's really nothing else I can do."

Most of that was bluster, designed to protect himself from the sort of criticism that had nearly killed him twice. Algren did see himself as a tradesman, but he did more than make a living; he kept creating literature, as he defined it. In 1964, he published a sort of sloppy autobiography called *Conversations with Nelson Algren*. And he wrote two travel books, *Who Lost an American?* and *Notes from a Sea Diary*, in '63 and '65, respectively. In '73, a collection of Algren's magazine writing, essays, and short fiction was published as *The Last Carousel*. These later books were uneven—sometimes lazy, often brilliant—but not one of them elided Algren's conviction that it was his responsibility as a writer to challenge authority with "conscience in touch with humanity."

Algren was still living in his West Evergreen flat in 1974 when the American Academy of Arts and Letters called to say it had voted unanimously to present him with the Award of Merit for the Novel—an honor shared only with Dreiser, Mann, Hemingway, Huxley, O'Hara, and Nabokov. He was in his mid-sixties, almost retired, and unwilling to become excited by an honor that would not enhance his ability to publish. Algren accepted the award graciously, in writing, but on the day of the awards ceremony he lectured to a garden club in Chicago. Years later, when Kurt Vonnegut, a friend and member of the Academy, asked what happened to the medal, Algren said it must have "rolled under the couch."

Algren spent part of 1974 in Paterson, New Jersey, on assignment for *Esquire*. The magazine wanted a story about Rubin "Hurricane" Carter, a middle-weight boxer who had been convicted of multiple homicides. Carter's guilt was unquestioned at the time, and *Esquire* wanted an Algrenesque piece about the psychology of a murderer. After reporting the story, Algren wrote a feature suggesting Carter's innocence. *Esquire* rejected it on those grounds, and in so doing delivered Algren his last lost cause.

Despite his recent award, by 1975 Algren was sinking ever deeper into obscurity. Chicago was no longer the "drafty hustler's junction" he had helped define, and few people living in the affluent present were interested in Algren's tales of the shabby past. Though he had, during his travels, found his books in libraries in Asia and Europe, he couldn't find a single one in Chicago's main library. And when *Playboy* hosted a Chicago writers' conference, he wasn't even invited. Using the Carter case as his cover, Algren decided to leave the only city he really knew and exile himself to Paterson, a city he could still understand. Shortly after leaving Chicago, Algren was caught on camera at a party, deadpanning with Studs Terkel about his move. "Downtown Paterson is really… something you shouldn't see after midnight," he says. "It's my kind of town. I like it, I like it."

Four years into his exile, Algren, by then a poor old man, had a heart attack, which he hid from his friends. He had started shopping around a nonfiction book documenting the miscarriage of justice in the Carter case, but no publisher wanted journalism from Algren; they wanted fiction. He rewrote it as a novel, but when the time came to part with the manuscript, he refused to sell for the amount he was offered. (It was eventually published posthumously.) Hurting from rejection, sick from a bad heart and a shelved book, with no projects on the horizon, Algren left Paterson to enter unofficial retirement in Sag Harbor, Long Island.

Algren rented a small bungalow hard by the Atlantic, and kept his writing desk clear. Free from the pressure to outwrite his younger self, he was happier than he had been in decades. He spent weekends holding court at a small local bookstore, and reconnected with Kurt Vonnegut, who introduced him to Peter Matthiessen. Betty Friedan lived across the street, and often drove Algren around in a hundred-dollar wreck of a car that once spilled him onto the street when she took a sharp turn.

Fat and happy was how the American Academy and Institute of Arts and Letters found Algren when they called in February 1981, this time to say he had been inducted as a full member. It was an honor he had felt entitled to for decades, and however belatedly, it returned him to the spotlight. A German press bought his book about Rubin Carter, as well as the rights to republish all his major works. And the *New York Times* and *Newsday* called for interviews. "I'm going on half a century in this ridiculous business," he said. "You know, Hemingway said the main point is to last. And I guess I'm still here," he finished, with his signature mix of spite, pride, and self-effacement.

Algren had often compared himself to Melville, who had been "banished" for writing *Moby-Dick* and died earning less then twenty-five dollars a week as a customs inspector. Like Melville, Algren insisted, he would be denied the recognition he deserved from the literary establishment during his lifetime.

And he was right, if just barely.

On May 8, 1981, Algren felt chest pains. He visited a doctor, who insisted he check in to the hospital for observation, a demand Algren refused. He was hosting a party to celebrate his induction into the Academy the next day, and he was not going to miss it. That night he gave a long, stressful phone interview. A few hours later, at 6:05 am on May 9, he had another heart attack, this one deadly. There was no will and no known next of kin. Algren's body went unclaimed for two days. Chicago friends, not knowing whom else to contact, called Joe Pintauro, who had known Algren well for only a year, to express their sympathies. Candida Donadio, Algren's agent, had to order the headstone, and when it arrived, Algren's name was misspelled. His name is correct on the replacement, which sits on a plot near the edge of the cemetery, chosen by Pintauro so Algren could be "near the people." And below his name is an epigraph perfect for a man who preferred fighting to winning, and gambled without regard for the consequences: THE END IS NOTHING. THE ROAD IS ALL.[9] ✴

---

9. This quote is often attributed to Willa Cather, but it belongs to Jules Michelet. One of Cather's characters in *Old Mrs. Harris*, a novella published in 1932, quotes Michelet in the original French and then translates. The phrase has evermore been attributed to Cather, who often used it in her speech.

RACHEL POLIQUIN

HOW TO SCRUTINIZE
A BEAVER

DISCUSSED: *A Fountain of Live Flounder, Death by Dog,*
Secretions from the Castor Sacs Used in Puddings, An Inducement
to Miscarry, Fabled Self-Castration, Isidore of Seville, The First
Beaver Dissection at the Bibliothèque du Roi, The Great Fissure,
To See Well What One Wishes to Represent

I. THE SUM TOTAL OF THE BEAVER

The great British collector, naturalist, and physician Sir Hans Sloane kept a young female beaver in his garden in the fashionable Bloomsbury District at the center of London. She was a paunch-bellied beast and only half-grown, measuring thirty inches from the tip of her nose to the end of her tail. She lived mainly on bread, which she held with both paws, sitting on her haunches like a squirrel. Occasionally she nibbled the willow boughs that were brought for her, but she preferred the vines growing in Sloane's garden and gnawed several of them down to the roots. She was never heard to make any noise, except a few short grunts when chased or angered. Most of all she loved to swim in a fountain filled with live flounder, which she ignored. Her excrement was jet

Engraving from Claude Perrault's Description anatomique

black and extraordinarily fetid. Her urine was turbid, white, and pungent. Where the beaver hailed from, who sent her to Sloane, and when she came to the garden are lost to time, but she was decidedly dead three months after her arrival, when Cromwell Mortimer, Sloane's neighbor and good friend, dissected her remains, in 1733. The beaver had suffered a bout of convulsive fits. She recovered and was well enough until the day she was torn apart by a dog.

This much we know from a paper Mortimer published in *Philosophical Transactions*. At the time of the beaver's death, Mortimer and Sloane were at the heart of London's scientific community. Sloane was president of the Royal Society of London for Improving Natural Knowledge, succeeding Isaac Newton in the position. Mortimer was the society's secretary, and, as secretary, he was responsible for circulating any and all noteworthy observations, experimentations, and innovations in the society's journal, none other than *Philosophical Transactions*.

Taken on its own, Mortimer's sketch of a beaver ambling about an English garden hardly constituted useful knowledge for his enlightened readers. After all, this was the eighteenth century. Daniel Gabriel Fahrenheit invented the mercury thermometer in 1714. Edmond Halley had discovered the proper motion of the stars in 1718. And Carl Linnaeus would publish the first edition of his revolutionary ordering system, *Systema Naturae*, in 1735. The new natural philosopher discovered the world and its laws by investigation and experiment, accumulating natural facts by slow and precise observation. Which is to say, properly scrutinizing a beaver, by eighteenth-century standards, required an exhaustive description of the sum total of the beaver, or, as Mortimer entitled his paper, "The Anatomy of a Female Beaver, and an Account of Castor Found in Her."

II. FALSE TESTICLE-TALES

Castor, more commonly known as castoreum, is the potent-smelling, yellowish, sticky secretion from a beaver's castor sacs, mashed together with the dried and macerated sac itself. Beavers actually have two sets of scent organs: a pair of anal scent glands—common to most animals, including humans, and used to attract a mate or mark territory—and their castor sacs, which are unique to beavers. The sacs are not glands but distinctive pouches of dense epithelial layers that pack a heady pong, particularly when mixed with beaver urine. Castoreum has been used extensively in perfumery and as a fixative in soaps and lotions. It is also used as a vanilla flavoring in baked goods, frozen dairy products, candy, puddings, nonalcoholic beverages, and chewing gum. (The United States Food and Drug Administration estimates the daily intake per capita of castoreum is around 0.01261 milligrams.) However, for most of human history, castoreum has been highly prized for its fabled medicinal properties.

The ancient Roman Pliny the Elder claimed that castoreum induced miscarriage—if a pregnant woman stepped over a jar of it, or over a beaver itself, abortion would be the sure result. Castoreum was an excitant for patients suffering from lethargy, an antispasmodic, and—if used as a suppository—it dispelled hysterical suffocations. (A footnote from my 1857 translation of Pliny's text observes that "castor is still given to females to inhale, when suffering from hysteria.") Pliny claimed castoreum helped with vertigo, fits of trembling, affections of the sinews, sciatica, stomachic complaints, and epilepsy. Taken with vinegar, it cured hiccups. When beaten with oil and injected into the ear, it cured a toothache on the same side.

Pliny also narrates the dark little tale of self-castrating beavers. Confusing a beaver's organs for testicles, a myth spread that a cornered beaver would bite off his own testes, rolling them toward the hunter in the hope of escaping with his life.

Pliny was aware that physician-philosopher Quintus Sextius had discredited the myth. However, the story had been around too long and was too deliciously perverse to expire just from the words of one careful observer. Among the earliest versions of the tale is "The Beaver and His Testicles," included in Aesop's fables, which concludes with this pithy moral: "If only people would take the same approach and agree to be deprived of their possessions in order to live lives free from danger; no one, after all, would set a trap for someone already stripped to the skin." The seventh-century scholar Isidore of Seville added an etymological elegancy to the tale by erroneously claiming that the word *castor* was derived from the Latin verb *castrare*, "to castrate." (In fact, the Greek word for "beaver," *castor,* is derived from the ancient Sanskrit word for "musk," *kasturi.* The original Latin word for "beaver" is *fiber.* For better or worse, Carl Linnaeus gave the Eurasian beaver the binomial name *Castor fiber,* translatable as "beaver beaver.") Sometime before his death, in 1566, from a surfeit of figs, the French physician Gulielmus Rondeletius finally dissected a beaver with sufficient accuracy to determine that the castoreum was not held in a beaver's testicles but produced by a pair of stink pouches *inside* the beaver's abdomen, making them anatomically impossible to nip off in a pinch. Yet almost a hundred years later, the myth was still prevalent enough for Thomas Browne to include it in his encyclopaedic debunking of ancient errors and spurious notions, *Pseudodoxia Epidemica Or, Enquiries Into Very many Received Tenets, And commonly presumed Truths,* first published in 1646. Interestingly, Browne seems to think that the confusion between testicles and scent organs was a more egregious error than the idea of a beaver biting anything off to save his life.

The only medicinal virtue Mortimer mentions in his paper (both he and Sloane were physicians) is that wearing a beaver cap and anointing one's head with castor oil would so strengthen one's memory that nothing read would ever be forgotten. However, Mortimer is quick to qualify that "this seems to be only a superstitious Fancy, yet I mention it, because probably such a Notion might have first brought the Use… of this Animal into Request for making Hats." Mortimer had better things to do than debate the merits of ancient wisdom. In the true scrutinizing spirit of eighteenth-century anatomy, Mortimer set out to detail the anatomical particularity of the female beaver, something which had yet to be systematically inspected.

III. INSIDE THE BODY
OF A FEMALE BEAVER

Beavers had once been plentiful throughout the British Isles, but the last words on British beavers came in 1188. In his *Itinerary through Wales,* Giraldus Cambrensis claimed beavers were extinct in England and could be found only in the River Teivi in Wales and one river in Scotland. After Cambrensis, we hear no more of the beaver in Britain. By the seventeenth century, Eurasian beavers seemed destined for the same fate. With their scaly tails and aquatic lifestyle, beavers were deemed to be fish by the Roman Catholic Church, which meant they could be eaten on non-meat Fridays and throughout Lenten abstinence. Perhaps more devastatingly, a rage for broad-brimmed beaver hats eradicated beavers from most rivers in Europe and Russia. Mortimer notes they were long gone from the Biber River, named for its beavers, and from the Danube. By the early eighteenth century, Eurasian beavers survived only in a few rivers in Switzerland, Poland, Russia, and Austria. With Eurasian beavers in sad decline, the discovery of a new continent teeming with beavers was astounding good fortune for European furriers.

Although beavers were hardly unknown or unusual, by the early eighteenth century only a few descriptions existed of beaver anatomy. Ancient and medieval authors had barely explored beyond the powers of castoreum, and beavers from North America usually arrived at European ports as skins for hats, not as living creatures. One of the first beaver dissections was performed on a deceased male beaver at the Bibliothèque du Roi in the late seventeenth century. The beaver had been taken from the Saint Lawrence River, and had lived at Versailles for several years, although he was never allowed in the fountains. Claude Perrault's account of the dissection was published by the Académie Royale des Sciences in 1671, accompanied by illustrations of the left paw, brain, reproductive system, and sharp-pointed penis bone.

With the fresh body of a dead female beaver, Mortimer hoped to make a similar contribution to the anatomical sciences. However, nothing much was left of the beaver after the dog attack. "She was so torn," he writes, "that we could see nothing Particular in the Heart, or in the Lungs. In the *Abdomen* the *Liver* and *Kidnies* were quite torn a-pieces. There were several Holes bit through the Stomach." Luckily for Mortimer, the beaver's "Parts of Generation" were sufficiently unharmed by the attack to allow detailed observations of the exact size, shape, and location of the beaver's uterus, ovaries, bladder, castor sacs, anal glands, vagina, anus, and cloaca, the last described by Mortimer as the "great *Fissure*."

The beaver's bowels and ovaries resembled those of a female dog, while her bladder was the size of a wrinkled walnut. Her two castor sacs were like two pears, each about an inch and three quarters long and filled with a dark, syrupy, musky tar with the extreme pungency of smelling salts. The membranes of the sacs were tough, "full of Wrinkles and Furrows and of a livid dirty Colour," and able to contain about an ounce of water. The beaver's wizened anal glands were oblong, and the pale, fleshy color of a pancreas. Each anal gland was connected to a castor sac above by a narrow canal and to a separate orifice below, beset with long black hairs, which in turn was connected to the cloaca.

Mortimer's article is accompanied by his own illustration of the beaver's inward parts. Surely the beaver's body was a bloodied clutter of tubes and organs, but Mortimer's drawing is a wonder of clear-eyed scrutiny. In the words of Perrault (the author of the Parisian beaver dissection), the importance in anatomical illustration "was not to represent well what one sees, but to see well what one wishes to represent." Mortimer certainly succeeded. The illustration neatly delineates all the parts, just as Mortimer described them: the irregularities of the ovaries, the wrinkled furrows, the dark cavern of the anus, and the long black hairs. He even included a portion of her tail so readers could orient themselves, anatomically speaking.

And in case anyone desired to scrutinize the truth of these matters for herself, Mortimer—or Sloane, or both—skinned what was left of the beaver and preserved her reproductive tract in alcohol. Listed among the vertebrate specimens in the catalogs of Sloane's collection are "the case [skin] of a beaver I kept alive in my garden for some time" and "the inward parts in spirits." ✱

FRANCISCO GOLDMAN

THE UNRESILIENT

DISCUSSED: *Unimaginable Grief, A Promise, A Libro Unico,*
A Reprehensible Phrase, Café le Roy, Hybrid Tags for Prose,
Deceit, Courage, Face-Burning Immediacy,
The American Zeal for Classification, A Sacred Relic

...And suddenly a hare ran across the road.
One of us pointed to it with his hand.

That was long ago. Today neither of them is alive,
Not the hare, nor the man who made the gesture.

O my love, where are they, where are they going
The flash of a hand, streak of movement, rustle of pebbles.
I ask not out of sorrow, but in wonder.

—"Encounter," Czeslaw Milosz

Illustration by Tony Millionaire

My wife, Aura Estrada, died in Mexico City on July 25, 2007, after breaking her neck the day before while bodysurfing at a beach on the Pacific Coast. She was thirty, and we'd been together for four years, married for two. Aura's mother and an uncle blamed me for the accident, and even threatened me with prison. It is understandable that her mother, having lost her only child, in her unimaginable grief, maybe even maddened by grief, would blame me. But I was close to mad with grief myself.

The day of Aura's funeral I scribbled a note that I intended to put into her coffin, but then I couldn't, because the coffin was sealed, a window over her face. In the note I thanked Aura for the happiest years of my life, asked her forgiveness for failing to protect her from that wave that killed her, and promised that instead of killing myself, I would fulfill these promises: I would get a book of her writing published. I would start a literary prize in her name. I also vowed to live each day in a way that would honor her.

I still have that note. It wasn't until I started writing this, and I looked at it again, that I realized one of the promises I'd remembered making wasn't, in fact, written there. I'd promised Aura that I was going to write a book about her and about us, a book *for* her.

Why write a book at all? Because I had no other way of processing what had happened. According to grief experts, if you've witnessed the death of your beloved in an unexpected, sudden, and violent way, and if that beloved was what they call "an attachment figure," the person who really was the greatest source of happiness and meaning in your life, then you are prone to traumatic or complicated grief; if your beloved's family also blames you for the death, inevitably causing you to internalize that burden of guilt—which you may well have done even without the blame—that will probably complicate matters even more. Neurological imaging reveals the lesions trauma inflicts on the brain's pathways. That is one reason why traumatic grief, when you are really inside it, harrowing as it is, is so trippy. The wall between night and day, between subconscious and conscious, breaks down. Over a year, I was diagnosed not just with PTSD and situational major depressive disorder, but also with minor psychotic episodes. "Don't worry, it doesn't mean I think that you're schizophrenic," my therapist reassured me. The key word was *situational.* It had been brought on by a situation, not by my own predetermined biology. I could get over it.

So that was the mental and emotional state in which I began to write my—our—own *libro unico.* "What is a *libro unico?*" asked Roberto Calasso, the Italian writer and editor at the publishing house Adelphi, in an essay about the founding of the Libro Unico line of books. I am not sure how to translate *libro unico* precisely—a unique, a singular, an only or an isolated book, an exception, a book that is a complete departure from a writer's more aesthetically self-aware books, or in some cases an author's only book. "Definitely," wrote Calasso, "a *libro unico* is one in which it is immediately noted that something has happened to the author, and he has ended up depositing that something in a text."

"A book that was written from inside a delirium" is how Calasso described Alfred Kubin's *The Other Side,* the first in the Libro Unico collection. "Nothing like it in the life of Kubin before it," he wrote, "nothing like it after."

I don't remember the moment I began to write what became *Say Her Name.* It was December, six months since Aura's death. I'd fled Brooklyn for Berlin, a city I'd never been to before, though Aura had. Recently I found an email that I sent to a friend on the day after Christmas.

> i'm here in berlin… have actually started writing a bit, am writing a novel about aura, so far its pretty much the way things happened but its rigged up to merge into beautiful fiction I hope, its the first writing I have done since july. if I am going to feel this sad all the time, I might as well dance with that sadness, and see what comes out of it. its not as if I would be capable of writing anything else.

I especially regret the reprehensible phrase *dance with that sadness,* but it's what I wrote. The email is interesting to me in that—unlike the note I had meant to slip into Aura's coffin—it doesn't contradict my own memory. I'd thought of the book as a novel from the start. The disgusting jauntiness of *dance with that sadness* also shows that I had no notion of what lay ahead, and that I might even have believed that, after six months, I was over the worst of grief. Recent experts who've written about grief as experienced by so-called "resilient grievers," who they say constitute the majority of grievers, describe the "resilients" as returning to normalcy relatively quickly, even within six months. But so-called "complicated" grief is a different animal. Little did I know that the second year of grief would be much harder than the first, and the third not much better.

When I wrote that my book was "rigged-up to merge into beautiful fiction," I meant that I was aiming to merge our story (in which "I," or a version of me, was the narrator) with the novel Aura had been working on during the last year of her life. While working toward her PhD in Latin American literature, at Columbia, Aura was secretly, so as not to put her Columbia scholarships at risk, enrolled in the Hunter College MFA program. Her novel—the "beautiful fiction" I was referring to— was tentatively titled *Memoirs of a Grad Student.*

From the beginning of *Say Her Name,* my plan was for my narrative, about two-thirds in, to merge with Aura's unfinished manuscript, which I was going to try to carry forward for her. Novels, however, rarely turn out the way they were originally intended. In the end, only the last chapter of *Say Her Name* is set in La Ferte, where part of Aura's novel is set. Only for a moment, on almost the last page, does my narrator step into Aura's novel and become Marcelo Díaz Michaux, one of her characters, but then my narrator steps out again, back into "myself."

For more than three years, until October 2010, the book was with me every day. I used every writerly tool I knew how to use, and some that I'd never tried before. I wanted, in *Say Her Name,* not only but most of all, to write about Aura. I wanted to tell her whole short life story, and to make a portrait of her, and to bring that portrait "to life." To do all that, I needed both memory and imagination. I wanted to find Aura's voice, and somehow make, from language, from her words and mine, a place where we could surprise each other and love each other again. I will give one tiny example. In the novel, I wrote:

...fifteen months later I still hadn't gone back to Café le Roy, the neighborhood restaurant Aura and I went to most often, especially on weekends for brunch. Aura was sure the name must be a reference to the Triste-le-Roy of the Borges story "Death and the Compass," but no, it turned out the owner's name was Leroy.

Café le Roy is a fictional place. So Aura, in real life, could not have thought the café's name must be a Borges reference. Aura could easily have said of herself what Roberto Bolaño said of himself, that she could happily "live under a table reading Borges," so it was definitely the kind of thing Aura might have said had she come across a Café le Roy. When I wrote it, I laughed out loud, and I could hear perfectly how Aura would have laughed at herself when she found out about Leroy.

A novel is a search—to paraphrase Adorno—for a form that overtakes what is expressed, and changes it. The book, I eventually realized—after I was finished, actually—had found the form of a wave. It builds and builds, tracking both of our lives, until that moment when Aura and I are in the ocean together and the wave that will kill her rises to meet her. Everything we were led to that wave. I found no other way to see it. Everything led up to that one inexplicable, freakish, hideous catastrophe of chance.

I did not submit or sell *Say Her Name* to my publisher until I'd finished it, though later, working with my agent and editors, I did do some revising. That was when I was first confronted with the why-isn't-this-a-memoir question. Memoirs supposedly sell better than novels. But I'd never even considered calling it a memoir. Why can't I just call it "prose?" I finally said, citing Sebald's dismissal of genre as strictly defined by the book business. "My medium is prose, not the novel," Sebald told an interviewer, yet his prose books were published as novels nonetheless. Book-length prose works have to be categorized as either "fiction" or "nonfiction," they can't just be "prose" or "a book." With my editors, we kicked around such hybrid tags as *memoir novel* or *novelized memoir* before rejecting what seemed like a straining toward self-justification. *Novel* is a very capacious term, after all. It can include almost anything. "The word *novel,* when it entered the languages of Europe, had the vaguest of meanings; it meant the form of writing that was formless, that had no rules, that made up its own rules as it went along." That is J. M. Coetzee, as quoted in David Shields's *Reality Hunger,* which argues for a renewed embrace of such roots. We decided that *Say Her Name* would be published as a novel, but in such a way that readers would know it was about a real person, and about what had happened. There were myriad ways for a potential reader to know or discover that the book was about something that had happened to real people. We would simply state it in the flap and back-cover copy and in everything sent to the media. What readers then made of it would be a matter of the persuasiveness of the book itself.

When *Say Her Name* was published, in April of 2011, most readers and reviewers accepted my calling it a novel. But a few, though only in the United States, were bewildered that I'd called it a novel. I had done a disservice to my readers, one argued. Another, the *New York Times* daily reviewer Dwight Garner, wrote that I had made a "puzzling" choice in calling my book a novel. He was bothered that he had no way of knowing what was factual and what wasn't. "By robbing this version of its grainy authenticity," Garner wrote, "he's robbed it of something essential. You're too busy wondering which details and dialogue are real—the scenes from her childhood? from the early days of her parents' marriage?—to submit to the spell being cast." If this book had been a memoir, would it have relieved Garner's suspicions of inauthenticity?

It's this conflation of fact with authenticity, and of nonfact with inauthenticity, that Maggie Nelson explores in her book *The Art of Cruelty.* She cites daily *Times* critic Michiko Kakutani's piece, called "Bending the Truth in a Million Little Ways," about James Frey's discredited memoir, *A Million Little Pieces.* Frey had indeed been dishonest, and Kakutani, writes Nelson, ascribed Frey's lies "to our 'relativistic culture,'" which she faulted for a variety of ills, ranging from reality TV, historians who argue that history depends on who is writing the history, the Bush administration's lies, and creative nonfiction. Nelson concludes that as long as people "keep using 'fact' and 'truth' as interchangeable terms that need no definition or clarification, and so long as they continue to smear out the differences between dishonesty and relativism, or between political lies aimed to bring us into an unjust war and, say, the art of creative non-fiction, no clarity of thought is likely to emerge."

A naive or impressionable reader might draw the conclusion that publishing a fact-based personal narrative as fiction and lying in a memoir are equivalent crimes. The problem, however, resides in the "fact" that memoirs are considered factual at all. Given that subjective memory itself can be the most inventive of fictionalizers without even trying, some argue that all memoirs should be classified as fiction. (The influential Mexican writer Luigi Amara recently argued that all personal essays should be published as fiction, as well.) In the Mexican poet Julián Herbert's autobiographical prose account of the life and death of his prostitute mother, he explained that he was calling the book fiction because parts of it were written in the present tense, "a voluntary suspension of grammatical credibility." As for creative nonfiction, something Tobias Wolff said last spring turned up in my Twitter feed: "There's just fiction and nonfiction. Creative nonfiction is what we used to call fiction."

In other countries, the memoir doesn't have the same privileged stature as personal-truth-conveyor that it has in the United States. Roberto Bolaño was harsh about memoirs, harsher than I wish to be. In an essay on the subject, he wrote: "Of all books, memoirs are the most deceitful because the pretense in which they engage often goes undetected and their authors are usually only looking to justify themselves. Self-congratulation and memoirs tend to go together. Lies and memoirs get along swimmingly." You don't have to make things up to commit what feels like a lie. The grieving me in *Say Her Name* doesn't have all that much in common outwardly with the real-life griever others saw. Imagine my narrator writing such words as "I kept my promises! I started a prize in Aura's name... I compiled a book of her writings and got it published!" Oh, what a noble widower! I'd done those things in real life, but had I written about them in *Say Her Name*, they would have felt to me like the kinds of smarmy lies Bolaño was referring to. My narrator, the fictionalized me, quits his job to live off Aura's savings, as, in reality, I did not. Why did I write about myself in this way? Why did I want to demean myself with lies? Because sometimes—in the context of an autobiographical novel, especially—lies tell the truth, and the "truth" (as in factuality) doesn't.

Everywhere I went in the United States on my *Say Her Name* book tour, there was not a single public event or media interview in which I was not asked, "Why did you call it a novel?" or "Why isn't this a memoir?" People asked out of curiosity and sometimes, I'm sure, confusion. I really hadn't anticipated that it was going to be such an issue. When I went abroad to do events for the book, I was hardly ever asked why it wasn't a memoir; nor did the foreign reviews, so far as I know, question my genre choice.

"Why would you make into fiction a true story that has a very accepted and widely manifested form?" wrote an editor, meaning to prod my thinking on this matter. The "rise of the memoir" as a literary form, the thriving existence of a "memoir movement," are, I now understand, fixtures of US literary culture. This imperative that if you are going to write about your own life it should be in a memoir exists nowhere else but in the United States. We have critics who police writers' compliance with the genre's presumed rules, which apparently are routinely, even comically, violated. Many readers here now feel mistrustful or confused when an autobiographical book is published as a novel instead of as a memoir. Where did this really come from? Like so much else in our particular culture, it seems rooted in capitalist economics. An executive at a major publishing house recently explained to me that in the 1980s, publishers realized that the rise of daytime television talk shows offered a great platform for promoting authors who'd written about their lives and who could go on the shows and talk about their lives some more, and "the rise of the memoir" was born. I've heard stories about writers who wanted to publish personal narratives as novels but were forced by their publishers to publish them as memoirs. Other editors told my editor that they would have insisted I publish *Say Her Name* as a memoir, and congratulated her on her "courage." Obviously, writers who've done spectacular and innovative work in the memoir form in recent decades have helped to give the form its current literary legitimacy. But the American insistence on a division between genres, as if to insure clarity in product placement, seems related in spirit—I know this is a stretch, but it's not a violation of essay rules to *stretch*—to the conservative mania for privatization: privatized education, privatized prisons, privatized health care, privatized life stories. (We *own* the way you're to write these now.)

For most of the '80s I lived outside the United States, in Central America, mainly, and in Spain. I've existed somewhat outside American literary culture, and wasn't all that aware of the memoir phenomenon. When I began *Say Her Name*, I wrote the way I wanted to write. Still, I'm not averse to the idea that I should now take responsibility for the choice I made to "reject" the memoir form. When, as an undergrad in the mid-'70s, I took creative-writing classes at the University of Michigan and elsewhere, conventional realist fiction seemed to be under universal assault. Writers such as Gaddis, Gass, Barthelme, Pynchon, and, of course, Nabokov, were the era's American heroes of narrative complacency demolition and of ambitious experimentation. They, and their Latin American and Eastern European contemporaries, Grass, Calvino, and a few others, were the writers I learned to admire. I holed up in the library, seeking out such precursors as Raymond Roussel and the Oulipo writers. It seemed to me, back then, that it was embarrassing for a young person to aspire to write realist fiction. But then I read Peter Handke's *A Sorrow Beyond Dreams,* a narrative reflection on his mother's life, written only seven weeks after her suicide. I'd had no personal experience of loss, but was devastated by the book, and thought it so beautiful that I brought it into my creative-writing class to read out loud. I think one of my reasons for doing this was to give my classmates (yes, I was pretty obnoxious) an example of the kind of innovative writing that was still possible in the realist mode: a fragmented, spare, at times abstract and speculative, reticent yet so emotionally powerful autobiographical realism. Beginning my own writing career, I saw myself as tussling with all those colliding influences of unforgettably intense reading, searching for my own way.

If I had published *Say Her Name* twenty years ago as a novel, would my not calling it a memoir have been an issue for anyone? Handke's *A Sorrow Beyond Dreams,* in its recent reissue by New York Review

Books Classics, is described as a memoir, but in fact it was originally published, in German, as a novella, a semiautobiographical novella. In the NYRB Classics catalog's product details for *A Sorrow Beyond Dreams*, I found, hidden in tiny print: "Subject: Personal Memoirs; Subject: General Fiction." Does that offer a clue?

In 1992, Leonard Michaels published *Sylvia*, his 126-page autobiographical account of his harrowing relationship and marriage, in the early '60s, to a violently unstable though riveting woman who finally, in her early twenties, committed suicide. Michaels had first written about the relationship in a personal essay for *Vanity Fair*, which he'd afterward expanded into a short memoir. But *Sylvia* was published as a novel. From the few reviews from 1992 that I've been able to find, Michaels's calling it a novel was uncontroversial. But one reviewer, the poet Tom Clark, in the *Los Angeles Times,* did wonder about the choice:

> In styling his "fictional memoir," Michaels seems to be trying
> to touch a fact-based, occasionally journalistic reminiscence
> with the novelist's magic wand—a curious stroke considering
> that Michaels makes no bones about the verisimilitude of
> his tale to an ill-starred personal relationship conducted in
> the turbid hipster depths of 1960s Greenwich Village. This
> brief, sad story (advertised in the publicity copy as a rewrite
> of an autobiographical memoir published in Michaels' 1990
> collection "Shuffle"), delivered in a detached, dispassionate
> and spare first-person recounting, has a palpable ring of truth.
> Indeed, that's the best thing about it.

Clark, as did the *New York Times* reviewer, focused much of his attention on the book as a ("journalistic") documenting of the early-'60s counterculture in New York—Kerouac, Ginsberg, and Lenny Bruce have cameos. Clark considered *Sylvia* part of a "reactionary backlash" against '60s nostalgia, and wrote that Michaels was implying in his book that the "moral chaos and social confusion" of the times—when "R. D. Laing and others sang praises to the condition of being nuts…"—was to blame for Sylvia's tragically "wasted life." My own recollection of *Sylvia* was that it immersed the reader, with face-burning immediacy, in the young narrator's bewildered, helpless, and lacerating love for a woman seemingly possessed by demons but also sometimes by angels, and who was seriously mentally ill, though the narrator, up to his neck in it, doesn't, can't, comprehend that. The book certainly does, appallingly and heartbreakingly, have "a palpable ring of truth." *Sylvia* was reissued in 2007, after Michaels's death, mostly to praise, but reviewers were now less interested in its documentary value. A new concern was in the air. "Written in 1990, before the current vogue in memoirs…" (Paul Wilner, the *San Francisco Chronicle*); "Michaels had a broader, more inclusive idea of genre. He insisted on calling *Sylvia* first 'a fictional memoir,' then 'a novel,' though it was, from what I gather, entirely factual. In any case, I read it as a memoir" (Phillip Lopate, the *Nation*); "What does it mean to write a 'fictional memoir'—or a 'memoir,' or 'fiction'—anyway? Does the answer determine whether this is a cowardly book or a brave one?… And, of course, who cares?" (Alex Abramovich, *Bookforum*); "Though finally not as realized as Peter Handke's great memoir, *A Sorrow Beyond Dreams*, about his mother's suicide, *Sylvia* nonetheless resonates with the grim misery… of incomprehensible loss" (Mona Simpson, the *New York Times*); "*Sylvia: a novel* was first 'Sylvia,' the story-length memoir… Where publicists seek ways to pitch books to readers, Michaels transgressed serially against every manner of classification" (Garth Risk Hallberg, the *Millions*). In *Harper's*, Wyatt Mason, after describing *Sylvia*'s previous incarnations, wrote, "The facts do not change from version to version, but Michaels's fictional account tells them best."

It was now impossible to write about *Sylvia* without at least mentioning its not being a memoir. Though some reviewers seemed unsettled by that choice, they resisted policing it. ("Who cares anyway.") Some of the reviews do reveal, perhaps, a touch of that well-known American zeal for classification, compartmentalization. The one reviewer who raised the cowardice issue did so equivocally, raising and quickly dismissing it. (Who or what is it, anyway, that the writer supposedly so fears and that can also be, presumably, so easily evaded merely by calling a book a novel? I don't doubt that Michaels faced fears, but I also feel pretty certain that none were dispelled by his genre choice.) Some, like Lopate, insisted on reading *Sylvia* as a memoir anyway. (I got used to seeing *Say Her Name* described as a memoir in the media, and resigned myself to it. I understood that readers responded that way because they knew or sensed or believed that the story was "factual.") Finally, Michaels's celebrated skill and *Sylvia*'s emotional force provided their own self-justification. Wyatt Mason's response was spot-on. In the end, the facts, even when presented faithfully, matter less than what the writer has made of them.

In the UK—or the non–US English-language countries, i.e., the Booker territories—very well-known authors have long been blurring barriers between fiction and nonfiction, especially autobiographically, including V. S. Naipaul (*The Enigma of Arrival*) and, in his later writings, J. M. Coetzee (*Youth, Diary of a Bad Year, Summertime*). *The Enigma of Arrival*, published as a novel, seemed as straightforwardly autobiographical as could be, except that Naipaul decided not to mention his wife even once, though she was apparently with him during the English countryside sojourn that much of the book evokes. When Coetzee gave the Tanner Lectures at Princeton University, in 1997 and 1998, his lectures on "The Lives of Animals" were delivered in the voice of a fictional stand-in, an Australian novelist named Elizabeth Costello. Princeton University Press published the lectures as a book with commentary by Princeton faculty members. "Not surprisingly," wrote David Lodge in the *New York Review of Books*, "most of the commentators felt somewhat stymied by Coetzee's meta-lectures, by the veils of fiction behind which he had concealed his own position from scrutiny. There was a feeling… that he was putting forward an extreme, intolerant, and accusatory argument without taking full intellectual responsibility for it." Coetzee incorporated the lectures into his novel *Elizabeth Costello*. In their enriched, fictional context, according to Lodge, "'The Lives of Animals' no longer seems vulnerable to such criticism."

Though I write in English, I read about as many books and magazines in Spanish as I do in English. In Spanish, the two most celebrated autobiographical works of recent years have been Héctor Abad Faciolince's memoir, *El olvido que seremos*, about his father, an activist physician killed by an assassin, and the poet Julián Herbert's *Canción de tumba*, about the life and death of his prostitute mother. Abad Faciolince, in his book, evokes his father's life and death in the context of a diligently reported history of the Colombian politicial situation and the violence that entangled his father. It seems the obvious choice to publish a book as nonfiction when its personal story also aims to provide an authoritative account of a specific time and place, of historic events and of prominent people. (Patti Smith's wonderful *Just Kids* is another example of that kind of book.) Herbert's novel, on the other hand, is obsessively personal, subjective; it is a portrayal of twin deliriums: his mother's on her deathbed, and his own, often drug-fueled. "What's important," he meta-reflects in the book, "is not that the acts be true, but that the illness or madness be." The writer is trying to write about a time when his grasp of the world was unstable, when his usual sense of self was unreliable, or absent.

Aura and I talked about books and about writing constantly, but never about memoirs. The only memoir I can recall Aura ever mentioning or buying was Bob Dylan's. Before Aura's death, the few memoirs I'd read were mostly by famous writers: books about their upbringings and how they became writers. There is *The Life of Henri Brulard*, of course, which opens with Stendhal's recollection of being an infant suckling at his mother's breast. Naipaul's *Enigma of Arrival* could be counted as one of those books. (I, too, read parts of it, anyway, as a "memoir," which did not seem to contradict its being a novel.) I also enjoyed Martin Amis's *Experience*, Gabriel García Márquez's *Living to Tell the Tale*, and, of course, Vladimir Nabokov's *Speak, Memory*. Nabokov, in that book's publication history, also ignored boundaries: at least one of its chapters, "Mademoiselle O," was published separately as a short story, and is included in his collected stories. In *Speak, Memory*, Nabokov writes about his life from 1903 until his immigration to the US in 1940. His biographer Andrew Field wrote that in the parts about his life with his wife, Vera, and their child, he wrote with absolute fidelity, while giving reign to "a puppet show of memories" in other, at least partly fictionalized, chapters. In *Say Her Name*, I also wrote with absolute fidelity about my life with Aura, apart from a few playful instances like the one I mentioned earlier (Café le Roy). But I fictionalized elsewhere, including in the "before Aura and I," where, drawing on a remembered fragment of something Aura had told me, or a few lines in her childhood diaries, I would imagine an episode.

Nabokov called his book a memoir but published at least one chapter as fiction. I called mine a novel and published one chapter, in the *New Yorker*, as "Personal History," or memoir. That was the magazine's decision. The excerpt centered on Aura's accident in the waves at Mazunte, and on her death. Among other things, it is a journalistic investigation and reconstruction of her death. It turns up the fact that the waves at Mazunte were more dangerous than I'd thought they were, which I'll never forgive myself for not having known, and includes other extremely painful moments and revelations. Those are the most difficult pages I've ever had to write. I had no objection to publishing those pages as nonfiction in a magazine, because that was what they were. I never insisted that *Say Her Name* was strictly nonfiction, or strictly fiction. It was because it included both that it seemed correct to publish it as a novel, while also wishing, like Sebald, that I could just call it prose.

During the second year after Aura's death, I rode the subway from Brooklyn to Columbia University to take part in an experiment headed by the clinical psychologist George Bonanno, who has conducted the most prominent "resilient griever" studies. It was an encounter between the world of scientific fact and the other, of absence and delirium. I was carrying a mood of heavy sadness that day. While an assistant observed from behind a one-way window, I sat alone in a room at a computer, watching a stream of blotchy, Rorschach-like images, trying to discern a pattern, obediently clicking on the images I recognized as recurring. But I couldn't concentrate on the images. I fell asleep at the keyboard. Later, the assistant explained that the experiment's hypothesis was that grievers would click on happy images, those that suggested smiles and such, a sign of optimism, hope, and resilience.

I was to be paid two hundred dollars for participating. The assistant held up a brand-new Columbia University coffee mug. If I wanted to buy it, I could offer whatever amount I wanted, and it would be deducted from my pay. I offered twenty-five dollars. He explained, after I asked, that my desire to purchase the mug and pay that amount was a sign of a practical and optimistic outlook, of resiliency.

I felt bewildered. When he'd held the coffee mug up, I'd known I had to have it. I thought later that I would have been willing to pay any amount for it. How could it be, I'd thought, that Aura, though a Columbia student, had never bought a Columbia mug? And how could I not have realized that until now? It seemed like something that belonged to her and that she'd left behind, or that I had to retrieve for her, and for myself. It seemed like one more sacred relic, one more piece of her to hold on to. ✳

MONTE REEL

HOW TO EXPLORE LIKE A REAL VICTORIAN ADVENTURER

DISCUSSED: *Counting Cats in Zanzibar, The Strange Disease of Modern Life, Hog's Back v. Sugar-Loaf, The Care Bestowed Upon the Bees, Efforts to Create Happier Carpenters, RadioShack's Zero-Tolerance Policy Regarding Serifs*

I n Zanzibar, late in 1856, Richard F. Burton and a caravan of porters prepared to venture into the heart of Africa's interior to search for the source of the Nile River. A ropy knot of scar tissue shined on Burton's cheek—a souvenir from his most recent expedition, upon which he caught a spear to the face during an ambush by Somali tribesmen.

An English diplomat on the island tried to warn Burton against pressing his luck a second time. The diplomat told Burton that a wandering French naval officer recently had been taken prisoner by tribal warriors. The natives had tied the luckless pilgrim to a tree and lopped off his limbs, one by one. The warriors, after dramatically pausing to sharpen their knives, relieved the Frenchman of his misery by slicing off his head. A true story, the diplomat insisted.

Illustration by John Murray from Francis Galton's The Art of Travel

Burton wasn't fazed. Severed limbs, rolling heads—even the grisliest of portents couldn't deflate his spirit, not before a journey into uncharted territory. He'd spent his life cultivating a world-worn persona that confronted anything resembling naïveté with open hostility, but a blank space on a map could reduce him to giddiness: "Of the gladdest moments in human life, methinks, is the departure upon a distant journey into unknown lands," he wrote in his journal before that trip inland. "The blood flows with the fast circulation of childhood."

Africa, as it turned out, would wring much of that blood out of him. In the months ahead he would suffer partial blindness, partial paralysis, and sizzling fevers. Hallucinations crowded his brain with ghosts. A swollen tongue got in the way of eating. But the bottom line: he would survive to explore again. And years later, flipping through that worn journal from 1856, he would pass retrospective judgment on his pre-expedition enthusiasm: "Somewhat boisterous," he concluded, "but true."

This kind of aimless gusto for all things unexplored defined the golden age of inland travel, which roughly coincided with Queen Victoria's reign (1837–1901) in England. It's no coincidence that these were the same years when steamships and telegraphs began to shrink the globe. Industrialization transformed urban landscapes and fueled the expansion of colonial empires. Railroads standardized the world's clocks, and a new strain of hurried angst—what poet Matthew Arnold labeled "this strange disease of modern life"—began to devour souls by the millions.

Enter a new breed of adventurous explorer, which Burton perfectly exemplified. These men filled the membership rolls of the "geographical societies" that started to pop up in London, New York, Paris, Berlin, and most other capitals of the industrialized world. Geographical expeditions became the antidote to an increasingly ordered, regulated, and unmysterious way of life.

But what purpose would be served if the person who finally entered terra incognita couldn't handle its unpredictable challenges? What was the point of travel if the person who finally laid eyes on the previously unseen didn't really know how to look at it?

It quickly became clear that far-flung voyagers, even those as hearty as Burton, needed focus when confronting the riddles of undiscovered worlds. They needed guiding hands. They needed how-to manuals.

Victorian adventurers rarely took a step into the wild without hauling a small library of how-to-explore books with them. Among the volumes Burton carried into east Africa was a heavily annotated copy of Francis Galton's *The Art of Travel: or, Shifts and Contrivances Available in Wild Countries*. Originally conceived as a handbook for explorers, and sponsored by England's Royal Geographical Society, the book was required reading for any self-respecting Victorian traveler. Before rolling up his sleeves and getting down to the hard business of exploring, he could turn to page 134 to learn the best way to do exactly that:

> When you have occasion to tuck up your shirt-sleeves, recollect that the way of doing so is, not to begin by turning the cuffs inside-out, but outside-in—the sleeves must be rolled up inwards, towards the arm, and not the reverse way. In the one case, the sleeves will remain tucked up for hours without being touched; in the other, they become loose every five minutes.

The amiably neurotic Galton left nothing to chance. His index is studded with gems like "bones as fuel" and "savages, management of." If Burton couldn't find the advice he was looking for in Galton, he could always consult one of the other books in his trunk that were written with explorers in mind. The stated aim of Randolph Barnes Marcy's *The Prairie Traveler: The 1859 Handbook for Westbound Pioneers*, which Burton himself edited in later editions, read like a manifesto for every handbook of this kind: "With such a book in his hand," Marcy writes, "[the explorer] will feel himself a master spirit in the wilderness he traverses, and not the victim of every *new* combination of circumstances which nature affords or fate allots, as if to try his skill and prowess."

All of the books advertised practical intentions: if adventurers are compelled to wander the globe, why not teach them how to take note of details—be they geographical, anthropological, or whatever—that might prove useful to science, industry, or empire?

I stumbled upon *The Art of Travel* while researching a book about African exploration, and continued on to the other titles, all of which are available for free on the internet. After reading them, I can confidently report that the scientific, industrial, and political developments of the intervening century have thoroughly undermined the original intentions of most of their authors. These titles won't help powerful nations lay claim to new territories and exploitable populations. As literary genres go, this one is about as dead as they get.

But it deserves a resurrection.

It's true that the authors are generally eccentric, habitually obsessive, and at times comically misguided. A modern reader will find plenty of hopelessly dated assumptions to indulge a sense of cultural superiority. You might chuckle when someone writes about the best place to buy a pith helmet in London. But that stuff has little to do with these books' contemporary relevance, which goes beyond entertainment value.

While no one was looking, this neglected genre transcended its crudely utilitarian origins to occupy a higher sphere: the books are instruction manuals for the senses, lovingly compiled tip sheets on the acquired art of paying attention.

They're not quick and easy reads. Arcane language and compulsive punctuation force the reader to decelerate. But that is exactly what many of the explorers of the period identified as the most important first step of any successful expedition.

"While traveling in a strange country [I] should always prefer making my observations at a rate not quicker than five or six miles an hour," wrote Richard Owen, the superintendent of the British Museum's Natural History Departments and a scientific patron for many of the period's most far-reaching expeditions. History has judged him harshly for opposing Darwin's ideas, but when it came to the subject of travel, his philosophy represented the vanguard of his generation's views.

The crux of that philosophy—"Slow down; it's the journey, not the destination," etc.—has ripened into soft travel-guide cliché. Modern writers tend to sound like humorless scolds when they preach about this stuff, but the Victorians avoided the trap of bland sanctimony because they were never content to stop at generalized advice. They always pushed it further. After advising travelers to reduce their speed, they offered hyper-specific instructions about exactly what travelers should observe, and how they should observe it.

The obvious titles illustrating this tendency are Harriet Martineau's *How to Observe Morals and Manners*, published in 1838, and *What to Observe: The Traveller's Remembrancer*, written by Colonel Julian R. Jackson three years later. Jackson, a secretary at the Royal Geographical Society, explains in his preface that he has "endeavored to excite a desire for useful knowledge by awakening curiosity. The intending traveller, it is hoped, will, from a perusal of the present work see what an immense field of physical and moral research lies open to his investigation..."

Everything that meets the eye tells a story, but if viewed skillfully, it also can crack open a Russian-doll wonderland of stories within stories. When looking at a mountain peak, for example, Jackson emphasizes that care must be taken to determine if it's a "saddle-back" or a "hog's back" or a "sugar-loaf"—because the structure might reveal the landscape's geological composition, which in turn can explain its vegetative potential, which can in turn... and so on.

Jackson spends thirty pages advising travelers on how to look at a river. (Is the surface of the water flat, or does it actually appear slightly convex? What sort of debris does it carry?) There is no such thing as an insignificant detail. After reading a few dozen pages of this stuff, his book works like a mind-altering drug. You look up from the page and notice that the world around you is popping into new dimensions. Suddenly the tree outside your window is demanding attention. You start to notice the subtle temperature differences between the air circulating around your head and the soil beneath your feet. If you're not careful, you can get lost on runaway trains of thought.

Jackson recognizes this danger, and he gently reminds his readers to stay on track, to maintain a discipline of focus. When he suggests that travelers should determine if native populations practice beekeeping (among many other things), he cautions against jumping ahead. First, the skillful explorer must fully observe the matter at hand before moving on to related concerns: "The care of bees is seldom an exclusive occupation, and although the honey, and particularly the wax obtained are important objects, we are here to consider merely the care bestowed on the bees themselves."

Martineau's *How to Observe* limits its attention to the proper manner of perceiving humans and their behavior. Like Jackson, she goes to great lengths in listing what travelers should notice—their treatment of criminals, the aspirations of children, beliefs about marriage—and she's a stickler for concrete details. But she also exhibits a respect for the distorting potential of point of view that's downright postmodern.

She urges the voyager to dismantle his assumptions and to always remain vigilant against "the affliction of seeing sin wherever he sees difference." It takes a lot of practice to learn how to see the world clearly, but learning how to gauge the fun-house-mirror refractions of a foreign land is the duty of all who find themselves stumbling into disorienting territory: "A child does not catch a gold fish in water at the first trial, however good his eyes may be, and however clear the water; knowledge and method are necessary to enable him to take what is actually before his eyes and under his hand. So it is with all who fish in a strange element..."

The cameras of this era were cumbersome, delicate, and hellishly tricky to use in the field. Most explorers didn't even bother. But often they were still expected to provide their sponsoring geographical societies with visual representations of the people and lands they had encountered.

Burton, our tour guide into this lost world, turned to writers like Jackson and Martineau to broaden the scope of his attentions, but he delved deeper into his makeshift bookmobile when he needed to zoom in for a tighter focus. An essential handbook was *The Elements of Drawing in Three Letters to Beginners,* by John Ruskin. Upon publication, in 1857, it immediately found a place in the luggage of explorers in every corner of the world.

Other travel handbooks, including the Royal Geographical Society's

Hints to Travellers (1854), had previously emphasized the importance of drafting and sketching, but Ruskin provided detailed, practical know-how. His book simply cannot be cracked open without intensifying a reader's visual acuity. Without cameras to record the details for them, explorers needed to develop the eyes of an artist. *The Elements* aimed to refine their vision:

> The victorious beauty of the rose as compared with other flowers, depends wholly on the delicacy and quantity of its colour gradations, all other flowers being either less rich in gradations, not having so many folds of leaf; or less tender, being patched and veined instead of flushed.

Ruskin didn't envision his audience as frustrated painters indulging ambitions to hang a canvas in the Louvre: "My efforts are directed not to making a carpenter an artist, but to making him happier as a carpenter." Encouraging such eclecticism seems strange, not to mention vaguely irresponsible, in our age of hyper-specialization. But the Victorians were unembarrassed about dipping from one discipline into another.

Consider Burton. He spoke more than twenty languages, wrote books on subjects ranging from bayonet technique to gold mining, was a spy and a consul, and was generally regarded as the most accomplished ethno-sexologist of his generation. Before disguising himself as a dervish to complete a pilgrimage to Mecca, he apprenticed himself to a blacksmith—just in case he came across some available steeds during the journey and needed to make horseshoes. He was an enthusiastic amateur in an era when the word wasn't a slur.

Dedicated travelers didn't limit their aesthetic studies to the visual arts. William Gardiner's *The Music of Nature* (1838) was a treasury of creative listening techniques to be applied in the field. Every sound, as heard by Gardiner, can reveal and instruct.

Using standard musical notation, he transcribed everything from the canter of a horse to the cry of a child. He charted the musical differences between the "yelp of a cur, whose foot has been trod upon" and "the whine of a dog tied up." He encouraged readers to apply a musical ear to every sound they might encounter out in the great wide open, even the speech of the natives. He concluded that the sounds of the Nordic languages are "less pleasing" than those found in milder climates, for example, because "the severity of the regions in which they are spoken keeps the mouth constantly closed, and the act of speaking is principally performed in the throat."

In the ragged chorus of nature, where insects provide the dominant sound track, we find Gardiner at his most enthusiastic. "The lively note of the cricket… consists of three notes in rhythm, always forming a triplet in the key of B," he writes.

Remember how Jackson suggested that explorers should notice whether or not a native population keeps bees? With Gardiner, this field of inquiry bursts open with newfound potential. He informs readers that within every hive, certain bees called "fanners" ventilate the premises by the incessant motion of their wings.

"If the ear is placed on the outside of the hive," Gardiner advises, "you may distinguish the mezzo tones that emanate from the host of fanners, who shed a mellow music from their odorous wings, which, on listening, will be found to be in the key of F."

"It is not worth the while to go round the world to count the cats in Zanzibar…" That's Henry David Thoreau, gently mocking the fellows of the geographical societies in the pages of *Walden*. When he goes off on this subject, Thoreau sometimes sounds as if he's responding to passages in the handbooks of Galton or Marcy. Other times he sounds as if he's shouting directly into Burton's ear:

> What does Africa—what does the West stand for? Is it not
> our own interior white on the chart?… If you would learn to
> speak all tongues and conform to the customs of all nations,
> if you would travel farther than all travellers, be naturalized
> in all climes, and cause the Sphinx to dash her head against
> a stone, even obey the precept of the old philosopher, and
> Explore thyself.

Screw Zanzibar, in other words.

But here's something Thoreau neglected to admit in that book: no one was more incurably addicted to expeditionary literature and the how-to-travel books than HDT himself. Not only did he devour the travelogues of Burton and other contemporary explorers, but he energetically consumed the works of almost every author referred to above. Martineau, Owen, Ruskin, Gardiner—references to each of them appear in Thoreau's journals.

Thoreau's love of these books can be reconciled with his stay-at-home instinct, because he recognized the durable potential of the how-to-explore genre even better than its authors did. The lessons of the books could be applied to Zanzibar, but they held up equally well in the bustling hamlet of Concord, Massachusetts—or pretty much anywhere else in a world growing more tired, crowded, and worn with every passing year.

"It is worth the while to see your native village thus… as if you were a traveler passing through it," Thoreau wrote in his journal.

There's an idea.

Before I turned sixteen and got a driver's license, I spent a lot of time in the Cross County Mall in Mattoon, Illinois. Within my compressed conception of the universe, the mall was roughly analogous to the Silk Road: a place that marked the eastern edge of the world, where they sold imported goods. I dared go no farther on my bike. Beyond the mall, there was nothing but an interstate and a lot of corn. This was my ultima Thule.

My world has since expanded. My parents still live in Mattoon, and I visit occasionally, but the mall exerts little pull on me. I spent more hours inside the mall during an average day playing video games as a preteen than I've spent there in the past twenty years. It's no longer a destination for me; it's a forlorn piece of architecture that I drive past on the way out of town. One of roughly fifty thousand shopping malls crowding roadsides in America, according to the Bureau of the Census. I could ignore it for another twenty years, and it would still feel like the most familiar place in the world.

On a recent morning, I pulled into the mall's parking lot with a Kindle full of downloaded guides: *The Art of Travel, What to Observe, How to Observe, Hints to Travellers, Elements of Drawing, The Music of Nature,* and *The Prairie Traveler.*

I started by following Jackson's advice to place the area in its broadest context by surveying the surrounding geography, which was ironed flat by a mile-thick glacier that rolled through about twenty thousand years ago. Now the landscape imposes rigid Newtonian laws on anything that messes with its uniformity—if you see the mild rise of an interstate overpass (like the one within eyeshot of the parking lot), a small man-made pond of inverse dimension will be found nearby, a couple hundred yards away.

The mall is a three-hundred-thousand-square-foot retail space anchored by a JCPenney at one end and a Sears at the other. Faithfully observing Owen's speed limit, I walked at a relaxed pace from the entrance of one store to the other. The journey took exactly two minutes, three seconds.

Following Galton's advice, I was sensitive to my first impressions. Evidence of recent economic troubles screamed for immediate attention. Of thirty-eight leasable spaces, sixteen were vacant. But instead of giving off a hollow, abandoned vibe, the mall felt mildly claustrophobic. A dozen separate vendors had set up cafeteria tables in the main concourse, hawking everything from hunting knives to pewter dragons to collectible dolls. You could still find nice stuff in the remaining stores, but these tables represented a lower rung on the retail ladder, and they were clearly taking over.

In place of the landmarks of my youth, like the video-game arcade and the ice-cream parlor, I saw a General Nutrition Center and something called "Community Blood Services." Before I made it to Sears, I began to feel as if I were strolling through a world robbed of joy.

But I checked myself. I returned, took a seat on a grated metal bench in the middle of the concourse, and reached into my backpack for my Kindle full of PDFs. Martineau was waiting to remind me to turn my attentions outward. She urges her readers to assess the "character of the Pride" of a region—figure out what inspires them to make public proclamations, and you're on the way to cracking their moral code. A T-shirt table in the middle of the mall attracted my eye. The first shirt I saw featured the letters *GPS*, with smaller letters around them. With exploration on the brain, I naturally gravitated toward it. It read, IF LOST, USE GPS – GOD'S PLAN OF SALVATION.

I remembered that Jackson, in his chapter about exploring the religion of an unknown locale, advises explorers to look for hints that might answer this question: "What do they hold necessary to be done in this life to receive happiness in the next?" I found some clues on the T-shirt table. TO GET TO HEAVEN, YOU NEED TO GET THE HELL KNOCKED OUT OF YOU.

In my pocket notebook, under a few lines of first impressions, I wrote: "Christianity rules here, and it seems to be a combative, hard-won strain." The author of *Hints to Travellers* advises that explorers label all field notations as "good," "very good," "doubtful," etc. I confidently scribbled "v. good" in the margin.

I now think of the first page of that notebook as a necessary warm-up, full of disposable insights. Few who visit could fail to note that whenever this Midwestern town doesn't wear its faith on its sleeve, it often wears it emblazoned across its chest. But it was around this time, as I wandered away from the T-shirts, that the tireless focus these books help to instill started to reveal less-obvious patterns.

Jackson insists that the ways a society engraves letters, for example, are "cognate and characteristic of the national mind, and are therefore, as such alone, highly worthy of the traveller's attention." I ducked into the Kirlins Hallmark store and found that cursive fonts, particularly those designed to suggest the lightest of pen strokes, could be found on almost all of the sympathy cards. Bold, blocky letters—many inscribed with a caveman sort of imprecision—almost always meant the cards were either meant to be funny, or else were for children.

These bare facts led me to really read the signs throughout the mall, and I traced undisguised symbolism everywhere. Thin-bodied letters were used to sell beauty products (you won't find many fat, inky fonts in Bath & Body Works). RadioShack seemed to observe a zero-tolerance policy regarding serifs, which are reserved for products that appeal to classicism and tradition (see the Lands' End clothing section at Sears). Every letter in the mall seemed to exude purpose, as if hand-chiseled by market-testers.

Suddenly the mall didn't seem quite as simple as it had just a couple minutes before. Instead of being a vacuous purgatory that deserved pity, the mall grew in complexity with each stride. The point that the how-to-explore books collectively hammered home is this: if you sincerely investigate it, every detail hides reason, and any environment is far more sophisticated than our senses can appreciate. You have no justification for feeling world-weary; even if the modern world bombards you with a million images per second, you have not seen it all. Ruskin writes:

> There was always more in the world than men could see, walked they ever so slowly; they will see it no better for going fast. And they will at last, and soon, too, find out that their grand inventions for conquering (as they think) space and time, do, in reality, conquer nothing; for space and time are, in their own essence, unconquerable, and besides did not want any sort of conquering; they wanted *using*.

For a while, I tried to inventory all of the smells I could detect and trace them to their sources: the dyed fabrics in Maurices clothing store, the brushed suede in Payless Shoes, the jasmine and sandalwood of the cosmetics counter in the Elder-Beerman department store. While concentrating hard to identify the characteristic smell of an electronics aisle in Sears (did I really detect the subtle tang of burning circuits?), a three-year-old boy accompanied his mother to inspect the DVD players. The kid wouldn't shut up. "I want this one! I want this one!" Every ten seconds or so, for reasons only he could grasp, he'd shriek like a beluga whale—three high, raspy squawks. My concentration shattered into a hundred pieces. I lost the scent.

But I remembered that I was carrying an electronic voice recorder—a device that I believe the author of *The Music of Nature,* had he lived into our century, would have carried on his person at all times. I fished it out of my pocket and covertly began recording the boy's voice.

For the next half hour or so, I digitally captured the discrete units of sound that collectively composed the mall's soundscape. The hum of the refrigerator at Mom's Legendary Foods. The splash of the decorative water fountain in the geographic center of the concourse. The squeaky wheel of one of the race-car-shaped strollers available near the main entrance. The rapid-fire percussion of a cash register.

Some things, surely, deserve to be ignored, for sanity's sake. At times, I worried I might have been too loose with my attentions at the mall. Emerson had warned against this sort of thing, believing that indiscriminate observation could turn a person into a mere child—"the fool of his senses, commanded by every sight and sound, without any power to compare and rank his sensations, abandoned to a whistle or a painted chip, to a lead dragoon or a gingerbread-dog, individualizing everything, generalizing nothing, delighted with every new thing..."

It's true that the techniques outlined in these books can be abused, and they should be applied sparingly, medicinally. But I was discovering unexplored territories within the commonplace, and it felt as if I was beginning to correct an imbalance that had taken hold years before, when I'd pedal out to the mall to pump tokens into *Galaga* and *Tempest*, losing hours staring into a digital display. Video games train players how to react quickly to abrupt changes in the visual field, something that researchers now call "target vision." Young gamers—the ones who don't have to go to arcades, but can play at home, token-free, for hours—are really good at it. But that skill, if overdeveloped, can erode a person's "field vision," which is the ability to register what's going on before and after those abrupt changes happen. Field vision requires proactive, not reactive, awareness. Without it, the bigger picture is lost.

The Victorians valued that way of looking at the world, considering it a critical skill when wandering into strange and bewildering territories. It still is. Behind a trash can near Sears, a single-serving carton of milk lay partially spilled. After reading Galton, the image was infused with intrigue: he tells us that milk, when applied to paper and subjected to a low flame, works as invisible ink, useful to explorers in hostile territories. The carefully designed GNC storefront display, with its labels advertising protein supplements and antioxidants, read like a sociological essay. The ragged chorus of the mall's concourse, captured on my digital recorder, then analyzed using music-studio software, revealed itself as music in the key of B-flat major, and the screech of a toddler, instead of being something that annoys and distracts, rang out in a perfectly pitched D. ★

THE IMMORTAL HORIZON

DISCUSSED: *An Escaped Assassin, Raw Chicken Meat, Unimaginable Physical Exhaustion, A License Plate from Liberia, Duct-Tape Pants, Novels Hidden in Tree Trunks, Testosterone Spread Like Fertilizer, Rattlesnakes as Large as Arms, Arms That Baptize Cats, A Bunch of Guys in the Woods Talking about Something Called the Bad Thing*

On the western edge of Frozen Head State Park, just before dawn, a man in a rust brown trench coat blows a giant conch shell. Runners stir in their tents. They fill their water pouches. They tape their blisters. They eat thousand-calorie breakfasts: Pop-Tarts and candy bars and geriatric energy drinks. Some of them pray. Others ready their fanny packs. The man in the trench coat sits in an ergonomic lawn chair beside a famous yellow gate, holding a cigarette. He calls the two-minute warning.

The runners gather in front of him, stretching. They are about to travel more than a hundred miles through the wilderness—if they are strong and lucky enough to make it that far, which they probably aren't. They wait anxiously. We, the watchers, wait anxiously. A pale wash of

Photo by Leslie Jamison

light is barely visible in the sky. Next to me, a skinny girl holds a skinny dog. She has come all the way from Iowa to watch her father disappear into this gray dawn.

All eyes are on the man in the trench coat. At precisely 7:12, he rises from his lawn chair and lights his cigarette. Once the tip glows red, the race known as the Barkley Marathons has begun.

I.

The first race was a prison break. On June 10, 1977, James Earl Ray, the man who shot Martin Luther King Jr., escaped from Brushy Mountain State Penitentiary and fled across the briar-bearded hills of northern Tennessee. Fifty-four hours later he was found. He'd gone about eight miles. Some might hear this and wonder how he managed to squander his escape. One man heard this and thought: I need to see that terrain!

Over twenty years later, that man, the man in the trench coat— Gary Cantrell by birth, self-dubbed Lazarus Lake—has turned this terrain into the stage for a legendary ritual: the Barkley Marathons, held yearly (traditionally on Lazarus Friday or April Fool's Day) outside Wartburg, Tennessee. Lake (known as Laz) calls it "The Race That Eats Its Young." The runners' bibs say something different each year: SUFFERING WITHOUT A POINT; NOT ALL PAIN IS GAIN. Only eight men have ever finished. The event is considered extreme even by those who specialize in extremity.

II.

What makes it so bad? No trail, for one. A cumulative elevation gain that's nearly twice the height of Everest. Native flora called saw briars that can turn a man's legs to raw meat in meters. The tough hills have names like Rat Jaw, Little Hell, Big Hell, Testicle Spectacle—this last so-called because it inspires most runners to make the sign of the cross (crotch to eyeglasses, shoulder to shoulder)—not to mention Stallion Mountain, Bird Mountain, Coffin Springs, Zip Line, and an uphill stretch, new this year, known simply as "the Bad Thing."

The race consists of five loops on a course that's been officially listed at twenty miles, but is probably more like twenty-six. The moral of this slanted truth is that standard metrics are irrelevant. The moral of a lot of Barkley's slanted truths is that standard metrics are irrelevant. The laws of physics and human tolerance have been replaced by Laz's personal whims. Even if the race was really "only" a hundred miles, these would still be "Barkley miles." Guys who could typically finish a hundred miles in twenty hours might not finish a single loop here. If you finish three, you've completed what's known as the Fun Run. If you happen *not* to finish—and, let's face it, you probably won't—Laz will play taps to commemorate your quitting. The whole camp, shifting and dirty and tired, will listen, except for those who are asleep or too weak to notice, who won't.

III.

It's no easy feat to get here. There are no published entry requirements or procedures. It helps to know someone. Admissions are decided by Laz's personal discretion, and his application isn't exactly standard, with questions like "What is your favorite parasite?" and a required essay with the subject "Why I Should Be Allowed to Run In the Barkley." Only thirty-five entrants are admitted. This year, one of them is my brother.

Julian is a "virgin," one of fifteen newbies who will do their damndest to finish a loop. He has managed to escape the designation of "sacrificial virgin," officially applied to the virgin each year (usually the least experienced ultra-runner) whom Laz has deemed most likely to fail in a spectacular fashion—to get lost for so long, perhaps, that he manages to beat Dan Baglione's course record for slowest pace. At the age of seventy-five, in 2006, Baglione managed two miles in thirty-two hours. Something to do with an unscrewed flashlight cap, an unexpected creek.

It's probably a misnomer to talk about "getting lost" at Barkley. It might be closer to the truth to say you begin lost, remain lost through several nights in the woods, and must constantly use your compass, map, instructions, fellow runners, and remaining shards of sanity to perpetually unlose yourself again. First-timers usually try to stay with veterans who know the course, but are often scraped. "Virgin scraping" means ditching the new guy. A virgin bends down to tie his shoelaces, perhaps, and glances up to find his veteran Virgil gone.

IV.

The day before the race, runners start arriving at camp like rainbow seals, sleekly gliding through the air in multicolored bodysuits. They come in pickup trucks and rental cars, rusty vans and camper trailers. Their license plates say 100 RUNNR, ULT MAN, CRZY RUN. They bring camouflage tents and orange hunting vests and skeptical girlfriends and acclimated wives and tiny travel towels and tiny dogs. Laz himself brings a little dog (named "Little Dog") with a black spot like a pirate's patch over one eye. Little Dog almost loses her name this year, after encountering and trying to eat an even smaller dog, the skinny one from Iowa, who turns out to be two dogs rather than just one.

It's a male scene. There are a few female regulars, I learn, but they rarely manage more than a loop. Most of the women in sight, like me, are part of someone's support crew. I help sort Julian's supplies in the back of the car.

He needs a compass. He needs pain pills and NO-DOZ pills and electrolyte pills and Ginger Chews for when he gets sleepy and a "kit" for popping blisters that basically includes a needle and Band-Aids. He needs tape for when his toenails start falling off. He needs batteries. We pay special attention to the batteries. Running out of batteries is the *must-avoid-at-all-costs worst possible thing that could happen*. But it has happened. It happened to Rich Limacher, whose night spent under a huge buckeye tree earned it the name "Limacher Hilton." Julian's coup de grâce is a pair of duct-tape pants that we've fashioned in the manner of cowboy chaps. They will fend off saw briars, is the idea, and earn Julian the envy of the other runners.

Traditionally, the epicenter of camp is a chicken fire kindled on the afternoon before the race begins. This year's fire is blazing by 4 pm. It's manned by someone named Doc Joe. Julian tells me Doc Joe's been wait-listed for several years and (Julian speculates) has offered himself as a helper in order to secure a spot for 2011. We arrive just as he's spearing the first thighs from the grill. He's got a two-foot can of beans in the fire pit, already bubbling, but the clear stars of this show are the birds, skin-blackened and smothered in red sauce. The chicken here (as legend has it) is served partway thawed, with only skins and "a bit more" cooked.

I ask Doc Joe how he plans to find the sweet spot between cooked and frozen. He looks at me like I'm stupid. That frozen chicken thing is just a myth, he says. This will not be the last time, I suspect, that I catch Barkley at the game of crafting its own legend.

At this particular potluck, small talk rarely stays banal for long. I fall into conversation with John Price, a bearded veteran who tells me he's sitting out the race this year, wait-listed, but has driven hundreds of miles just to be "a part of the action." Our conversation starts predictably. He asks where I'm from. I say Los Angeles. He says he loves Venice Beach. I say I love Venice Beach, too. Then he says: "Next fall I'm running from Venice Beach to Virginia Beach to celebrate my retirement."

I've learned not to pause at this kind of declaration. I've learned to proceed to practical questions. I ask, "Where will you sleep?"

"Mainly camping," he says. "A few motels."

"You'll carry the tent in a backpack?"

"God, no," he laughs. "I'll be pulling a small cart harnessed to my waist."

I find myself at the picnic table, which has become a veritable bulimic's buffet, spread with store-bought cakes and sprinkle cookies and brownies. It's designed to feed men who will do little for the next few days besides burn an incredible number of calories.

The tall man next to me is tearing into a massive chicken thigh. His third, I've noticed. Its steam rises softly into the twilight.

"So that whole frozen thing?" I ask him. "It's really just a myth?"

"It *was* one year," he says. "It was honest-to-god frozen." He pauses. "Man! That year was a great race."

This guy introduces himself as Carl. Broad and good-looking, he's a bit less sinewy than many of his fellow runners. He tells me he runs a machine shop down in Atlanta. As best I can gather, this means he uses his machines to build *other* machines, or else he uses his machines to build things that aren't machines—like bicycle parts or flyswatters. He works on commission. "The people who ask for crazy inventions," he says, sighing, "are never the ones who can afford them."

Carl tells me that he's got an ax to grind this time around. He's got a strong history at Barkley—one of the few runners who has finished a Fun Run under official time—but his performance last year was dismal. "I barely left camp," he says. Translated, this means he ran only thirty-five miles. But it was genuinely disappointing: he didn't even finish a second loop. He tells me he was dead-tired and heartbroken. He'd just gone through a nasty breakup.

But now he's back. He looks pumped. I ask him who he thinks the major contenders are to complete a hundred.

"Well," he says, "there's always Blake and A.T."

He means two of the "alumni" (former finishers) who are running this year: Blake Wood, class of 2001, and "A.T.," Andrew Thompson, class of 2009. Finishing the hundred twice would make history. Two years *in a row* is the stuff of fantasy.

Blake is a nuclear engineer at Los Alamos with a doctorate from Berkeley and an incredible Barkley record: six for six Fun Run completions, one finish, another near finish that was blocked only by a flooded creek. In person, he's just a friendly middle-aged dad with a salt-and-pepper mustache, eager to talk about his daughter's bid to qualify for the Olympic marathon trials, and about the new pair of checkered clown pants he'll wear this year to boost his spirits on the trail.

Andrew Thompson is a youngish guy from New Hampshire famous for a near finish in 2005, when he was strong heading into his fifth loop but literally lost his mind when he was out there—battered from fifty hours of sleep deprivation and physical strain. He completely forgot about the race. He spent an hour squishing mud in his shoes. He came back four more times until he finally finished the thing, in 2009.

There's "J.B.", Jonathan Basham, A.T.'s best support crew for years, at Barkley for his own race this time around. He's a strong runner, though I mainly hear him mentioned in the context of his relationship to A.T., who calls him "Jonboy."

Though Carl doesn't say it, I learn from others that he's a strong contender, too. He's one of the toughest runners in the pack, a DNF (Did Not Finish) veteran hungry for a win. I picture him out there on the trails, a mud-splattered machinist, with mechanical claws picking granola bars from his pockets and bringing them to his mouth. There are some strong virgins in the pack, including Charlie Engle, already an accomplished ultra-runner (he's "done" the Sahara) and inspirational speaker. Like many ultra-runners, he's a former addict. He's been sober for nearly twenty years, and many describe his recovery as the switch from one addiction to another—drugs for adrenaline, trading that extreme for this one.

If there's such a thing as the opposite of a virgin, it's probably John DeWalt. He's an old man in a black ski cap, seventy-three and wrinkled, with a gruff voice that sounds like it should belong to a smoker or a cartoon grizzly bear. He tells me that his nine-year-old grandson recently beat him in a 5K. Later, I will hear him described as an animal. He's been running the race for twenty years—never managing a finish or even a Fun Run.

I watch Laz from across the campfire. He's darkly regal in his trench coat, warming his hands over the flames. I want to meet him, but haven't yet summoned the courage to introduce myself. When I look at him I can't help thinking of *Heart of Darkness*. Like Kurtz, Laz is bald and charismatic, leader of a minor empire, trafficker in human pain. He's like a cross between the Colonel and your grandpa. There's certainly an Inner Station splendor to his orchestration of this whole hormone extravaganza, testosterone spread like fertilizer across miles of barren and brambled wilderness.

He speaks to "his runners" with comfort and fondness, as if they are a batch of wayward sons turned feral each year at the flick of his lighter. Most have been running "for him" (their phrase) for years. All of them bring offerings. Everyone pays a $1.60 entry fee. Alumni bring Laz a pack of his favorite cigarettes (Camel Filters), veterans bring a new pair of socks, and virgins are responsible for a license plate. These license plates hang like laundry at the edge of camp, a wall of clattering metal flaps. Julian has brought one from Liberia, where—in his non-superhero incarnation as a development economist—he is working on a microfinance project. I asked him how one manages to procure a spare license plate in Liberia. He tells me he asked a guy on the street and the guy said, "Ten dollars," and Julian gave him five and then it appeared. Laz immediately strings it in a place of honor, near the center, and I can tell Julian is pleased.

All through the potluck, runners pore over their instructions, five single-spaced pages that tell them "exactly where to go"—though every single runner, even those who've run the course for years, will probably get lost at least once, many of them for hours at a time. It's hard for me to understand this—*can't you just do what they say?*—until I look at the instructions themselves. They range from surprising ("the coal pond beavers have been very active this year, be careful not to fall on one of the sharpened stumps they have left") to self-evident ("all you have to do is keep choosing the steepest path up the mountain"). But the instructions tend to cite landmarks like "the ridge" or "the rock" that seem less than useful, considering. And then there's the issue of the night.

The official Barkley requirements read like a treasure hunt: there are ten books placed at various points along the course, and runners are responsible for ripping out the pages that match their race number. Laz is playful in his book choices: *The Most Dangerous Game, Death by Misadventure, A Time to Die*—even *Heart of Darkness*, a choice that seems to vindicate my associative impulses.

The big talk this year is about Laz's latest addition to the course: a quarter-mile cement tunnel that runs directly under the grounds of the old penitentiary. There's a drop through a narrow concrete shaft to get in, a fifteen-foot climb to get out, and "plenty of" standing water once you're inside. There are also, rumor has it, rats the size of possums and— when it gets warmer—snakes the size of arms. Whose arms? I wonder. Most of the guys here are pretty wiry.

The seventh course book has been hung between two poles next to the old penitentiary walls. "This is almost exactly the same place James Earl Ray went over," the instructions say. "Thanks a lot, James."

Thanks a lot, James—for getting all this business started.

V.

Laz has given himself the freedom to start the race whenever he wants. He announces the date but offers only two guarantees: that it will begin "sometime" between midnight and noon (*thanks a lot, Laz*), and that he will blow the conch shell an hour beforehand in warning. In general, Laz likes to start before dawn.

At the start gate, Julian is wearing a light silver jacket, a pale gray skullcap, and his homemade duct-tape chaps. He looks like a robot. He disappears uphill in a flurry of camera flashes.

Immediately after the runners take off, Doc Joe and I start grilling waffles. Laz strolls over with his glowing cigarette, its gray cap of untapped ash quaking between his thick fingers. I introduce myself. He introduces himself. He asks us if we think anyone has noticed that he's not actually smoking. "I can't this year," he explains, "because of my leg." He has just had surgery on an artery and his circulation isn't good. Despite this he will set up a lawn chair by the finish line, just like every year, and stay awake until every competitor has either dropped or finished. Dropping, unless you drop at the single point accessible by trail, involves a three-to-four-hour commute back into camp—longer at night, especially if you get lost. Which effectively means that the act of *ceasing to compete* in the Barkley race is comparable to running an entire marathon.

I tell him the cigarette looks great as an accessory. Doc Joe tells him that he's safe up to a couple packs. Doc Joe, by the way, really is a doctor.

"Well, then," Laz says, smiling. "Guess I'll smoke the last quarter of this one."

He finishes the cigarette and then tosses it into our cooking fire, where it smokes right into our breakfast. I am aware that Laz has already been turned into a myth, and that I will probably become another one of his mythmakers. Various tropes of masculinity are at play in Laz's persona—badass, teenager, father, demon, warden—and this Rubik's cube of testosterone seems to be what Barkley's all about.

I realize Laz and I will have many hours to spend in each other's company. The runners are out on their loops anywhere from eight to thirty-two hours. Between loops, if they're continuing, they stop at camp for a few moments of food and rest. This is both succor and sadism; the oasis offers respite and temptation at once. It's the Lotus Eaters' dilemma: hard to leave a good thing behind.

I use these hours without the runners to ask Laz everything I can about the race. I start with the start: how does he choose the time? He laughs uneasily. I backtrack, apologizing: would it ruin the mystery to tell me?

"One time I started at three," he says, as if in answer. "That was fun."

"Last year you started at noon, right? I heard the runners got a little restless."

"Sure did." He shakes his head, smiling at the memory. "Folks were just standing around getting antsy."

"Was it fun to watch them agonize?" I ask.

"Little bit frightening, actually," he says. "Like watching a mob turn ugly."

As we speak, he mentions sections of the course—Danger Dave's Climbing Wall, Raw Dog Falls, Pussy Ridge—as if I'd know them by heart. I ask whether Rat Jaw is called that because the briars are like a bunch of little rodent teeth. He says no, it has to do with the topographic profile on a map: it reminded him of—well, of a rat jaw. I think to myself, A lot of things might remind you of a rat jaw. The briar scratches are known as rat bites. Laz once claimed that the briars wouldn't give you scratches any worse than the ones you'd get from baptizing a cat.

I ask about Meth Lab Hill, wondering what its topographic profile could possibly resemble.

"That's easy," he says. "First time we ran it we saw a meth lab."

"Still operating?"

"Yep," he laughs. "Those suckers thought they'd never get found. Bet they were thinking, Who the *fuck* would possibly come over this hill?"

I begin to see why Laz has been so vocal about his new sections: the difficulty of the Bad Thing, the novelty of the prison tunnel. They mark his power over the terrain.

Laz has endured quite a bit of friction with park officials over the years. The race was nearly shut down for good by a man named Jim Fyke, who was upset about erosion and endangered plants. Laz simply rerouted the course around protected areas and called the detour "Fyke's Folly."

I can sense Laz's nostalgia for wilder days—when Frozen Head was still dense with the ghosts of fled felons and outlaws, thick with undiscovered junkies and their squirreled-away cold medicine. Times are different now, tamer. Just last year the rangers cut the briars on Rat Jaw a week before the race. Laz was pissed. This year he made them promise to wait until April.

His greatest desire seems to be to devise an un-runnable race, to sustain the immortal horizon of an unbeatable challenge with contours fresh and unknowable. After the first year, when no one even came close to finishing, Laz wrote an article headlined: THE "TRAIL" WINS THE BARKLEY MARATHONS. It's not hard to imagine how Laz, reclining on his lawn chair, might look to the course itself as his avatar: his race is a competitor strong enough to triumph, even when he can barely stand.

He used to run this race, in days of better health, but never managed to finish it. Instead, he's managed to garner respect as a man of principle—a man so committed to the notion of pain that he's willing to rally men in its pursuit.

VI.

There are only two public trails that intersect the course: Lookout Tower, at the end of South Mac trail, and Chimney Top. Laz generally discourages meeting runners while they're running. "Even just the sight of other human beings is a kind of aid," he explains. "We want them to feel the full weight of their aloneness."

That said, a woman named Cathy recommends Chimney Top for a hike.

"I broke my arm there in January," she says, "but it's pretty."

"Sounds fun," I say.

"Was it that old log over the stream?" Laz asks wistfully, as if remembering an old friend.

She shakes her head.

He asks, "Was Raw Dog with you when you did it?"

"Yep."

"Was he laughing?"

A man who appears to be her husband—presumably "Raw Dog"—pipes in: "Her arm was in an S-shape, Laz. I wasn't laughing."

Laz considers this for a moment. Then he asks her, "Did it hurt?"

"Think I blocked it out," she laughs. "But I heard I was cussing the whole way down the mountain."

I watch Laz shift modes fluidly between calloused maestro and den father. "After nightfall," he assures Doc Joe, "there *will* be carnage," but then he bends down to pet his pirate dog. "You hungry, Little?" he asks. "You might have got a lot of love today, but you still need to eat." Whenever I see him around camp, he says, "You think Julian is having fun out there?"

I finally say, "I fucking hope not!" and he smiles. *This girl gets it!*

But I can't help thinking his question dissolves precisely the kind of loneliness he seems so interested in producing, and his runners so interested in courting: the idea that when you are alone out there, someone back at camp *is thinking of you alone out there*, is, of course, just another kind of connection. Which is part of the point of this, right? That the hardship facilitates a shared solitude, an utter isolation that has been experienced before by others and will be experienced again, that these others are present in spirit even if the wilds have tamed or aged or brutalized or otherwise removed their bodies.

VII.

When Julian comes in from his first loop, it's almost dark. He's been out for twelve hours. I feel like I'm sharing this moment of triumph with Laz, in some sense, though I also know he's promiscuous in this sort of sharing. There's a place in his heart for everyone who runs his gauntlet, and everyone silly enough to spend days in the woods just to watch someone touch a yellow gate.

Julian is in good spirits. He turns over his pages to be counted. He's got ten 61s, including one from *The Power of Positive Thinking*, which came early in the course, and one from an account of teenage alcoholism called *The Late Great Me*, which came near the end. I notice the duct tape has been ripped from his pants. "You took it off?" I ask.

"Nope," he says. "Course took it off."

In camp he eats hummus sandwiches and Girl Scout cookies, barely manages to gulp down a butter pecan Ensure. He is debating another loop. "I'm sure I won't finish," he says. "I'll probably just go out for hours and then drop and have to find my way back in the dark."

Julian pauses. I take one of his cookies.

He says, "I guess I'll do it."

He takes the last cookie before I can grab it. He takes another bib number, for his second round of pages, and Laz and I send him into the woods. His rain jacket glows silver in the darkness: brother robot, off for another spin.

Julian has completed five hundred-mile races so far, as well as countless "short" ones, and I once asked him why he does it. He explained it like this: he wants to achieve a completely insular system of accountability, one that doesn't depend on external feedback. He wants to run a hundred miles when no one knows he's running, so that the desire to impress people, or the shame of quitting, won't constitute his sources of motivation. Perhaps this kind of thinking is what got him his PhD at the age of twenty-five. It's hard to say. Barkley doesn't offer a pure form of this isolated drive, but it comes pretty close: when it's midnight and it's raining and you're on the steepest hill you've ever climbed and you're bleeding from briars and you're alone and you've been alone for hours, it's only you around to witness yourself quit or continue.

VIII.

At four in the morning, the fire is bustling. A few front-runners are in camp preparing to head onto their third loops, gulping coffee or taking fifteen-minute naps in their tents. It's as if the thought of "the full weight of loneliness" has inspired an urge toward companionship back here, the same way Julian's hunger—when he stops for aid—makes me feel hungry, though I have done little to earn it. Another person's pain registers as an experience in the perceiver: empathy as forced symmetry, a bodily echo.

"Just think," Laz tells me. "Julian's *out there* somewhere."

"Out there" is a phrase that comes up frequently around camp. So frequently, in fact, that one of the regular racers—a wiry old man named "Frozen Ed" Furtaw (like Frozen Head, get it?) who runs in sunset orange camo tights—has self-published a book called *Tales from* Out There: *The Barkley Marathons, The World's Toughest Trail Race.* The book details each year's comet trail of D.N.F.s and includes an elaborate appendix listing other atrociously difficult trail races and explaining why they're not as hard.

"I was proud of Julian," I tell Laz. "It was dark and cold and he could barely swallow his can of Ensure and he just put his head in his hands and said, 'Here I go.'"

Laz laughs. "How do you think he feels about that decision now?"

It starts to rain. I make a nest in the back of my car. I type notes for this essay. I watch an episode of *The Real World: Las Vegas* and then turn it off—just as Steven and Trishelle are about to maybe hook up—to conserve power for the next day and also because I don't want to watch Steven and Trishelle hook up; I wanted her to hook up with Frank. I try to sleep. I dream about the prison tunnel: it's flooding, and I've just gotten a speeding ticket, and these two things are related in an important way I can't yet fathom. I'm awoken every once in a while by the mournful call of taps, like the noises of a wild animal echoing through the night.

Julian arrives back in camp around eight in the morning. He was out for another twelve hours, but he managed to reach only two books. There were a couple hours lost, another couple spent lying down, in the rain, waiting for first light. He is proud of himself for going out, even though he didn't think he'd get far, and I am proud of him, too.

We join the others under the rain tent. Charlie Engle describes what forced him back during his third loop. "Fell flat on my ass going down Rat Jaw," he said. "Then I got up and fell again, got up and fell again. That was pretty much it."

There's a nicely biblical logic to this story: it's the third time that really does the trick, seals the deal, breaks the back, what have you.

Laz asks whether Charlie enjoyed the prison section. Laz asks everyone about the prison section, the way you'd ask about your kid's poem: *Did you like it?*

Charlie says he did like it, very much. He says the guards were friendly enough to give him directions. "They were good ol' Southern boys, those guys," and I can tell from the way he says it that Charlie considers himself a good ol' Southern boy as well. "They told us, 'Just make yer way up that there holler...' and then those California boys with me, they turn and say, 'What the fuck is a holler?'"

"You should have told them," says Laz, "that in Tennessee a *holler* is when you want to get out but you can't."

"That's exactly what I said!" Charlie tells us. "I said: when you're standing barefoot on a red ant hill—that's a holler. The hill we're about to climb—that's a holler."

The rain is unrelenting. Laz doesn't think anyone will get the full hundred this year. There were some stellar first laps, but no one seems strong enough now. People are speculating about whether anyone will even finish the Fun Run. There are only six runners left with a shot. If anyone can finish, everyone agrees, it will be Blake. Laz has never seen him quit.

Julian and I share a leg of chicken slathered in BBQ sauce. There are only two left on the grill. It's a miracle the fire hasn't gone out. The chicken's good, and cooked as promised, steaming in our mouths against the chilly air.

A guy named Zane, with whom Julian ran much of his first loop, tells us he saw several wild boars on the trails at night. Was he scared? He was. One got close enough to send him scurrying off the edge of a switchback, fighting stick in hand. Would a stick have helped? We all agree, probably not.

A woman clad in what looks like an all-body windbreaker has packed a plastic bag of clothes. Laz explains that her husband is one of the six runners left. She's planning to meet him at Lookout Tower. If he decides to drop, she'll hand him his dry clothes and escort him down the easy three-mile trail back into camp. If he decides to continue, she'll wish him luck as he prepares for another uphill climb—soaked in rainwater and pride, unable to take the dry clothes because accepting aid would get him disqualified.

"I hope she shows him the dry clothes before he makes up his mind," says Laz. "The choice is better that way."

The crowd stirs. There's a runner coming up the paved hill. Coming from this direction is a bad sign for someone on his third loop—it means he's dropping rather than finishing. People guess it's J.B. or Carl—*must* be J.B. or Carl, there aren't many guys still out—but after a moment Laz gasps.

"It's Blake," he says. "I recognize his walking poles."

Blake is soaked and shivering. "I'm close to hypothermia," he said. "I couldn't do it." He says that climbing Rat Jaw was like scrambling up a playground slide in roller skates, but otherwise he doesn't seem inclined to offer excuses. He says he was running with J.B. for a while but left him on Rat Jaw. "That's bad news for J.B.," says Laz, shaking his head. "He'll probably be back here soon."

Laz hands the bugle over. It's as if he can't bear to play taps for Blake himself. He's clearly disappointed that Blake is out, but there's also a note of glee in his voice when he says: "You never know what'll happen around here." There's a thrill in the tension between controlling the race and recognizing it as something that will always disobey him. It approximates the pleasure—pleasure?—of ultra-running itself: the simultaneous exertion and ceding of power, controlling the body enough to make it *run* this thing but ultimately offering it to the uncontrollable vagaries of luck and endurance and conditions, delivering oneself into the frisson of this overpowering.

Doc Joe motions me over to the fire pit. "Hold this," he says, and shoves a large rectangle of aluminum siding in my direction. He balances a fallen tree branch against its edge to make a rain roof over the fire, where the single remaining breast of chicken is crisping to a beautiful charred brown. "Blake's chicken," he explains. "I'll cover it with my body if I have to."

IX.

Why this sense of stakes and heroism? Of course, I have been wondering the whole time: why do people *do* this, anyway? Whenever I pose the question directly, runners reply ironically: I'm a masochist; I need somewhere to put my craziness; type A from birth; etc. I begin to understand that joking about this question is not an evasion but rather an intrinsic part of answering it. Nobody has to answer this question seriously, because they are *already* answering it seriously—with their bodies and their willpower and their pain. The body submits itself in utter earnest, in degradation and commitment, to what words can speak of only lightly. Maybe this is why so many ultra-runners are former addicts: they want to redeem the bodies they once punished, master the physical selves whose cravings they once served.

There is a gracefully frustrating tautology to this embodied testimony: why do I do it? I do it because it hurts so much and I'm still willing to do it. The sheer ferocity of the effort implies that the effort is somehow worth it. This is purpose by implication rather than direct articulation. Laz says, "No one has to ask them why they're out here; they all know."

It would be easy to fix upon any number of possible purposes—conquering the body, fellowship in pain—but it *feels* more like significance dwells in concentric circles of labor around an empty center: commitment to an impetus that resists fixity or labels. The persistence of "why" is the point: the elusive horizon of an unanswerable question, the conceptual equivalent of an un-runnable race.

X.

But: how does the race turn out?

Turns out J.B. manages to pull off a surprising victory. Which makes the fifth paragraph of this essay a lie: the race has nine finishers now. I get this news as a text message from Julian, who found out from Twitter. We're both driving home on separate highways. My immediate thought is, Shit. I wasn't planning to focus on J.B. as a central character in my essay—he hadn't seemed like one of the strongest personalities or contenders at camp—but now I know I'll have to turn him into a story, too.

This is what Barkley specializes in, right? It swallows the story you imagined and hands you another one. Blake and Carl—both strong after their second loops, two of my chosen figures of interest—didn't even finish the Fun Run.

Now everyone goes home. Carl will go back to his machine shop in

Atlanta. Blake will help his daughter train for the trials. John Price will return to his retirement and his man-wagon. Laz, I discover, will return to his position as assistant coach for the boys' basketball team at Cascade High School, down the highway in Wartrace.

XI.

One of the most compelling inquiries into the question of *why*—to my mind, at least—is really an inquiry *around* the question, and it lies in a tale of temporary madness: A.T.'s frightening account of his fifth-loop "crisis of purpose" back in 2004.

By "crisis of purpose," he means "losing my mind in the full definition of the phrase," a relatively unsurprising condition, given the circumstances. He's not alone in this experience. Another ultra-runner named Brett Maune describes hallucinating a band of helpful Indians at the end of his three-day run of the John Muir trail:

> They watched over me while I slept and I would chat with
> them briefly every time I awoke. They were very considerate
> and even helped me pack everything when I was ready to
> resume hiking.
> I hope this does not count as aid!

A.T. describes wandering without any clear sense of how he'd gotten to the trail or what he was meant to be doing there: "The Barkley would be forgotten for minutes on end although the premise lingered. I *had* to get to the Garden Spot, for... why? Was there someone there?" His amnesia captures the endeavor in its starkest terms: premise without motivation, hardship without context. But his account offers flashes of wonder:

> I stood in a shin-deep puddle for about an hour—squishing
> the mud in and out of my shoes....
> I walked down to Coffin Springs (the first water drop).
> I sat and poured gallon after gallon of fresh water into my
> shoes.... I inspected the painted trees, marking the park

boundary; sometimes walking well into the woods just to look at some paint on a tree.

In a sense, Barkley does precisely this: forces its runners into an appreciation of what they might not otherwise have known or noticed—the ache in their quads when they have been punished beyond all reasonable measure, fatigue pulling the body's puppet strings inexorably downward, the mind gone numb and glassy from pain.

By the end of A.T.'s account, the facet of Barkley deemed most brutally taxing, that sinister and sacred "self-sufficiency," has become an inexplicable miracle: "When it cooled off, I had a long-sleeve shirt. When I got hungry, I had food. When it got dark, I had a light. I thought: *Wow, isn't it strange that I have all this perfect stuff, just when I need it?*"

This is benevolence as surprise, evidence of a grace beyond the self that has, of course, come *from* the self—the same self that loaded the fanny pack hours before, whose role has been obscured by bone-weary delusion, turned *other* by the sheer fact of the body losing its own mind. So it goes. One morning a man blows a conch shell, and two days later— still answering the call of that conch—another man finds all he needs strapped to his own body, where he can neither expect nor explain it. ✶

THE FICKLE NEEDLE
OF FATE

DISCUSSED: *A Solid '60 Plymouth, The Pitiless Judgment of Youth, Dashboard Jukeboxes, Horn-Rims and Brylcreem, Optimistic Overestimation in Marketing Copy, That Damn Rock-and-Roll Noise, Purchases Made by Howard Hughes, Inventors and Madmen, Custom Presses, The Hard Sell*

 rackle.)
(Crackle.)
(Crackle.)
(Crackle.)
"Howdy, this is Steve Allen. No—wait a minute, don't go looking in the glove compartment. I'm not there. I'm not really in the car at all. Not personally, that is. But you have to admit, that RCA Auto Victrola's a fooler.

"You know, I enjoy sitting at my piano. I guess, uh, any musician does. But you! Man, you're really in solid—sitting behind the wheel of a new, solid '60 Plymouth.... Solid, man. Really solid!"

(Crackle.)
"Solid, man. Really solid!"

Promotional photo courtesy of Daimler Chrysler National Training Center

(Crackle.)

"Solid, man. Really solid!"

(Crackle.)

"Soli..."

(Click.)

You're working in the parts department of a Plymouth dealership, car demo disc in your hand, campaign coverage of Nixon and Kennedy chattering away from another car in the garage.

And you're wondering: who the hell puts a turntable in a car's dashboard?

Five years earlier, the verdict of Peter Goldmark's son had been pitiless: "Boring."

The radio in the Goldmark family's Chrysler had no stories to listen to, no good music—why, the boy demanded, couldn't they bring their own stuff to listen to in the car? By 1955, Peter Goldmark had plenty to work on already—the Hungarian émigré was an inventor of the 33 rpm LP for CBS Laboratories, and had created the nation's first color TV system. But now, he admitted, "I kept thinking of my son's question."

Their car already had a radio, something almost unthinkable before the 1950s. Prior to transistor radios, getting music in your car meant installing a vacuum-tube set so monstrous that it required sawing apart the dashboard. But now Goldmark sensed an opportunity: why not hook a dashboard-mounted jukebox up to these sleek new audio systems?

Sure, there were problems—after all, the 33 rpm LP that Goldmark helped invent was too big for a dashboard. He needed something smaller yet capable of running for an hour without skipping or switching records. Goldmark had his lab shrink the grooves down to cram three where one normally sat; they slowed the rotation; they buffered out potholes with rubber pads; they jammed the needle so hard into the record that it wouldn't skip. The resulting "ultra-microgroove" 16⅔ rpm record—a thick vinyl platter the size of a 45, but so slow and densely pressed that it took an hour to play—tested beautifully in a CBS exec's jet black Ford Thunderbird.

Goldmark pitched the invention to Detroit, and within days found himself at a Chrysler test track. Horn-rimmed execs swapped records in and out of the player as the auto giant's president wildly drove a car over a torture-track of cobblestone, speed bumps, and washboard test strips. Goldmark, tossed around the backseat, was on the verge of throwing up. But his player performed perfectly, and the car swung into the test garage with music swelling from its windows.

"I must have it for the Chrysler," one executive barked to Goldmark. As the men stepped out, company managers gathered around their bosses in what one can only imagine was a haze of Brylcreem fumes and cigar smoke.

Yes, they chanted in corporate unison. *Yes, we must have it.*

The fall '55 advertising was ecstatic.

"It's another Chrysler Corporation first!" the ads blared. "The Highway Hi-Fi record player slides in and out easily and can be operated without taking your eyes off the road." If the wisdom of changing records while driving was debatable, the price was not: Chrysler was pushing the seventy-five-dollar option, along with what it called "The Forward Look '56," with a barrage of buzzwords like "magical Pushbutton PowerFlite."

The press quickly followed. "You'd have to drive up a wall to make the needle skip a groove," *Popular Science* marveled. *Billboard* reported that CBS was even testing out the system for use in taxicabs, DC-7 passenger planes, Washington, DC, buses, and on the Pennsylvania Railroad.

But the fickle needle of fate, alas, was about to skip.

Highway Hi-Fi units, still ruinously under warranty, started pouring back into service departments. It hardly helped that Chrysler had also installed them in its cheaper Dodge and Plymouth lines, whose suspensions were harder on the units. And someone else was a little hard on the players, too: namely, CBS chief William Paley.

"He felt that record players installed in cars might cause drivers to turn off the radio to listen to records," Goldmark recalled years later, "and thus CBS would lose listeners."

Despite car ads promising "a complete modern record library on wheels," Columbia Records' proprietary 16⅔ rpm format left buyers at the mercy of a perversely scattershot catalog. Chrysler drivers puzzled over titles like *Ken Griffin at the Wurlitzer Organ*, Irving Berlin tunes, and a dramatic reenactment of the signing of the Magna Carta. Part of the problem, Goldmark admitted, was William Paley himself: "He didn't think pop music was a market at all." Even worse, Chrysler brass agreed with Paley, imagining the market was full of people like themselves—executives tired of all that damn rock-and-roll noise.

"If you want to listen to classical music and relax and you can't get anything on the radio but rock and roll, it can be irritating," one Chrysler VP explained. "Did you ever try to get classical music on your radio at three in the afternoon?"

For a round disc, Highway Hi-Fi was hopelessly square. It took two model years to unload the first hopeful production run of eighteen thousand sets. Columbia Records stalled at just forty-two album releases in the 16⅔ rpm format—with a number of the final records all by the deeply obscure "Lee Raine and His Orchestra." Though salesmen snared a final few unwary buyers (including Howard Hughes, who bought one in a blue '57 Imperial convertible), it seemed the song for Highway Hi-Fi was already over.

But—like a record on repeat—the idea just wouldn't go away.

THE MUSIC YOU LOVE IN THE CAR YOU LOVE, announced ads in 1960, showing a beaming Steve Allen clutching a handful of records. These, though, were 45s. After the fiasco of Columbia's proprietary format, Chrysler went to RCA and had it produce a dash-mounted record player that could play a stack of fourteen 45 rpm singles—be they Elvis, Sinatra, or Bill Haley. A California knockoff (the A.R.C. 2500) soon appeared, while in Europe the Dutch manufacturer Philips came up with its own version, the Auto Mignon AG 2101. But for all the clever padding and stylus tweaks made by RCA engineers, the machine was still dogged by the same existential crisis of automotive phonographs everywhere.

It skipped.

In the end, the RCA Victor Auto Victrola had an even shorter run than the Highway Hi-Fi, vanishing by 1961. The following year would bring the next serious attempt at car audio, a precursor to the 8-track deck by inventor Earl Muntz—"Madman" Muntz, as he was known. But what could ever be half so mad as a dash-mounted turntable?

There is quite possibly only one man left in the world still pressing records for the Highway Hi-Fi, and he lives in Minneapolis.

"I first had a guy come to me years ago who had an old Highway Hi-Fi, asking about making a record," says Kim Gutzke of Custom Records. Vintage car owners email Gutzke a music file, and he custom presses whatever they want onto a 16⅔ rpm acetate disc. And what they want, he says, is simple: "'50s rock and roll. Not the crappy music Hi-Fi put out."

The old machines are collectors' items now; even a rusted-out unit can fetch hundreds at auction. But a few YouTube videos circulate of restored dashboard phonographs in all their glory—and if you look hard enough, you can still find an otherwise-inexplicable Steve Allen 45 labeled *Solid Plymouth 1960*. Pressed by the specialty label Hanover-Signature Record Corp., it may be the very last record ever made purely for the doomed audio species of *Motor Victrola*.

(Crackle.)

"...Say, I'm getting carried away. This car doesn't need selling, it needs driving.... Yessir, your own reaction to the drive you're taking is the best salesman Plymouth could possibly have on the payroll.

"So, I guess I'll cut out. But let me leave you with a little thought. If you're looking for the best of the low-priced three, you're in it. When that fellow with you shows you the dotted line, sign, man, sign.

"So long. See you on television."

(Crackle.)

(Crackle.)

(Crackle.)

(Click.) ✳

MY PATRON

DISCUSSED: *A Career Ladder, Training for the Shrinkhood,*
Young Korean Sales Executives, The Locomotion,
An Urgent Need, A Job Well Done, The London Office,
A Proverbial Dog Show, Somebody Else

In 1988, I was thirty-one years old. I was a writer in all the
senses that count, apart from one: I hadn't sold a thing, and
there seemed to be no real prospect of me selling anything,
either. I was working as a teacher in a language school in Soho,
London; it was, I feared, exactly the sort of job you drifted into
at that age, when you had no real chance of doing the work you really
wanted to do. I was afraid of the future—of telling younger colleagues in
the year 1999 or 2009, age forty-two or fifty-two, that I was a writer, but
a writer whose stuff never got made or published. In the kinds of jobs
I had been doing, I met people like that all the time, writers, actors, the
occasional ancient musician. They scared me. Meanwhile, the friends
I had made at university were all on a career ladder. They were academics
or diplomats or journalists or accountants, and they were starting to

Illustration by Tony Millionaire

make money. When I arranged to meet them, I was embarrassed by my own lack of advancement—embarrassed, too, that evenings out couldn't involve food, because restaurants were too expensive.

If someone had told me that I was a couple of years away from being given a book contract that would change my life, then of course I'd have been happy enough to sit and wait it out. (And I'd have been amazed, too. I'd hardly written a paragraph of prose—all my efforts hitherto had gone into scripts, terrible things intended for the movies but which could just as easily have been performed on the radio, consisting as they did of a handful of conversations between two people.) But I didn't know that. My suspicion was that I was kidding myself, and that the smart thing to do would be to give up the writing and find myself a proper teaching job, if only so that I could pay for my own pizza sometimes.

The principal of the language school was a few years older than me, a smart, dry, interesting man who, years later, for reasons too involved to explain here, became my psychoanalyst, a job he has held down to this day. He was still training for the shrinkhood back then, although it seemed entirely indicative of our respective prospects that his make-do, pay-the-way job was as a principal of a school, and mine was as a part-time, non-contract teacher. One day he offered me a little bit of extra work at the offices of a large Asian trading company that had just set up in London. "They'll pay well," he told me, and he was right: they offered me forty pounds for two hours' teaching a week, an amount that probably amounted to about a quarter of my weekly wage.

I nearly didn't take the job. They wanted me to work on Saturday mornings, and I couldn't think of anything worse. (That is almost certainly true, I now realize. I've learned very little over the last couple of decades, but I do now know, regrettably, that there are worse things than setting an alarm clock on a weekend.) I played five-a-side football on Saturday mornings, I explained. They asked me what time the game took place, and I told them eleven o'clock, and they laughed—there was no scheduling clash, as far as they were concerned. They wanted me in at eight, before their day's work started. (This was the first thing I learned about them: they worked extraordinarily hard, these young Korean sales executives, much harder than anyone in England. Their contracted hours were 8 am until 8 pm, Monday to Friday, and 8 am to 2 pm on Saturday. When the recession kicked in, a couple of years later, they were told to combat it by working Sundays, too. But those were just the contracted hours. Anyone with any ambition couldn't be seen knocking off at eight, just as my friends with proper jobs couldn't leave the office at five.)

I really, really didn't want to work at eight o'clock on a Saturday morning. Friday nights were always late—my friends and I would often go to a cheap but utterly great nightclub in Kentish Town, the Locomotion, until two or three in the morning. (The music they played at the Locomotion I borrowed wholesale for the club that my narrator Rob ran in my first novel, *High Fidelity.*) And then there was the five-a-side, and then, every other Saturday, my team, Arsenal, played at home, and even watching football was tiring in those days: you stood, for two and a half hours, on concrete terraces, buffeted by fellow fans. But forty quid…

So I took it, and walked into their offices in Holborn still blinded by sleep and sometimes reeking of booze. I used to prepare a little bit, but mostly, I was told, they wanted conversation, so I would take in photocopied articles from the *Guardian* and the *Economist,* and sometimes we would get around to reading them, studying the vocabulary, talking about the pieces and the week's news. More often than not, though, the lessons didn't happen in the way I planned them, and sometimes they didn't happen at all. Most of them were too busy, at eight o'clock on a Saturday morning, to learn English, and the ones who did turn up needed urgent help with something practical—a letter to a solicitor about a patent or a terminated contract or something else I didn't really understand. I presumed that they needed my help because the local staff didn't and wouldn't work on a Saturday morning, but later on I discovered that there wasn't really a local staff. The company had so recently arrived, it hadn't yet really gotten around to employing anyone.

After a few weeks of being asked about planning permission and the local council and the prevailing economic weather, an idea began to form. What if I offered my services on a regular part-time basis? Like, what if I came in every afternoon and helped them with anything that was going on, anything where it was easier to be English than Korean? My nationality was my main talent, as far as they were concerned, and I could see that, in this place, at that time in the company's history, my main talent had an economic value. I went to see one of the managers, gave an oral version of the job description, and got offered a job on the spot.

My roommate was a management accountant, and he was paid what seemed to me to be a preposterous amount of money. I told them that I'd work every afternoon for half the salary he earned. They didn't even blink. And if I had to isolate the single most important moment in my writing career, then that would have to rank in the top two or three. The eternal, moral-sapping question of how to earn money while writing had been answered, without any apparent deliberation on the part of those in a position to pay it. And I did write, too: I was disciplined about it. The first story I ever sold was written in the mornings I had available, and the first chapters of my first book, and a lot of book reviews in newspapers… I had a patron, and my patron paid for all that. But between 2 pm and 6 pm, I was an Asian yuppie. On the Tube home, I could feel the ulcers developing, and I know that if I'd been asked to work in the mornings, leaving the afternoons free for writing, I'd just have put a cold flannel over my face and laid down on the floor of a darkened room. No stories or reviews or early chapters would ever have been written.

On the first afternoon, I sat down at the desk that had been found for me, and started to go through the day's newspapers. I was told to photocopy anything that might be of professional interest and fax it to Head Office. I was happy. This seemed like the sort of job an English graduate who wanted to write should be doing—something that involved literacy, nothing too stressful, an entirely appropriate job for a would-be man of letters who needed money but didn't want to break a sweat getting hold of it. After a pleasant hour or so reading the sports pages and idly circling an article about inflation, the company secretary called me in to his office.

"Mr. Nick." (They never did drop the "mister," in the three years I was there.) "We need the plans for the gardens of Hampton Court Palace. Urgently."

I gaped at him.

"Why?"

This was an inappropriate question, one that I would eventually learn not to ask. Curiosity was permissible, at some point in the job, but my immediate, knee-jerk "Why?" was a snotty "Why": it implied, as I meant it to, that I'd do the job only if someone could provide me with a good reason. It was the "Why" of a free-spirited arts graduate, not a company man, and if I was going to do this job I had to be a company man.

I was new, so he answered me anyway.

"The chairman is building a replica in Seoul."

This was my introduction to the character and interests of the chairman, a man whom I would come to hear a lot about over the next couple of years. As far as I could work out, he owned the company, one of the biggest trading companies in the world. When he spoke, he was heard in a thousand different cities. Sometimes I felt sorry for him, because his whims and musings, it seemed to me, became solidified and real and troublesome when perhaps he didn't mean them to be. Had he really said, "I want to build a replica of Hampton Court?" Or had he said, "Hey, it would be cool if we had a replica of Hampton Court here," and then chuckled, the way that you or I might have done, possibly when stoned? It never would have occurred to him that he would thus be causing trouble and stress for somebody half a world away.

I took a train down to Hampton Court, which is in the southwestern suburbs of London. It was Henry VIII's favorite palace. Its gardens are famous, a tourist attraction; there's a maze that has been there for hundreds of years. When I got there, I wandered around aimlessly, asked the person in the gift shop if the plans were for sale, bought a guidebook, and went back to the office.

"I couldn't find them," I said cheerfully. Job done. Well, undone, anyway. But, you know, done as far as I was concerned. Done because it couldn't be done, so it was now someone else's problem.

"Tomorrow, please," said the company secretary, with an awful finality.

I should point out at this point that there was no internet back then. There were faxes and telephones, although nobody had a cell phone. Research was laborious, and invariably involved going somewhere.

I should also point out that I am a can't-do person. If a job is hard, then my philosophy is that it's best to give up on it straightaway, especially if it contains the potential for embarrassment. Writing was fine; you just had to write. Selling the work to anyone—an agent or publisher or producer—was impossible, though, because that might at some point involve a phone call that only a big-head or a show-off or someone with some sense of his own self-worth would make. (I may well have taken the afternoon job because it would allow me to write forever: I could stick my work in a brown envelope, send it to some people who would never read it, and then start on something else without ever having to speak to anyone.) I suddenly saw that this job might have the potential for endless, permanent, excruciating embarrassment. It might involve pestering people, for example—soon enough I would find out that it would involve phoning people who'd hung up on you ten minutes previously—and I could always see the reasons why they wouldn't want to give me something I was asking for. Maybe this sympathy would be useful in my morning job, but it wasn't much use to me here. When you're an Asian company man, the ability to see another person's point of view is a disadvantage.

In the year or so that had elapsed between my starting the Saturday-morning teaching job and the part-time office job, my weekly football had moved to a Monday-night slot. People had started having kids, and their weekend time was more precious. Coming out of the Underground station, I bumped into one of my teammates, a guy I didn't know that well, and on the way to the sports hall, I started telling him about my new job. He was mystified by it, probably because I couldn't really understand it myself.

"Like, what sort of thing?"

"Today they asked me to find the plans for the grounds at Hampton Court. I mean—"

"Oh, we've got them," he said.

I looked at him. He was serious.

"I'm a landscape architect," he said. "We've got all that stuff."

I called in to his office on my way to work the following day, and then marched in to my office brandishing the photocopies they needed. I was gleeful and somewhat amazed: I'd actually achieved the hard-looking thing they had asked me to achieve. They were politely grateful, but not amazed in the least. This was what they had paid me to do, and I had done it. It was no big deal.

At the beginning of the following week, they asked me to buy an equestrian center. There was a note on my desk, waiting for me. "PLEASE BUY EQUESTRIAN CENTER," it said. (Why? Because the company was going to be sponsoring its country's equestrian team at the next Olympics, and England, it had been decided, was the best place for training.)

When you're a can't-do kind of a guy, this isn't a message you want to read. And, as luck would have it, they'd picked another area of life about which I knew literally nothing. I thought of a couple of counties in the southern half of England where, it seemed to me, equestrianism might be going on, phoned a couple of estate agents, asked if they had any equestrian centers for sale. They didn't. I went back to reading the sports pages and circling the inflation articles.

Two hours later, my boss called me in.

"Have you found an equestrian center?" he asked me.

"No," I said. "But, you know. Early days."

This was supposed to be a piece of comical understatement, a joke about how he was expecting an equestrian center less than one hundred and twenty minutes after asking for one, but it was a joke that could work only if my boss and I shared the same sense of time passing. We didn't. These were not early days to him. These were late days. I, meanwhile, had privately estimated that this job would take between six months and forever. My plan was to leave messages with a couple of estate agents every week for a while or as long as I could be bothered, and the word would get out that, in the unlikely event of an equestrian center coming on the market, we would snap it up. What more could be done?

"So what will I say to Head Office tonight?"

"Tonight?"

"I must give a report tonight."

This was now officially hilarious. I was working for people who saw no reason why an equestrian center couldn't be located and bought in a day. And they had employed me, a man who could only just manage to locate and buy a packet of cigarettes in a day.

"Tell them we're scouring the country." My boss didn't know the word *scoured*. He was pleased to make its acquaintance, and I went home feeling as though I'd achieved something.

I was learning quite a lot about the company quite quickly, if only because I had to recruit local secretarial staff for the Asian sales managers. Quite often, I had conversations like this:

"So… you need an assistant?"

"Yes."

"What shall I say you do?"

There would be a long sigh and a shake of the head.

"Ah, very bad job. Sports shoes and pianos."

I stared at him, to see if he was pulling my leg, but it wasn't a leg-pulling kind of place. He really was supposed to sell sports shoes and pianos. His competitors were Nike and Steinway, both at the same time, and he was entirely on his own, although I was about to provide him with a seventeen-year-old assistant. Once I spoke to a man who was running the company advertising agency. He was on his own, too. No creatives, no account directors, no basketball hoops, nothing, apart from a smallish desk in an open-plan office. Head Office was expecting him to poach business from Saatchi, Saatchi, Ogilvy, and Mather. Back home, the company sold everything there was to sell, and it had its own chain of department stores to sell it in. The London office was beginning to make me sad: it reminded me of King Lear, robbed of his power, unable to understand quite why the entire country wouldn't jump to attention when told to. In a way, it was good that they'd employed a can't-do guy, because it seemed to me that they had to learn that some things can't be done. The manager running the ad agency was as can-do as you can get, but it wasn't going to help him.

I phoned my half brother, who had grown up in a different place from me, and went riding a lot when he was a kid.

"I have to buy an equestrian center," I told him.

He laughed for a long time. He knew I had no interest in horses, and he also knew that I had absolutely no ability to accomplish anything that men in suits accomplished during their working days. (I wore a cheap suit to work, by the way. A cheap suit, a cheap tie, and a cheap shirt.)

"So what should I do?" I asked when he had stopped laughing.

"I don't know. Phone the guy at the place where I used to ride. He probably knows about other equestrian centers."

So I phoned him, and he laughed, too. But he was laughing, it turned out, because he'd been dreaming for years of receiving a phone call like this one. He was desperate to get rid of his establishment. By the end of the week, my employers had visited him and had an offer accepted. (A few months later, it turned out that they had bought the wrong size of equestrian center, and they had to sell up and buy another one.)

Once Head Office found out that I was working there, I began to receive faxes addressed to me personally. These faxes were always marked "TOP URGENT," and would frequently contain a request that seemed so extraordinarily eccentric that on occasions I began to feel like a Candid Camera victim. "WHAT IS DEFINITION OF DRINKING WATER IN UK?" "WHAT WAS SCIENTIFIC BACKGROUND OF WRITER JONATHAN SWIFT?" "WHAT IS A GOOD SPACE IN A MUSEUM?" "HOW MUCH DOES ORPAHANGE COST?" And invariably it turned out that I knew someone who knew something, just as I had done in the Hampton Court case, and the equestrian-center panic. I discovered that my friend Sarah, for example, was friends with a museum consultant. (I discovered at exactly the same time that this was an actual job.) But we employed him, and he wrote us a report on the space that was being offered for sponsorship in a prestigious London museum. They never read it. They looked at its thirty or forty pages with some alarm, and said to him, "Good space? Or bad space?" There was never time for nuance.

It was all weird, and stressful, and sort of satisfying, and then, one day, there was a message on my desk that changed everything. "PLEASE BUY PEDIGREE DOGS," it said. "CRUFTS WINNERS ONLY." Our chairman, I discovered, was one of the most avid dog breeders in South Korea. He loved his pedigree dogs, and he wanted to buy the best. Crufts is our big dog show. In the UK, it's proverbial. Owners groom their dogs and train them and send them to the hairdresser and put little cardigans on them and teach them to talk, and the BBC puts the whole thing on TV, or used to, anyway. Now it probably has its own cable channel.

I am not a big fan of the dog, but then I hadn't been a big fan of Jonathan Swift or horses or water or any of the other things I'd been doing. It didn't matter. It was just another job. I went to the newsagent, bought a magazine about dogs, turned to the classified ads at the back, and started ringing around.

This was probably sometime in 1990, a couple of years after the Seoul Olympics, and it seemed that people had retained two facts from the entire event. The first was that Ben Johnson took drugs to make him run faster; the other was that Koreans ate dogs. My conversations with owners of Crufts-pedigree puppies went like this:

"Oh, hi. I'm ringing on behalf of a Korean multinational company, and we're interested in…"

Click.

"Oh, hi, I'm ringing on behalf of a multinational company, and we're interested in buying any puppies you might have for sale."

"What's the name of the company?"

(I told them the name of the company.)

"Where are they from?"

"South Korea."

Click.

These puppies would have cost tens of thousands of pounds. And though the chairman of our company was rich, even he wasn't going to spend that kind of money on a meal. It never did any good, though, when I tried to explain that. The dog owners were not about to let their teased and blow-dried babies go off to make soup on the other side of the world.

Eventually, after weeks of embarrassment and pestering and calling people back who had just hung up on me, I opened a dialogue with a pedigreed-dog owner. He wouldn't sell us a dog; he would, however, be interested in talking to us about what we were prepared to do to outlaw Korean dog-eating. We opened a dialogue with an animal-rights organization. The animal-rights organization opened a dialogue with Head

Office. Two of my superiors flew over the Arctic in a helicopter to see the work that the animal-rights organization was doing in the field of seal-clubbing. (They wanted me to go with them, but I couldn't see how a trip to the Arctic was going to fit in with my afternoon hours.) Within a few weeks of receiving the initial fax, I was overseeing an intricate web of discourse involving literally hundreds of people, animals, and welfare groups. Even my can-do Koreans were daunted, seeing as they all had day jobs as well, selling microchips and sports shoes and pianos.

Finally, after many, many hours of dinners and visits and top-urgent negotiations, we had done enough: we were allowed to buy a puppy. We collected it, put it in a little cage, and sent it to Seoul. And the chairman ate it! Just kidding. But the puppy we sent did provoke in him a huge hunger for more and more and more puppies. I was no longer an all-rounder, the guy who took care of the letters and the recruitment and the museum sponsorship; I was the full-time dog purchaser. My despair was real and profound, and ended only by an advance for my first book.

Soon after I'd left, the company stopped trying to sell everything and concentrated on selling electronic goods; within a few years, it had earned itself a household name. It was hard to see that happening while I was there, but then, I missed all the signs: the dedication to somebody else's cause, the hard work and discipline, the willingness to bury irritation and dissent. I just thought that everyone except me was nuts. In the meantime, my can't-do spirit remains undimmed, although luckily I work for myself, in the field of the arts, so any tantrums I throw have to be understood, tolerated, indulged.

And, like the business I worked for, South Korea's economy continues to grow. It grew 6 percent last year; it grew even during the global financial crisis. I'm sure there are many reasons why this should be so—most of them beyond the scope of this essay and the comprehension of the person writing it—while economies in the West lurch from crisis to crisis; I'm just as sure that one of the reasons is the recognition that, for a country to do well, its people, even those with education and ambition, have to do stuff they don't want to do. Meanwhile, my patron paid my rent, while I trained to be someone who could do what he wanted for the rest of his life. For a couple of years back there, afternoons only, I was somebody else. *

CONTRIBUTORS

COLIN ASHER's writing has appeared in nearly two dozen publications, a few reputable. Many of his waking hours are now spent writing a biography of Nelson Algren for W. W. Norton.

ZACH BARON has written for the *New York Times, Grantland,* and many other publications. He is presently a staff writer for *GQ.*

PAUL COLLINS lives in Portland, Oregon. His latest book is *Edgar Allan Poe: The Fever Called Living.*

BRIAN T. EDWARDS teaches at Northwestern University, where he is also director of the Middle East and North African Studies Program. He is the author of *Morocco Bound: Disorienting America's Maghreb, from Casablanca to the Marrakech Express.* His new book, *After the American Century: Ends of Circulation in Casablanca, Cairo, and Tehran,* is forthcoming.

RACHEL KAADZI GHANSAH is an essayist whose writing has appeared in the *Paris Review, Bookforum, Transition,* the *New York Observer,* and *Rolling Stone.* She has taught at Columbia University, Bard College, and Eugene Lang College. More of her work can be found at *the-rachelkaadzighansah.tumblr.com.*

FRANCISCO GOLDMAN is the author of *Say Her Name* (2011), winner of the Prix Femina Étranger, and *The Interior Circuit: A Mexico City Chronicle* (2014) as well as three novels and a work of non-fiction. Every year he teaches one semester at Trinity College in Hartford, Connecticut, and then hightails it back to Mexico City.

SARA GRAN is the author of five critically acclaimed novels, including the Claire DeWitt series.

LEV GROSSMAN is the author of the best-selling Magicians trilogy. He's also the book critic at *Time* magazine, and his essays on technology and culture have appeared widely in newspapers and magazines and on NPR.

NICK HORNBY is the author of six novels, the most recent of which is *Juliet, Naked*, and a memoir, *Fever Pitch*. He is also the editor of the short-story collection *Speaking with the Angel*. His screenplay for *An Education* was nominated for an Academy Award, and *Songbook* was a finalist for a National Book Critics Circle Award for music criticism. He lives in North London.

LESLIE JAMISON is the author of a novel, *The Gin Closet*, and a collection of essays, *The Empathy Exams*, which includes "The Immortal Horizon" alongside other examinations of pain and wonder. In October 2012, she completed a half marathon. She's still proud of it.

HEIDI JULAVITS is a founding editor of the *Believer* and the author of four novels, including the PEN Literary Award–winning *The Vanishers*. Her short fiction and essays have appeared in *Harper's*, *The Best American Short Stories*, the *New York Times*, *Bookforum*, and other places. An associate professor at Columbia University and the recipient of a Guggenheim Fellowship, she lives in New York City and Maine.

MICHAEL PAUL MASON is an author, journalist, and the founding editor of *This Land*, a literary magazine based in Oklahoma.

ED PARK is a founding editor of the *Believer* and the author of the novel *Personal Days*.

RACHEL POLIQUIN is dedicated to all things orderly and disorderly in the natural world. She is the author of *The Breathless Zoo: Taxidermy and the Cultures of Longing* and is writing *Beaver* for Reaktion Books' Animal Series. She lives in Vancouver, by the sea.

MONTE REEL is the author of *Between Man and Beast* and *The Last of the Tribe*, and he has also written for the *New York Times Magazine*, *Harper's*, and *Outside*.

KENT RUSSELL is a writer from Miami. His first book, *I Am Sorry to Think I Have Raised a Timid Son*, will be published in Spring 2015.

SUSAN STRAIGHT has published eight novels and two books for children. Her stories and essays have appeared in *The O. Henry Prize Stories, The Best American Short Stories*, the *New York Times*, the *Los Angeles Times*, *Harper's*, *McSweeney's*, *Salon*, *Zoetrope*, *Black Clock*, and elsewhere. She has been awarded the Lannan Literary Award for Fiction, a Guggenheim Fellowship, and the Gold Medal for Fiction from the Commonwealth Club of California. She is Distinguished Professor of Creative Writing at UC Riverside.

REBECCA TAYLOR studied and taught fiction at Columbia University. She is working on a book.

JEANNIE VANASCO has cleaned motel rooms, managed a citizen journalism project based in Sudan, volunteered at a carousel museum, taught creative writing at the university level, waitressed the night-shift, and ghostwritten for a French philosopher. Most recently, she's an Emerging Poets Fellow at Poets House.

ANNIE JULIA WYMAN is a writer and editor living on both coasts. She studies and teaches literature at Harvard University and runs a little business connecting other writers and artists with freelance work.

MOLLY YOUNG is a writer living in Manhattan. She writes for *New York* magazine, the *New York Times*, and other publications.

ACKNOWLEDGMENTS

Thanks to all the tireless *Believer* interns past, present, and future.

CONFIDENCE, OR THE APPEARANCE OF CONFIDENCE
THE BEST OF THE *BELIEVER* MUSIC INTERVIEWS
Edited by Vendela Vida & Ross Simonini

Thirty-four interviews with contemporary musicians, including such conversational treasures as Björk on e.e. cummings, Lucinda Williams on writing about sex, Trey Anastasio on improvisation games, M.I.A on the power of the internet, and Jack White on upholstering a couch.

REAL MAN ADVENTURES
by T Cooper

Now out in paperback, Cooper's bold and bracing exploration of his transition to male unfurls in a series of inspired vignettes, unsent letters, interviews, lists, and stories that capture the range of human experience. *Real Man Adventures* is a "sharp, hilarious, incredibly personal, and ingenuously honest look at what the hell it even means to be a man" (*Interview* magazine).

ALWAYS APPRENTICES
THE *BELIEVER* PRESENTS TWENTY-TWO CONVERSATIONS BETWEEN WRITERS
Edited by Vendela Vida, Ross Simonini, & Sheila Heti

"This enthralling collection contains twenty-two conversations between novelists, memoirists, poets, journalists, screenwriters, and combinations thereof about the craft of writing and the rewards (and torments) that it offers." —*Publishers Weekly*

"Reminds us how much the [*Believer*] magazine has contributed to the literary conversation." —*Chicago Tribune*

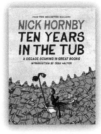
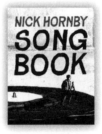

SUBSCRIBE
TO THE BELIEVER
AND RECEIVE A RECENT
BELIEVER BOOK FREE!

✮ ✮ ✮ ✮ ✮ ✮ ✮ ✮ ✮

Published six times a year, every issue of the *Believer* contains conversations and interviews, essays and book reviews, comics and illustrations, and original columns by Nick Hornby, Daniel Handler, Greil Marcus, and Lawrence Weschler. Three double issues come with ever-changing bonus items, such as vinyl records, DVDs, and temporary tattoos. Recent issues have included conversations between Judy Blume and Lena Dunham and Fred Armisen and Carrie Brownstein, as well as Anne Helen Petersen on the celebrity-gossip industrial complex, Leslie Jamison on medical acting, Lydia Millet on working as a copy editor at *Hustler*, and Sarah Marshall revisiting the Tonya Harding–Nancy Kerrigan off-ice drama of the early '90s. Subscribe with the form below and, in addition to a special discount, you'll get our new collection of interviews with musicians, *Confidence, or the Appearance of Confidence*, absolutely free!

visit us online at believermag.com
or fill out the form below for a special discount.

• •